LIVING UP WEST

Jewish Life in London's West End

by

Dr Gerry Black

'And Thou Shalt Spread to the West'
Genesis 28:14

THE LONDON MUSEUM OF JEWISH LIFE

1994

Published by The London Museum of Jewish Life

80 East End Road, London N3 2SY

ISBN 0 9511 613 6 9

Typesetting & Book Design : Ronald Stein

Printed by Aldgate Press

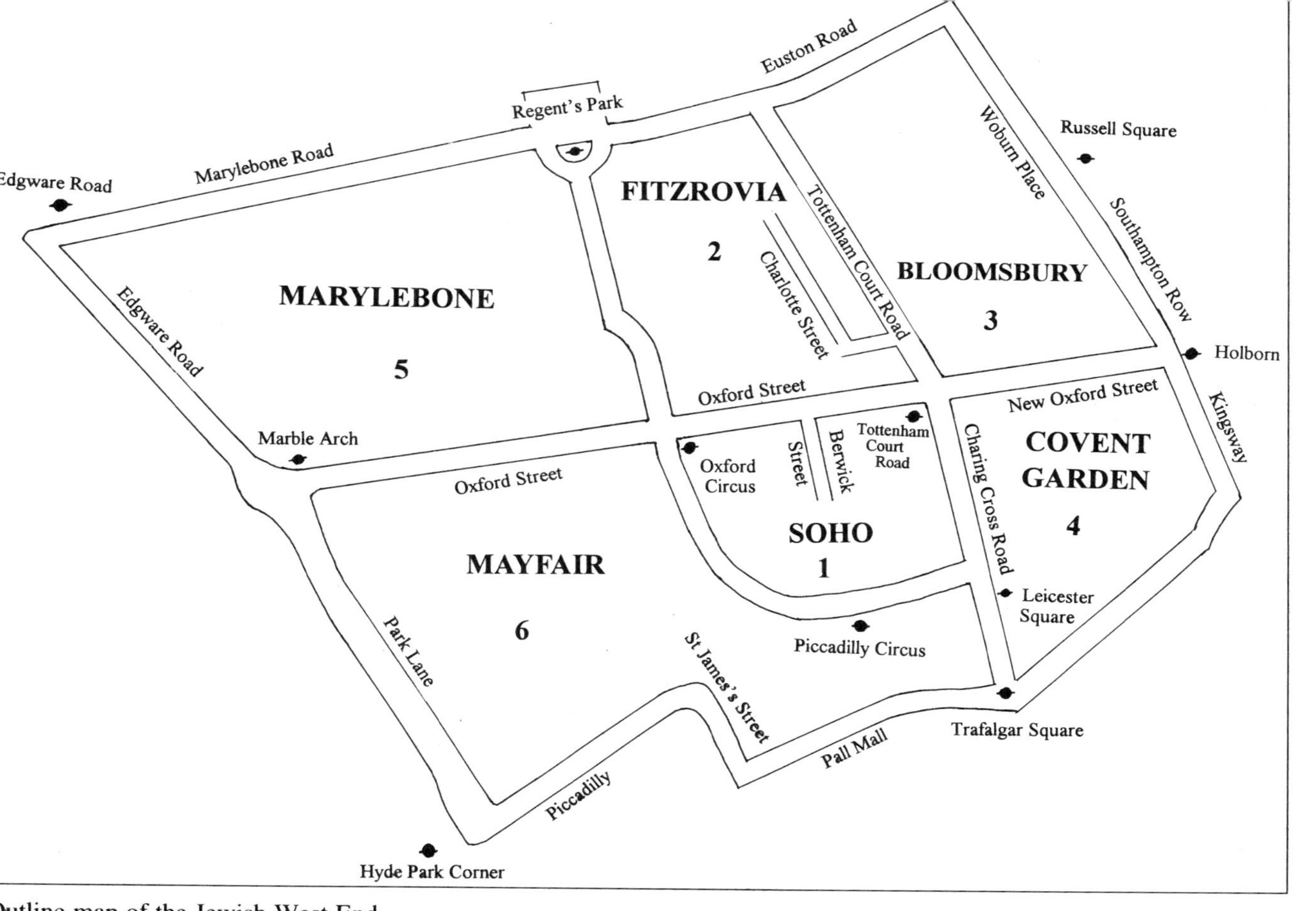

Outline map of the Jewish West End.

Contents

LIST OF ILLUSTRATIONS

IINTRODUCTION
By Sally Fiber

Chairperson and Founder of the Jewish West End Project

How does a four year project to uncover and record the history of the Jewish West End of London evolve and reach fruition? Firstly it is the realisation that there is an untold story which many people wish to hear (and some to tell) and secondly that there is an enthusiastic group of competent researchers, historians and fund-raisers who are prepared to dedicate themselves to the task.

My great fascination with the area arose from my own family connections. I am the grand-daughter of Judah 'Pop' Kleinfeld who founded the *Fitzroy Tavern* in 1919, and daughter of Annie and Charles Allchild who furthered its fame and prestige until their retirement in 1956. The *Fitzroy Tavern* became the haunt of famous artists, poets and writers of the Bohemian era and personalities of the 30s, 40s and 50s, establishing itself as the central shrine of the area to which it gave its name Fitzrovia.

Having heard so many intriguing anecdotes throughout my childhood, I set about recording my family's involvement in the *Fitzroy Tavern*. I also started to give talks about the Tavern and on every occasion members of the audience would recount stories of their own families and ask, 'Why can't the story of our Jewish West End Community be told?' I realised that a much wider story had never been fully recounted.

The need to grasp the 'living history' during the lifetimes of those who remembered, was emphasised by Henry Morris at a Service of Thanksgiving for the lives of my parents and grandparents organised by the Friends of Fitzrovia and the Ladies' Guild of the West End Great Synagogue in Dean Street. In June 1990, under the auspices of the London Museum of Jewish Life, the Jewish West End Research Committee was formed.

The project was officially launched in the following June when over 250 lively West Enders jammed into the Royalty Suite of the West End Great Synagogue, regaling us with splendid memories, memorabilia and money. This enthusiasm exceeded our expectations and confirmed our belief that the West End Story must be professionally recorded. Thereafter, members of the Research Committee gave unstintingly of their time - recording the personal memories of over 120 West Enders, and gathering photographs and memorabilia reflecting the everyday life of the Jewish community in London's West End from 1750 to the mid-1940s.

The committee organised two major fund-raising events. Benny Green generously and skilfully presented 'An Evening of Anecdotes and Song', and Harold Lester, ably assisted by Harry Rose, organised and performed the memorable 'West End Soirée'. We also held teas and lunches which not only helped to swell our funds but gave us the opportunity to reunite people who had not met for 50 or 60 years. These wonderful 'Living History' occasions revealed recollections of the past that would have been lost for ever.

We were most grateful to receive significant donations from the Clore Foundation, the Montagu Jewish Community Trust, Dame Shirley and Sir Leslie Porter and many generous West Enders. Through the good offices of the Museum we also received funding from the London Boroughs Grants Committee and the Area Museums Service for South East England.

I wish to place on record that this project would not have been possible without the belief, encouragement, professionalism and personal involvement of Rickie Burman, the Curator of the London Museum of Jewish Life.

Everyone involved in the project has been impressed by the dedication and expertise of Dr Gerry Black who describes himself as an 'Honorary West Ender'. His insight and skill as an historian in analysing and collating the mass of information has resulted in a masterly record of which we are all proud. I would also like to thank Sidney Budd and Ronald Stein who provided invaluable assistance to Gerry in preparing the book for printing.

To Rickie, Gerry; Judith Devons [the Museum's Exhibition Researcher] who compiled the major exhibition launched to coincide with the publication of this book; to Ian Lillicrapp, the Museum's photographer/designer, to the Trustees and staff of the Museum, and all members of the Research

Committee who have voluntarily devoted hours of their time and expertise to the project and the many generous contributors and supporters I acknowledge my sincerest gratitude.

I also thank the many sponsors of this book whose names are recorded in an Appendix which itself makes fascinating reading.

I am honoured to present this Introduction for our history of the West Enders and proud that I was the one destined to spearhead the project which I feel confident will establish the Jews of the West End in their rightful place in Anglo-Jewish history. True West Ender or not, I am sure you will be fascinated with our story.

Many great characters and personalities emerge in our story. The influence of 'Miss Lily', the Honourable Lily H Montagu on many of the West End girls and families stands out. The motto of her famed West Central Jewish Girls' Club, adapted from Hillel, could not have been more appropriate for our endeavours:

> *If I strive not after my own salvation*
> *who shall strive for me?*
> *and if not now, when?*

We have striven after our story, for us, our parents and for future generations, and if we had not, when, if ever, would this history have been preserved?

PREFACE

'We made a happy life for ourselves, considering we were poor'.

What was unique about the life of the Jews of the West End of London? The majority were lower income earners, or 'working class', and their experience in many ways mirrored that of the working class, both Jewish and non-Jewish, in other parts of London and in Britain as a whole. Between the wars, most working people who lived in large town centres could recount their experiences of buying a penny's worth of stale cakes, and having to use the public baths. The baths in Marshall Street and Whitfield Street evoke particular nostalgia for West Enders - twopence in hand, a towel and soap, calling out for hot water. But identical memories could be related by Jewish East Enders about Cheshire Street or Mile End Baths, or by non-Jews about West Ham Baths. Similarly tales could be told about how mother cooked for 10 people in a kitchen measuring just a few square feet, and how homes relied on outside toilets, and had no baths or hot water. Memories of these matters are important and valid, and need to be set out, but they were not unique to the West End.

Yet the West End was and remains unique. Its special quality stems from its location, the cosmopolitan composition of its inhabitants, and the cultural and recreational facilities with which it abounds. Nowhere else in Britain is there such a combined centre of entertainment, culture, shopping, parks, squares and institutional headquarters. Nowhere else covers such a wide diversity of nationalities, wealth and poverty, poor housing and mansions. Other areas may claim one or more of these attributes but only the West End has them all. Established wealthy families lived close by the majority of immigrant workers. In less than ten minutes' walk from Oxford Circus you can reach Grosvenor Square and Park Lane as well as Berwick Street, Hanway Place, and Cleveland Street. At the end of the 19th century Montefiores, Rothschilds and Mocattas lived around the corner from the tailors and small traders of Soho and Fitzrovia. Being in such a milieu gave its poorer inhabitants an immediate awareness of luxurious living and of a world outside their own.

The West End of London is also an area frequented by the rich and famous, whether or not they live within its boundaries. If you were, or indeed are, a newsagent, hairdresser, publican, tailor or restaurateur, then your clientèle could well include celebrities in a way unmatched elsewhere. The newsagent and tobacconist shop owned by Ronald Stein's family at 29 Rathbone Place numbered Sir John Martin Harvey and Nancy Cunard among its customers. The Fitzroy Tavern run by Sally Fiber's parents and grandparents in Charlotte Street had the painter Augustus John as a regular (and a guest at her parents' wedding). The international stars of stage and screen would eat and meet at Isow's restaurant in Brewer Street. When working in his father's restaurant in Moor Street, Jack Kahn served Charlie Chaplin. Harry Brahams, who had a shoe repair shop in Peter Street for 30 years after World War II, cobbled the shoes of Lauren Bacall, Tommy Steele, Danny La Rue and the the girls from the Windmill Theatre and Raymond's Revue Bar. A West End hairdresser could be called upon to attend to the hair of a leading politician, actor, film star, painter, musician or royalty. A humble West End tailor, toiling in a workshop set up in his home, made a suit for Churchill in the 1920s, and another for a prince. This did not happen on such a scale anywhere else.

Despite the fact that Jewish life in the West End spans some 250 years, starting in the middle of the 18th century, surprisingly little has been written about its history, particularly when compared with the literature available on the Jewish East End. This book aims to make a modest start in redressing the balance.

Its impetus came from a group of former West Enders who recorded memories of the formative years of their lives, mainly in Soho and Fitrovia, in the 1920s and 1930s. Their own recollections and their interviews with over a hundred other West Enders are reflected in this book, and set in historical perspective.

The interviews present a valuable but restricted viewpoint. It is restricted because the group resided in the West End mainly in the 1910s, 1920s and 1930s - a relatively short period in the life of the West End Jewish community - and almost all lived in Soho and Fitzrovia, only a small part of the West End as defined in this book. Moreover, some of their anecdotal recollections appear to be at odds with the prevailing conditions.

In his sermons, Rabbi Ferber of the West End Talmud Torah in Manette Street was able to reduce his congregation to tears, and there was much to cry about. Many West End families still had relatives in Poland and Russia, from which countries came heart-rending accounts of oppression, occupying the minds and thoughts of those here. The interviewees were living through one of the worst periods of unemployment, strikes, and recession that this country has ever experienced, and many were in the West End during both World Wars. Yet, almost without exception, they speak glowingly of their childhood - of the love and warmth of Jewish life, of the parks, theatres, museums, concert halls, dance halls and cinemas, all on their doorstep, of how safe and protected it was, of a warm village atmosphere where everyone knew everyone, where doors were ever open and the streets both safe and exhilarating, where they enjoyed a busy social life with their many relatives and friends, and had first-class schooling with outstanding teachers and first-rate clubs with remarkable leaders, and they spoke of how the many nationalities that composed the cosmopolitan community of the West End lived together in harmony. Was it really like that, or are they looking at the past through rose-coloured glasses, overwhelmed by nostalgia for things that were not quite what they remember?

Recollections are interesting, but are they reliable? Memory can be selective. People are delving back in their minds to events which occured 50 or 60 years ago, some indeed over 70 or 80 years. Distance sometimes lends enchantment, distasteful incidents or conditions can be pushed to the back of the mind, or forgotten. As one West Ender said 'We [mother and three daughters] lived in one room, but I can't bear to think about it now'. They may have been shielded from the rough edges of life by their parents, and may not even have been aware that they existed. Further, those who were prepared to be interviewed may not be representative, consisting mainly of people who wanted to talk about the West End because their overwhelming recollections were favourable. There were more women contributors than men. Where two or three different people gave accounts of the same incident or the same person, or the location of a shop, they often gave two or three conflicting versions. An historian must necessarily regard such recollections, if uncorroborated by any contemporary documentation, with extreme caution.

Despite all these factors leading to possible, indeed probable, distortion and exaggeration, I have come to the conclusion, based partly on the interviews, and partly on the sources which have been independently researched by myself and others, that the picture they present is largely true. The majority of West End children of the 1910s, 1920s and 1930s were the fortunate and privileged beneficiaries of an enviable education and upbringing, which gave them a wonderful grounding for their future. They *did* grow up in a vibrant, warm, loving environment, surrounded and protected by friends and relations.

How can this picture of West End life be reconciled with the economic realities of the time? The answer would seem to be that the interviewees were protected by their parents who bore the brunt of the poor wages and constant shortage of money at the end of the week, the grinding 70-hour or longer working week that then faced them, and the drudgery of housekeeping. The mothers, particularly, made sacrifices to ensure that no matter how hard life was for them, their children need not share the burden. It was the parents, themselves either first- or second-generation immigrants, who are the heroes and heroines of this period of the history of the Jews in the West End, as indeed was the case in the East End and in the provinces. Essentially, what the West Enders were doing in their interviews was paying a handsome tribute to them.

"I think that these people that came over, my grandparents and others of their generation, were the greatest in the world - to come to a foreign country where you didn't speak the language and did not have twopence to bless yourself with, and to then bring over and raise a family - I think there was no one in this wide world to compare with them. They are my ideal, wonderful, wonderful".

The rich, vivid, and vital lifestyle that undoubtedly existed, was by no means ideal. Much of the housing was substandard and overcrowded; privacy in the home was almost unknown; work was mostly seasonal. However, and without being overwhelmed by waves of nostalgia, it can be said that those who grew up in the West End enjoyed a fullness, richness and a satisfaction in life, and a sense of belonging. Being known and recognised in their tight community gave them a feeling of self-worth and dignity. Even compared with today's life in spacious suburbia, with all its modern comforts, it had much to commend it.

This book attempts, with a mixture of information and reminiscence, to define the Jewish West End, throw light on the numbers who lived within its boundaries, describe their housing, occupations, schools, synagogues, shops, clubs, societies, institutions, recreations and general life style, to place these in the context of the non-Jewish world which surrounded them, and to recreate as far as possible the atmosphere of the district and what it was like to live there, particularly in the first forty years of this century.

It was a painful choice as to what to include and what to omit. There were several outstanding personalities in the West End community in this century, and I have chosen just two to dwell upon at some length, The Honourable Lily Montagu and Rabbi Zvi Ferber who, I believe, were representative in their separate ways of much that was good in the West End and who beneficially affected the lives of thousands.

I have included as many quotations from the interviews as possible. There was, naturally, a certain amount of overlapping and repetition. Some people quite independently used almost identical words to express almost identical feelings or opinions, and it was an invidious task to choose between them. Some quotes comprise just a few words or only a sentence or two, while others are quite lengthy. In the light of this, it was decided not to attempt to attribute each and every quotation.

The original taped interviews and their transcriptions, together with photographs, articles, and a variety of documents, are now housed in the Londom Museum of Jewish Life's archives, where they are available for future researchers.

The catalyst has been Sally Fiber, fully supported by her husband Arthur, and to them the premier tribute must be paid. Without Sally's initiative and drive neither the exhibition, the archives nor this book would have come to fruition. Debbie Seedburgh was the principal interviewer, and Rickie Burman and Judith Devons the main contributors from the London Museum of Jewish Life. Judith's assistance far exceeded that of copy editor, and I am grateful to her for several valuable suggestions of content and order. Particular thanks are due to Sidney Budd, Zvia Ben-Horin, Rachele Kalman, Raymond Kalman, Henry Morris and Alex Rosenzweig for their important original research, and I should like to extend my gratitude to Alex Flinder and Sidney Spellman who not only shared their deep knowledge of the area with me, but took me on guided tours both south and north of Oxford Street. Without my wife, Anita's, usual forbearance and valuable assistance and suggestions my task could not have been completed.

All those individuals who made a contribution, by interviewing, being interviewed, providing documents and photographs, or writing special essays, are congratulated and thanked, and their names are listed in Appendix V.

As for my credentials for writing this book, I have always considered myself an honorary West Ender. My uncle had a stall in Berwick Street Market before World War I. Later, he and his brothers and my father ran the fun fair in the Haymarket. In the 1950s, for a season or two, I played for the West Central Club's football team, in the 1970s my wife and her sister had a shop in Berwick Street, and I have lived within easy walking distance of Oxford Street for the past 40 years. Most of my professional and business career was spent at my offices first in Wardour Street, then in St George Street, and finally in New Bond Street. The largest single section of my library, lovingly collected over the past 40 years, consists of books on Soho. It was, therefore, a special delight for me to be asked to write this book, and I hope it goes some way towards fulfilling the hopes expressed for it by Sally in her introduction.

I know from experience that after giving a talk lasting forty-five minutes, dealing with a topic which spans, say, two hundred years, at least one member of the audience will preface a question by saying 'I am surprised you did not mention X.' There may be readers of this book who will feel that too much space has been given to one topic, too little to another, or who are surprised that no mention has been made of a third. To them I say, 'All of you are right'. Perceptions of priorities vary with the individual, and this book can aspire only to give a taste of the West End story. I hope that other books will follow and fill in the many gaps - the West End communities of the past and present deserve no less.

I - THE WEST END DEFINED

What constitutes the West End of London? For many visitors it consists of the shops in Oxford Street and Regent Street, the restaurants of Soho, and the theatres of Shaftesbury Avenue; or perhaps Piccadilly Circus, Buckingham Palace, and the Horse Guards' Parade. For most of those who lived in the area during the 1920s and 1930s it meant either Soho or Fitzrovia, depending upon whether they lived south or north of Oxford Street. In the 19th century, Jews who moved to Bayswater, Notting Hill Gate, Maida Vale and St John's Wood all considered that they lived in the West End. Others will have their own definitions, but for the purposes of this book the West End is the area bounded on the **west** by Edgware Road and Park Lane, on the **east** by Southampton Row and Kingsway, on the **south** by St James and Piccadilly, and on the **north** by Euston Road and Marylebone Road.

Sidney Budd, whose paper on the Jewish population of the West End appears in Appendix I, subdivides this area into six zones - outlined and numbered in the map at the beginning of the book:

1)   **Soho**, bounded by Charing Cross Road, Oxford Street, Regent Street and Coventry Street

2)   **Fitzrovia**, bounded by Tottenham Court Road, Oxford Street, Regent Street/Portland Place, and Euston Road

3)   **Bloomsbury**, bounded by Tottenham Court Road, Euston Road, Woburn Place/Southampton Row, and New Oxford Street [but for certain purposes in this book reference is made to institutions as far east as Gray's Inn Road]

4)   **Covent Garden**, bounded by New Oxford Street, Kingsway, Strand, and Charing Cross Road

5)   **Marylebone**, bounded by Marylebone Road, Portland Place/Regent Street, Oxford Street, and Edgware Road

6)   **Mayfair**, bounded by Oxford Street, Regent Street/Haymarket, St James's Street/Piccadilly, and Park Lane.

THE GROWTH OF LONDON'S WEST END

The beginnings of the West End can be traced back to the 16th century. Many streets that later became so familiar to Jewish West Enders, in Soho in particular, can be found on 16th and 17th century maps and plans. **Wardour Street** is delineated on a plan of 1585 and was built upon in the 1680s, as was **Broadwick Street** (originally Broad Street at its western end and Edward Street at the narrower eastern part, both renamed Broadwick Street in 1936). **Berwick Street**, named after the Duke of Berwick, an illegitimate son of James II, was described in 1720 as 'a pretty handsome straight street, with new well-built houses much inhabited by the French'. There was a *Blue Posts* public house there then, and one has remained on the site ever since. North of Oxford Street, **Hanway Street** and **Hanway Place** were built up between 1720 and 1740, and **Cleveland Street** and **Windmill Street** were developed from 1745 to 1750 on land owned by Charles Fitzroy, the Duke of Southampton. **Charlotte Street**, named after Queen Charlotte, the wife of George III, was begun in 1787. Rocque's plan of 1746 shows how little the layout of Soho has altered in the past 200 years.

Bloomsbury Square was laid out in the 1660s. It attracted people of 'better qualitie' and many fine houses were erected in the late 17th century. The principal landowner was the Earl of Southampton who lived in a splendid house, with Sir Christopher Wren as a neighbour, just north of what is now **Great Russell Street**. He built extensively around it, and as the good dry Bloomsbury air was 'esteemed very healthful' it attracted many rich men who did not want to live too close to the polluted river and preferred to be on higher ground. The Fitzroy estate was rapidly developed in the years of the Regency, and **Fitzroy Square**, designed by Robert and James Adam, was built from the 1790s. **Alfred Place** began its life in 1806 and derives its name from the developer's son. The handsome squares and streets of the area were favoured by writers, painters and musicians, as well as by lawyers who found it very convenient for the Inns of Court. By the 1850s it had lost some of its fashionable status.

The area of the West End known today as **Fitzrovia** - **Charlotte Street, Cleveland Street** and their environs - has been described as cosmopolitan but fundamentally cheap and bohemian. Its streets only rarely provided fashionable addresses, it was more often a refuge for the impecunious and struggling artist, the self-employed cobbler, and successive waves of immigrants seeking cheap lodgings and employment in the service trades. **Fitzroy Square**, once an address of the rich, perhaps reached the low point of its reputation at the beginning of this century when Virginia Woolf felt it prudent to inquire of the local police whether it was a safe district for her to come to reside. The superintendant reassured her, and she moved in.

During the 16th century, the homes of bishops and noblemen were to be found in both **Covent Garden** and the **Strand**. By the early 17th century their large mansions had been replaced by smaller houses for fairly well-to-do citizens, and shops began to appear. The New Exchange built in the Strand in 1609, became a fashionable shopping centre, rather like the present-day malls.

Marylebone was developed from the beginning of the 18th century, largely by the Earl of Oxford who obtained the land through his wife Henrietta. Their daughter, Margaret Cavendish Harley, inherited the estate and married William Bentinck, the 2nd Duke of Portland, and they continued the expansion. The majority of the streets and squares took their names from members of the family, or from their titles - Portland, Mortimer and Bentinck - or from their estates - Wigmore, Wimpole or Welbeck. The area was to attract a strong Jewish presence.

Building in **Mayfair** began in the 1660s near the present-day Piccadilly Circus, advanced westward along the north side of **Piccadilly**, from where it extended northwards. By the mid-18th century almost the whole of modern Mayfair had been covered with houses, including **Hanover Square**, **Berkeley Square** and **Grosvenor Square**. The centre of gravity of aristocratic London shifted westward from the hitherto fashionable Covent Garden, and has maintained its position ever since, along with the later-developed Belgravia.

THE WEST END AS AN ENTRY POINT FOR IMMIGRANTS

The prime entry point for mass immigration into London has traditionally been the East End. Huguenots came at the end of the 17th century, Irish in the 1840s, and Jewish immigrants arrived in great numbers between 1880 and 1910 (although, of course, the Jewish community had established itself there on a smaller scale following the Resettlement of the Jews in 1656). They were succeeded by the Bangladeshi and other Asian communities.

It is sometimes overlooked that the West End, too, has been a major base for new arrivals escaping from religious persecution or economic hardship. Soho, in particular, has harboured small colonies of practically every European nationality including Huguenots in the 17th century, and other Frenchmen in the wake of the Franco-Prussian war. It was said that in the 1870s organ grinders in Soho's streets could earn more money by playing the *Marseillaise* than any other song. In the 1860s and 1870s there was an influx of Germans and Italians, many of the latter being cooks and waiters. The German Workers' Education Society established itself in Great Windmill Street, and a strong German settlement centred around Goodge Street and Mortimer Street from about 1877. The Swiss were in the neighbourhood of Cambridge Circus, and elsewhere in the area were Greeks and Chinese.

The principal immigration of Jews into Soho began in the 1880s and accelerated in the 1890s when large numbers, mainly of Polish and Russian origin, arrived. Most came directly from their native countries; some went first to the East End of London.

THE MOVEMENT OF LONDON'S JEWS FROM THE EAST END TO THE WEST END

The Jewish population of London increased from 750 at the start of the 18th century to 11,000 in 1791, 15,000 by the 1820s, and 18,000 in 1830. Until then, almost all of London's Jews lived in the East End, which contained three primary requisites for Jewish communal life - synagogues, Jewish schools and kosher butchers - together with charitable institutions that provided for the community's poor. By the second half of the 18th century, however, the rate books showed Jews living in Soho, in Rupert Street, Broad Street, Carnaby Street, Great Windmill Street, Greek Street and Berwick Street.   At the same time Jews were also residing in the Covent Garden, Strand and Leicester Square districts, in Long Acre, Panton Street, Denmark Court (off the Strand), Great Pulteney Court, Suffolk Street, Cockspur Street and St Martin's Lane. There was employment for tailors, cabinet makers, jewellers, fancy good dealers, and tobacco and snuff merchants, and Jews were among the first to take advantage of this opportunity.

There was a small and extremely poor Jewish community in Newport Market and Seven Dials in the 1830s, a district that they shared with the Irish, each in its own section. Flora Tristan gave a graphic picture of the poor 'Jewish Quarter' in her *London Journal* of 1840.

"The Jews of St Giles are shoemakers or old-clothes dealers. The streets ... are filled with shops where worn out shoes, old rags and old clothes are displayed ... It makes one shudder! ... The ground floor of all the old hovels in this quarter is given over to shops, so that the poor shopkeepers live in the kitchen located in the cellar; to reach it, a steep stairway, or rather a ladder, leads down from the street at so precipitous an angle that I have never seen its like on board the meanest merchant ship.   When one walks along the narrow sidewalks of the streets, the sight of these steep ladders makes one giddy. The cellars are nothing but kennels where the hapless people of Israel are crowded pell-mell.   In each one can be seen six, seven or eight dirty urchins, thin, gaunt, lying on the bare floor among the old shoes and filthy rags, crawling up and down the ladder like the slugs one sees crawling on cellar stairs".

The Irish quarter, she said, had filthy, wretched alleys from which fresh air and sunlight were completely blotted out, with men, women and children, all barefooted, ploughing through the nasty, filthy mire.

"If, before visiting the Irish quarter, I had gone to the Jewish quarter, the degradation of the people of Moses would have struck me as extreme, but compared to the Irish I had seen, the Jews in London enjoy a prosperous existence.What miracle keeps these children from breaking their necks going up and down the stairs a hundred times a day? It is a mystery. Poor creatures! There are thousands of human beings in these cellars, English subjects who speak English, and to whom no one pays any attention: one merely says with disdain: 'They are Jews'. Ah, how convenient it is for egoism in England when it can hide its cruelty under religious prejudice!

Flora Tristan appears to have based her account on a visit of only a few hours, and there certainly were not 'thousands' of Jews in St Giles at that time. Nonetheless there must have been more than an element of truth in her description. She thought Petticoat Lane was even worse.

From early in the 19th century, the distribution of London Jewry was in the throes of change. City merchants and brokers were no longer content to live above their shops or counting-houses in Devonshire Square, Finsbury Square or Wellclose Square, or in the many fine houses in such as Alie Street and Prescott Street. There was a stream of migration to the more desirable, newly built areas of residence outside the City, and wealthier members of the Jewish community were moving to the fashionable new thoroughfares in Westminster and Hyde Park. In so doing they were following the pattern of their non-Jewish neighbours.

The West End offered many attractions. It had cleaner air, larger and more magnificent houses, fashionable districts, and distinguished residents. Initially, some Jews moved to country areas such as Teddington, Twickenham and Richmond, where they lived in splendid isolation from their co-religionists, but from the second quarter of the 19th century it was the West End that attracted well-to-do City merchants and bankers. The wealthier Sephardim began moving to Bloomsbury and Mayfair, and the names of the famous families of 'the Cousinhood' became increasingly familiar in the West End. In 1825, Moses Montefiore and his wife moved from the City to Green Street, and shortly afterwards to 99 Park Lane. Nathan Mayer Rothschild and Edward Goldsmid moved to Piccadilly in the 1820s. Isaac Lyon Goldsmid went to Regent's Park at about the same time. Piccadilly Terrace, which stretched from the corner of Hamilton Place to Apsley House, became known as 'Rothschild Row'. In the course of time, Miss Alice de Rothschild lived at 142; Baron Ferdinand at 143; Baron Albert at 145; and Baron Lionel de Rothschild at 147/148, his double house actually joining Apsley House.

In his history of the Western Synagogue, Arthur Barnett wrote:

> The constant migration from the City westward had effected quite a phenomenal progress not merely in numbers but also in the standards of culture, opulence, and importance of this erstwhile tiny minyan. Apart from the relatively unimportant secession group which still worshipped in Maiden Lane, the Western Synagogue was the only sanctuary standing west of the Temple and Holborn Bars, and within its precincts were soon to be seen on Sabbaths and Festivals such famous families as the Goldsmids, the Sterns, Sir David Salomons, the Waleys, the Jessels, Henry Keeling, Samuel Ellis, Sidney Wolf Q.C., Simeon K.Salaman and many others who left their mark on Anglo-Jewish history. Here also you might have met Sir Moses Montefiore and Lady Judith who often attended together, and with their nephew Sir Joseph Montefiore and, still later, the Countess of Rosebery who, though the wife of a famous non-Jewish statesman still remained a Jewess and a member of the congregation.

Henry Keeling and Sir David Salomons were to become stalwart supporters of the Westminster Jews' Free School. In March 1836 the Western Synagogue was the fifth largest congregation in England, and was the first outside the City area to be regarded as of sufficient importance to be included within the Board of Deputies.

Disraeli's town house from 1839-73 was 93 Park Lane. When the *Jewish Chronicle* was first published in 1841 it appointed two of its five distributors in the West End, one in the Strand and one in Soho. By the 1840s the Mocattas had settled in the West End - Abraham in Woburn Place; Abraham junior (father of Frederick David Mocatta) in Endsleigh Street; Aaron in Burton Crescent (now Cartwright Gardens); David (the architect) in Brunswick Square, and his father, Moses, in Russell Square. The 1854 Annual Report of the Society for Supporting the Aged Needy showed that of its 40 life governors eight lived in the West End, as did more than 10 per cent of its subscribers.

THE EAST END SYNAGOGUES ATTEMPT TO STEM THE WESTWARD FLOW

The East End synagogues, the Great, the New, the Hambro and Bevis Marks, attempted to restrain the westward migration. They refused to countenance the formation of any fresh place of worship outside the traditional area, but had as much chance of achieving their objective as did Canute in his attempt to halt the sea tide. The reason for their efforts was clear. It was not only a question of dignity and jealousy but also of economics. If wealthier members living further west formed their own religious organisations, the financial burden on those who remained in the East End could become overwhelming. They feared that the community in the East End might not be able to maintain its collective responsibilities for the welfare of the poor, the burial of the dead, or even the upkeep of its own buildings.

The City synagogues forbad their members from holding or even attending services anywhere within six miles of the existing synagogues (ten miles in the case of the Great). Their purpose was to hold the congregation together, spiritually and physically, and avoid the danger of fragmentation. They contracted not to poach each other's members, and then brought the independent Western Synagogue, formed in 1761, into their agreement. The Western originally had no burial facilities of its own and had to depend upon an arrangement with the City synagogues. By a treaty of 1808 the condition was imposed that no one was to be admitted as a member of the Western unless he resided west of Temple Bar or Holborn Bar. The Western also agreed not to acquire its own burial ground. In return, the City synagogues offered burial facilities and undertook to prevent the foundation of any other West End congregation within six miles westwards of Denmark Court in the Strand, where the Western then stood. The combined effect of these restrictions was to make it difficult for other synagogues to open, or for members who wished to participate in Jewish religious rites to live beyond walking distance of their existing synagogue. In fact, the Western broke the treaty seven years later and acquired a burial ground at Queen's Elm, Brompton.

The West End pioneers considered it wrong that they should either have to forgo the pleasures of communal worship or walk several miles to synagogue, and they had sufficient wealth and influence to ensure their wishes were met. Inevitably they exerted pressure on the City synagogues to provide suitable arrangements in the West End and, equally inevitably, the City synagogues acquiesced, despite resistance from some of their more diehard members.

The strongest impetus for change followed the foundation of the Reform movement. In 1836, Moses Mocatta presented a petition to the Sephardi Council requesting changes in the form of service, but it was ignored. In 1838, the Elders were forced to convene a meeting, by which time the demands of the petitioners had changed. So many Bevis Marks members were now living in the West End that they wanted to establish a branch synagogue closer to their homes. Partly because of Bevis Marks' failure to accede to their requests, nineteen Sephardim joined five Ashkenazim to inaugurate a Reform Synagogue and, in January 1842, the West London Synagogue of British Jews opened in Burton Street, Bloomsbury. Bevis Marks reacted by opening a branch in Wigmore Street, but that was not until 1853 by which time the Reform had outgrown its Burton Street premises and was firmly established in Margaret Street in a building seating 400.

The Great was even slower. In 1848, its council reported that 'it is considered of the utmost importance that a place of worship in connection with this synagogue be established in the West End of the Metropolis'. They procrastinated, and it was not until 1855 that their first 'branch' synagogue, the Central, was opened in Great Portland Street.

TO BLOOMSBURY AND MARYLEBONE

In 1829, George Shillibeer, a young coach builder and livery stable keeper in Bloomsbury, started an omnibus route from Paddington Green to the Bank of England in the City. The 6d fare, as against the previous 2/-, made commuting to business more affordable. In the 1830s and 1840s, **Bloomsbury** became *the* Jewish residential district for the upper- and upper-middle classes. A random sample of 100 Jewish names in the 1848 Post Office Directory, which included only prominent individuals, showed that 25 per cent lived in the area bounded by Tottenham Court Road to the west, Euston Square to the north, Gray's Inn Road to the east, and Holborn to the south.

In the 1851 census, there were 13 Jewish householders in and around Gower Street, including Aaron and Jacob Mocatta; Lewis Levy, the turnpike contractor, Walter Josephs, founder of the Jews' Infant Schools; and James Lewis, solicitor (whose family included the future Sir George Lewis, then an articled clerk of 17).

In 1860, the tide of fashionable London Jewry spread even further westwards over the Edgware Road into **Bayswater**, then known as Tyburnia. The great age of **Maida Vale** was 1870-1900.

Despite the continuing westward tidal flow, the West Central District was far from deserted. In 1872 the *Jewish Chronicle* noted how many Jews still lived on the Bedford, Grafton, Portman, and Manchester estates. Many who attended the Central Synagogue came from the Russell Square area. The Central remained one of the larger constituents of the United Synagogue, although as the century progressed it was surpassed in the level of its wealth by the New West End, Bayswater and Hampstead synagogues.

By the middle of the 19th century, the West End reflected a combination of landed and merchant wealth and the craftsmen who supplied them with furniture, clothing, jewellery and other luxuries. The older parts of the West End, notably Soho and Covent Garden, provided a mixture of trade opportunities and cheap lodgings, which attracted the craftsmen there.

Booth's Poverty Map of 1889 was an attempt to gauge the wealth of the inhabitants in each street in London, from the very wealthy (marked in gold) to the very poor (dark blue). Some streets appeared in more than one category:

Gold (upper middle, upper classes, wealthy): Russell Square, Bedford Square, Tavistock Square, Gordon Square, Portland Place, Devonshire Street, Wigmore Street, Berkeley Square, Grosvenor Square, Park Lane, Bryanston Square, Bryanston Street, Upper Berkeley Street.

Dark Red (well-to-do middle class): Gower Street, Alfred Place, Store Street, Great Russell Street, Bloomsbury Square, Covent Garden, Sackville Street, Old Bond Street, Cork Street, Mount Street, Fitzroy Square.

Light Red (fairly comfortable, good ordinary earnings): Cleveland Street, Newman Street, Gerrard Street, Frith Street, Soho Square, Edward Street, Wells Street, Great Pulteney Street, Brewer Street, Wardour Street, Great Marlborough Street, Windmill Street, Charlotte Street, Howland Street, Whitfield Street.

Lilac (mixed, some comfortable, some poor): Grafton Street, Saville Street, Great Titchfield Street, Gosfield Street, Greek Street, Berwick Street, Broadwick Street, Marshall Street, Carnaby Street, Peter Street, Wardour Street.

Light Blue (Poor, 18/- to 21/- per week): Portland Street, Noel Street, St Anne's Court

Black (lowest class): Poland Street.

In the 1880s most Jews who settled in the West End came directly from Eastern Europe, but some moved there from the East End of London, particularly following the tailors' strike of 1889. The extent of the move from the East End to the West in this period becomes apparent from an examination of Admission Registers of the Westminster Jews' Free School and of the Pulteney School, now kept at the Greater London Record Office. Some include a column stating the new pupil's previous school. During the period 1870-1872, 8.4 per cent of the pupils at Westminster Jews' Free School had transferred from an East End school, whereas in the three years immediately following the strike the figure rose to 18.8 per cent, almost one in five of the school population. The percentage then dropped back again to five or six per cent.

The general population of St Anne's parish in Soho began to decline in the 1870s, and between 1881 and 1891 there was an even sharper drop from 16,608 to 12,317. This was partly due to the demolition of old houses in Newport Market and Charing Cross Road, and partly because Soho was becoming less residential and increasingly a centre of work or entertainment. So Jewish immigrants arrived in Soho at a time when the overall population was declining, and it necessarily followed that the percentage of Jews to the general population increased. By 1900, approximately 40 per cent of the inhabitants of St Anne's Parish were Jews.

The situation between 1891 and 1911 was well described by the Rev J H Cardwell, the vicar of St Anne's, in his book *Twenty Years in Soho*:

> The coming of the Jew to Soho ... began about 1891. Before that time there were comparatively few Jews in St Anne's and they were confined for the most part to one or two streets.   The tailors' strike was the cause of a considerable exodus of Israelites from Whitechapel to Soho. The increase in the number of Jewish residents may be gathered from the fact that whereas in 1891 there were very few Jewish children in St Anne's Schools they now [in 1911] form 25 per cent of the scholars. As an article in *Church and Synagogue* in 1898 stated 'The usual idea that the London "ghetto" is in Whitechapel and St George's-in-the-East is rapidly becoming incorrect. The Jews have arrived in the quarter which for 200 years was the French and Italian colony in London.'

THE TWENTIETH CENTURY

The Jewish community in the West End of London was approximately 15,000 in 1900 and about 25,000 from 1925 until the 1930s, according to Sidney Budd's estimate. Soho always accounted for less than half of these numbers, and through the period from 1900 to 1939 there was a significant reduction in the proportion living in Soho and an increase in the proportion living in Mayfair, Fitzrovia and Marylebone. At different times between 1900 and 1939 Sir Ernest Cassel, Adolph Tuck, Harry Sacher and Simon Marks lived in Grosvenor Square. Lord Duveen was in Grafton Street, Sir Edgar Speyer in Grosvenor Street, Sir Stuart Samuel MP in Hill Street, Arthur Cohen QC in Great Cumberland Place, Otto Schiff in Berkeley Square, Lord Jessel in South Street, Lord Mancroft in Montagu Square, Sir Rufus Isaacs in Park Lane and Curzon Street, Cyril Picciotto in Weymouth Street, Anthony de Rothschild in Hill Street, Sir Max Bonn (the banker) in Bryanston Court, Sir Felix Semon in Wimpole Street, Claude Montefiore in Portman Square, Sir Marcus Samuel in Hamilton Place, Leslie Hore-Belisha in Stafford Place, Lord Wolfson in Portland Place, and Sir Michael Balcon in Waterloo Place. Also in the area were Richard Tauber, Lord Wandsworth, and Sir Jules Thorn. During the same period there was a steady move out to Brondesbury Park, Cricklewood, and other north-western suburbs.

The Second World War saw the beginning of the end of the thriving West End community. Many of those who were evacuated or joined the forces did not return. Important institutions such as the Girls' Club and the Boys' Club, continued, but never again reached the heights of their pre-war heyday.

"I left the West End to be married in 1938, but I remember just after the war people began to move from the West End. They went to Highgate, Cricklewood, Golders Green: it was mostly the people who had their businesses there who remained in the West End. Those whose children married and left the West End, after a time moved and went to live nearer their children".

"I think the bombs that landed on the Club and Synagogue in 1941 heralded the end of an era of the vibrant Jewish community in the West End. We all went off to war and things were never the same on our return. Those who returned dispersed to other places, the great synagogues became empty, and grandiose names were attached to the shells they now are. The Clubs are closed. The Old Boys and the Old Girls - some of them now getting very old - still meet and remember with nostalgia our youth and our friends who, in the nature of things, are becoming fewer. But the well of recollection is bottomless".

II - AN EAST END IN THE WEST END?

Can substantial comparisons be made between the Jews of the West End and those of the East End? In numbers, the Jewish population of the West End could not match that of the East End. The East End peaked in about 1910 at some 110,000 Jews. Sidney Budd's figures [Appendix I] show the West End peaked later, probably in about 1925, did not exceed 25,000-28,000, and began its decline much later. Nonetheless, the West End Jewish population was of more than sufficient size to make comparisons meaningful.

The map of the East End in *The Jew in London* by Russell and Lewis, drawn in 1900, showed Old Montague Street, Flower & Dean Street, Wentworth Street, Plumbers Row, and others with 95-100 per cent Jewish occupation. Jewish concentration in the West End never reached such intensity, though such streets as Berwick and Broad[wick] Streets to the south and Cleveland and Hanson Streets to the north had a substantial Jewish majority.

Despite a significant movement of Jews from the East End to the West End from the 1890s there is no evidence of any comparable movement in the opposite direction. This is perhaps not surprising since there was little to draw Jews to the east. The East End had no special employment opportunities, its housing was generally inferior, and the West End was well supplied with schools, synagogues, and shops that catered for its Jewish needs.

Gertie Phillips' story of how her father moved from the East End to the West End is illustrative. He was offered accommodation in the East End and a job as a ladies' tailor more or less as he came off the boat. At the end of his first week he went for a walk, westwards.

"He saw the streets and the houses becoming better and better. He went on walking until he came to Oxford Street and when he got there he realised that London was not all like the East End, that there were other nice parts and lots of nice Jewish people. The following week he made up his mind that he would go back to the West End and see if he could get a job. The next Friday he left work early, got on a bus, looked around, and went into a shop in Regent Street called Nicholls which had dresses in the window. He went in and said he wanted a job, which he was given after he showed them his skill in padding a collar where the canvas joined the material. He found a room in the Berwick Street area for 5/- a week. He stayed there for many years and found himself making clothes for the Royal Family".

A main difference between the East End and the West End was, of course, the latter's unparalleled collection of theatres, museums, concert halls, parks, squares, large stores, restaurants, cafes, drinking places and clubs.

"You would walk out of Berwick Street and you were in the heart of the West End with all the big stores in Oxford Street and Regent Street".

"They could take buses to the West End, *but where we lived we could walk into culture*".

"We had access to the finest theatres, the finest plays, the music halls, variety shows, the concert halls. We were around the corner from the Queen's Hall. In addition we had the dance halls. We used to go to the Old Vic and sit up in the gods for 10d. *From the East End they would have to travel, and it wasn't part of them*".

The West End was also unrivalled in its parks.

"Within a mile we had Green Park, Hyde Park, St James' Park, and Regent's Park. We children had our nursery ground in these wonderful parks ... right in the heart of the West End".

The proximity of the houses of the wealthy in the West End added something to the lives of the poor.

"When I took a walk in Bruton Street or Grosvenor Square I lived, as it were, in my imagination the life of these affluent people who occupied these wonderful residences".

There was a widely accepted view, which may have been true, that West Enders were better off than the East Enders, but it is difficult to find hard evidence to support it. Tailoring was the dominant Jewish occupation in both areas. Wages were similar in both districts, and depended upon the level of skill involved. The lowest and highest skilled workers earned similar sums regardless of the area they worked in. However, because of the stores and Savile Row, there was more skilled work available in the West End, so in that limited sense the West End tailor earned more.

Certainly, some East Enders appear to have perceived that Jews living in the West End were wealthier. Some West End girls said that East Enders they met at dances clearly assumed this, doubtless leading to many a disappointment when the truth emerged.

It has been suggested that the East End community was more orthodox, and that West End Jews were more easily 'seduced' from religion by their surroundings. Chief Rabbi Hermann Adler said, in 1897, that the West Enders of Soho were surrounded by crowded streets full of snares and pitfalls, and they had the reputation of being generally irreligious. Both Lily Montagu and the leaders of the Boys' Club considered it their role to help their members avoid the particular temptations of the West End.

"It was more difficult to be *frum* in the West End. We couldn't go to *shul* on Saturdays because we had a business in Oxford Street. If we had lived in the East End we would have done the same as everybody else and closed on Saturday".

The West End contained a larger assimilated element, and possibly no synagogue in the East End was quite as anglicised as the Central Synagogue in Great Portland Street. 'My father', said Chaim Lewis, 'used to call them the *Englischer Yehudim*, the English Jews'.

"Many of the Jews who came into the West End began to show early signs of assimilation. They no longer observed the Sabbath. Well, it happened in the East End too, but because they had greater numbers there was always a strong reservoir of orthodox Jews who adhered to the strict tenets of Judaism. Whereas in the West End you saw the loosening of religious ties even among the newly arrived immigrants".

East End Jewish youths came to the West End on weekends.

"On Saturday evenings the East End boys came by bus from Aldgate to the West End dances and to the Lyons Corner House and you would see them all marching along Oxford Street towards Bloomsbury to go home to get the last bus or tram, back to the East End and Stamford Hill and Finsbury Park".

"I think the East Enders were a very smart community in their clothes. They used to meet by the Dominion, and go to the Astoria or the pictures. You could always tell the East End girls. They wore black stockings, and high heeled shoes. They were smart, smarter than we were. I think more street-wise. I think a little bit louder than the West End. They always looked the height of fashion, perhaps a little bit flash. As a child I was always interested in fashion sketching, and I used to notice these things. I used to love it if we could walk along and watch them as they got off the bus in New Oxford Street".

There was some traffic in the opposite direction. The Yiddish theatre flourished only in the East End. In the West End performances were occasional rather than regular. And some shopping was cheaper in the East End.

"I only went to the East End with my mother to Abrahams in the Lane for children's clothes and sometimes to the Houndsditch Warehouse".

"We used to go down the Lane every Sunday. It was interesting to us. We had a cup of coffee, knew all the boys who worked on the stalls and in the shops. We'd go there to buy handbags which were cheaper. There was a novelty about it".

"For the trousseau we went to the East End. When you got married, your mother bought you feathers, pillows, and daks, which they now call duvets. We used to go down the Lane for those".

Some thought they detected a difference in accents:

"The intonation of accents was different. You could tell: we weren't cultured by a long stretch of the imagination, and you could tell which people were Jewish, but the accents were different".

"The Eastenders were more cockney. It sounds odd, but they just spoke English differently. It was like a Jewish cockney. And it was very distinguishable. In the West End it was more of a normal London accent".

Some families had members in both camps, and there was obviously cross visiting. The Jewish clubs all belonged to the Jewish Athletic Association (later the Association for Jewish Youth) and there was inter-club mixing for both social and sporting activities.

But all these variations between East and West End neighbourhoods were minor. Their Jewish identity was a more powerful influence on them than the particular area of London in which they lived.

"When we met up after the war in North West London there were frankly no differences between East Enders and West Enders. I married an East End lady, and there was no difference in our backgrounds at all".

III - HOUSING

Housing in the West End varied from slums of the worst description (though these had almost completely disappeared by the beginning of this century), to fine houses and flats in Marylebone, to the mansions of the wealthy in Mayfair. There were also large houses originally erected for the middle- and upper-middle classes that were sub-divided vertically and horizontally into workrooms and rooms to let. What was remarkable was that examples of each style could be found almost cheek by jowl:

"I think that my standard of living in Cleveland Street was pretty low. It was poverty. Very harsh living. But you went 100 yards and you were at the Nash Terraces of Regent's Park and you saw how the other half lived. You went round the corner into Fitzroy Square, literally round the corner, and you saw another life. It didn't make me envious, but it made me fascinated that you might be able to end up with them or in those houses".

Jews were to be found occupying every type of house. The first Jew to live in Grosvenor Square was Samuel Lewis, the moneylender philanthropist, who in 1838 was born into abject poverty in a Birmingham slum. In 1880 he arrived at the Square, at number 23, on the corner with North Audley Street, accompanied by a butler, coachman, cook and several servants (the average in the Square at the time was 30 servants per household).

In 1901 his widow, Ada, purchased the 40 year lease of number 16 for £26,750, and this 'moderate sized' house, as the agents described it, had a frontage to the Square of 32 feet and a total depth of 160 feet. It was approached through a portico entrance into a marble-paved vestibule leading to the entrance hall, and was on four floors and also had a large basement. The first three floors were served by an Otis lift. There were eleven bedrooms, three bathrooms and two dressing rooms, a library, morning room and very large dining room. The front room measured 30 by 24 feet, and in addition to all this was the servants' hall, butler's bedroom, strong room, butler's pantry, a large kitchen (with a dressing room adjoining), scullery, spacious wine cellarage, coal cellars, larder and tradesmen's entrance. There was also property at the rear with a harness room, kitchen, two bedrooms, bathroom and stabling. Until her remarriage three years later, Ada Lewis lived there alone.

The houses in Devonshire Place and Portland Place ('the handsomest street in Europe') could almost match the Lewis residence. Miss Evelyn Waley reminded us that Solomon Jacob Waley, formerly Levy, the father of Jacob Waley, and one of the founders of the Jewish Board of Guardians, moved to 22 Devonshire Place in about 1840. Lionel van Oven wrote:

"It was one of the most delightful houses in London. They had a dinner party almost every Sunday, at which there was collected at dinner or in the evening afterwards, almost the greatest musical talent in London, to say nothing of artists and authors. Edward Bulwer (afterwards Lord Bulwer Lytton) used to come there to play whist with Mr Waley. Haussman, the violincello player was there contantly ... all the best English singers used to be there, and it was considered a great boon to any rising musician who came to London to get an introduction to be invited to Mrs Waley's house ... There was no house I ever knew or visited at, however wealthy the people might be, that was half so agreeable, or half so much in the style of the great houses you read of in the early part of the last century and the 18th century".

The house later became the home of Simon Waley and his wife Anna, née Salomons.

Sir George Lewis, England's leading society solicitor, whose clients ranged from the Prince of Wales to Lily Langtry, moved to number 88 Portland Place in 1876, and there his second wife Elizabeth created a salon that attracted the best of Bohemia and talented society. Whistler and John Sargent, Thomas Hardy and Oscar Wilde, W.S.Gilbert and Sir Arthur Sullivan, were among the regular guests.

At the other extreme, in the 1840s, were the slums of Seven Dials described earlier. Sixty years later, the West Central Ladies' Society could still find examples of Jews living in complete poverty in disgraceful, severely overcrowded conditions. Overcrowding was so much a part of Soho life that it was common to see signs in the windows of the old houses advertising 'Part of a room to let'. In 1896, houses in St Anne's parish were, on average, twice as overcrowded as those elsewhere in London, and rents were rising all the time, due largely to the success of the vice trade, but surprisingly few of those interviewees who lived in Soho or Fitzrovia in the 1920s considered the rents unreasonable.

The majority of Jewish West End families who came to Soho and Fitzrovia from 1890 onwards occupied one, two or three rooms , one of which was often used as a combined workroom and living room. Though crowded, and without the bathing facilities nowadays taken for granted, the families managed to create happy, clean (though sometimes bug-ridden) homes in which most children did not at the time feel in the least deprived. Many families started in one room and then expanded as other rooms in the house became available.

"We lived in Livonia Street on the top floor. We had one room for my mother and three children. Toilets? We had a 'po' upstairs or a bucket, and if we wanted to go to the loo we had to go right out downstairs. We were on the fourth floor. We had to go down into the yard, where there were two loos for four families".

"My mother had no help at home and we all helped, unwillingly, but we did help. Nine children, all that work! We had no inside toilet or water, just one lavatory in the yard for the whole family. When we were little my mother had a big zinc bath, and she used to line us up every Friday, until we graduated from that at about the age of 9 and went to Marshall Street baths. When we first went to the house, there was no electicity, just gas".

"I think time plays strange tricks with memories. I always thought of it as a big house, and it's still there, but seems to have become much smaller. It is in Windmill Street off the Tottenham Court Road, and is now an art gallery. I think we must have been comparatively comfortable. My parents and their four children occupied the whole upper part - that is the three floors.   Our front room on the first floor was unusually large with three windows. At no. 38 there was a huge vine, and every summer it grew an abundance of grapes - always an item in the newspapers. The lady who lived there used to lean out of the window surrounded with all this greenery - a lovely picture. My mother, like all the other women, helped in the tailoring workshop - a large room in the house, on the middle floor. We had a live-in help, Lizzie, who came from the Cut. She was with us for years, we all loved her. We had no fridges or freezers then, but my mother, with Lizzie's help, produced wonderful food daily. How did we manage? We had carpeted stairs, and you could always see Lizzie with a brush. She loved that carpet, and we didn't have a Hoover. How hard the work must have been".

"I lived in St James' Residences in Broad Street, now called Broadwick Street. My aunt who also lived in the building used to direct people by saying, 'It's opposite the *pishoska*' [public convenience]. It was a six-storey building on top of shops. Some families had two rooms and a sink outside on the landing halfway down the house. Mother had a bucket, and we would take it in turns to go and get water, only cold water. We used a tin bath in the kitchen. There were two lavatories between the six flats. We had a tin bucket behind a curtain in the room to wee in if we wanted to, and we'd take it down to empty once or twice a day. When my brother was born, we were up 53 stairs on the third floor, and my dad thought nothing of carrying the baby up and the pram. What man would do that now? You couldn't leave the pram downstairs because it would be taken in no time".

The grand houses of 18th and 19th century Soho which had been subdivided were well past their prime, and could be extremely uncomfortable to live in:

"They weren't so much cold as draughty. They had high ceilings, and the windows and floors didn't fit properly. If you sat in front of the fire your front was scorched and your back was freezing, and you had chilblains when you went to bed. We couldn't have a hot water system, even when the time came when we could afford one, because the walls weren't strong enough to fix anything to. The kitchen wall was so unsafe and flaky that my mother used to buy lining paper and pin it up with drawing pins. When the house was demolished they found the most beautiful panelling underneath, which was sold for a fortune to America. So it had been a good house once - which was why it had an indoor loo".

"My mother had the lavatory on the first floor all to herself. *That was her sole luxury*. She had the key to *her* toilet. Everyone else used the one upstairs".

"We lived in Grafton Way. I never saw a bug in the house, never. Maybe other people had, but we did not. Possibly we were better off than most of my school friends".

"We lived at 76 Berwick Street. We had bugs in the bedrooms. We went out and got the necessary fumigating agent, stripped or gave away old furniture, and put in new things, and only by doing this did we get rid of the plague".

"We lived at the corner of Whitfield Street and Howland Street. Over Launers the baker.

Did your father have his workshop elsewhere?

You must be joking!   His workshop was a partitioned part of the living room - part workshop, part living room, part bedroom. We all slept in one room, with Mummy and Daddy, all in one bedroom. Till we moved, and I think I was then nearly 14. And our kids today, if they don't have a bedroom each they think it is the end of the world, don't they?"

"There were plenty of places all over, you could move. Rent was cheap. I don't think it was much more than 30/- for a 2/3 bedroom flat in Broadwick Street or Berwick Street or Noel Street".

"My father left his job in the East End and started the new job the following Monday in the West End. He had to find a room to live. He walked around the Wardour Street, Berwick Street, and Dean Street area where there were a lot of Jewish people who wanted 5/- per week to let a room. So that is what he took".

"I lived at 5 D'Arblay Street. It was the tallest building in the street. It is now a film company place. We had a four- storey house on a very long lease. If we owned it today we would be worth a million".

"There was no bathroom in our house until we installed one after the war. People came up to have a look, neighbours, and then we would invite them in to have a bath".

"I don't know how we managed. It seemed to be a miracle, but we managed".

"I have the distinction of having been born in the house once occupied by William Blake, poet, painter and visionary, born 1757, but there the distinction ends. By 1919, it was no longer an elegant town house but a tenement occupied by two families, with the top floor let out as tailoring workshops. My family lived on the first floor - seven people in three small rooms - one room acting as living room and workroom combined, containing the last vestiges of grandeur of the prestigious former occupants, in the shape of two built-in glass fronted cupboards on either side of the fireplace - our library".

"I lived at 27 Clipstone Street. My father told me to paint my side of the room. I painted everything in sight, including a rather dirty fireplace. The house was badly damaged during an air raid and we had to move. Many years after the war I was astonished to read an article in a magazine, 'House and Garden' or some such title, by an author who had bought our house, and she described how she had put in several mirrors to create a more spacious atmosphere. She added that in a room on the second floor she had discovered an exquisite Adam fireplace 'which some idiot had painted over!'"

"It could not have been too long after my parents rented the shop that the first floor became available, and we all moved to 6 St Anne's Court.   How we managed I can only imagine, as we were three adults and three children in just the two rooms and downstairs tiny parlour. The only sink was on the landing between the first and second floors and the only toilet was an outside one in the back yard. Added to this was the fact that the latter two utilities were also shared by eight other people - two in each of the two rooms on the second and third floors. But manage we obviously did ...   As soon as they could afford to, my parents had the front basement room built up and decorated; at last we had our own 'family room' where not only did we have our very own sink, but we could wash, eat and even dance around the table to our wind-up gramophone.   The condensation ran down our wooden-painted walls, and we couldn't open the one blocked-up window, but we felt rich!   My memories are of a happy family; I cannot, in those happy years, recall ever having felt poor or deprived".

"For some years, some of my brothers boarded out. That was not unusual because there were families with five or six children".

"We went to live in Royalty Mansions in Meard Street. The flats were originally built in 1908 especially as dwellings for tailors so that one room could be used as a workshop. They were quite big, with four large rooms, self-contained with indoor sanitation. By the standards of Soho we lived very well".

A major effect of all this overcrowding was naturally a complete lack of privacy.

"I was one of seven girls. My older sisters were working and making their own clothes, so that in the evenings our home was buzzing. There were dresses being made, hats being designed, friends coming and going. No one could have any secrets because Pearl and I were always around. Under the table was the best vantage point, where we could hear all and not be seen and sent to bed".

IV - 'THE OTHER SIDE' - NORTH AND SOUTH
OF OXFORD STREET

There were quite separate *shtetls* either side of Oxford Street -   two villages each with its own facilities, cameraderie and unique atmosphere in which everybody knew everyone else. Those living north and south of Oxford Street referred to 'the other side' as though it were a foreign country.

The Jews who lived north of Oxford Street considered themselves somehow different from the Jews to the south of Oxford Street. Their housing was similar, as were the shops that provided for their needs. Perhaps the accommodation to the north was slightly more spacious, but not universally so. Each side had an abundant supply of kosher butchers, grocers, delicatessens and restaurants, and they mostly originated from the same areas of Poland or Russia. Yet they perceived themselves as different, and kept apart. Many crossed 'the great divide' only rarely, and if a family moved it was usually sideways.

"We took the plunge and moved north over to Rathbone Place.   It was unheard of."

"We usually played within sight of our own windows. South of Oxford Street was a foreign country when we were kids".

"We ran our fish business both sides of Oxford Street. Both sets of clientèle were Jewish but they mixed together very rarely".

Most West End Jews thought that the side on which they lived was the superior side.

"I didn't go to the south side except when I went with my parents to Folman's, because he was my father's pal. I didn't really have any friends from that side of Oxford Street. It was different, and we used to refer to it as the East End of the West End. No offence was meant, and they probably referred to us in the same way. We used to think we were a cut above them".

"We did not mix with those on the north side; they were far too snooty. It was a different territory".

"It wasn't that people to the north weren't as good as us. In fact they were in the main better off than we were. They lived in bigger houses, but they weren't a village community in the way we were. The market wasn't there, and that was the community's focus".

Despite general feelings of being different many things brought north and south together. The north had more synagogues - West London Reform, the Western, the Central and Whitfield Street Liberal - but for a more orthodox and *shtetl*-like *shul,* you had to go south to the Beth HaSepher in Soho Square or to the West End Talmud Torah and Bikkur Holim Synagogue in Manette Street where the service, rabbi, and the fervid atmosphere were more typical of the *heim.* Even then, so great were the numbers of Manette Street members who wished to attend High Holyday services, that from 1926 onwards they had to travel north to overflow services held in the Scala Theatre. On Sabbaths, the flow was from north to south, but on the High Holydays it reversed. Others crossed the divide to be married in a synagogue they considered more appropriate to the occasion.

Uniquely, the north had the highly popular West Central Jewish Girls' Club and West Central Jewish Lads' Club. Neither club had a counterpart in the south. The Jewish Lads' Brigade and the Scouts met at the Beth HaSepher, but they did not vie in importance with the clubs.

The Westminster Jews' Free School was in the north. It was the only 100 per cent Jewish school in the area, though schools such as Pulteney had a majority of Jewish pupils. The Jews' Free School drew its pupils from both sides of Oxford Street, but some parents regarded the journey from more distant parts of Soho as too far for their children, and others were unhappy that their children should cross busy Oxford Street.

Perhaps the greatest attractions to the south were the theatres, and Berwick Street Market with its particularly good fruit stalls. Berwick Street was also renowned for its smart and reasonably priced dress shops, provided you were not deterred by the *schleppers,* the salesmen who stood in the shop doorways, or even on the pavement or in the road, attempting to entice customers into the shops.

One northsider thought he spotted a difference:

"The people who came from Soho seemed racier ... more street-wise than we were. I could tell the difference between the Soho people and us. I can't put my finger exactly on the difference, but it revealed itself in their demeanour, their street language, that sort of thing. Because they lived in Soho, prostitution was on every street corner and the snooker halls were on their doorstep, not ours. And they were bunking into the cinemas through the back door every day of the week."

Despite all the talk of differences, these were more apparent than real. A stranger to the area, confronted with Jewish residents of both sides, would have been hard put to identify who came from where.

V - SOCIAL LIFE

"Very often on *Shabbos* afternoon, because people lived near each other, they didn't make an appointment like they do today. The men would play a game of cards, 66 or brag or whatever. People just came in, nicer than it is today. Everybody mucked in, and my mother always had cake and biscuits with tea. We always brought friends in and there were always people in the house".

"We always had to abide by our parents' wishes, whether we agreed or not, even at the age of 17 or 18; by about 21 things were a little easier".

"In those days we did not have much money, but there was great respect for others; not as it is today. You made friends and you appreciated them; today there is too much snob value".

"They were happy days, nothing was forced down your throat. You were not compelled to go to *shul*. You went out of respect to your home. We did little things that were silly or wrong, but never did anyone as far as I know ever disgrace their family name".

"Life was warm, and secure, and full of activity as I grew up".

"My part of Soho was a village comprising Broad Street, Dufours Place, Marshall Street, Ganton Street, and West Street [now Newburgh Street], bounded by Carnaby Street at one end, then a rather quiet backwater, and the bustling market of Berwick Street at the other. Almost all the residents and shopkeepers in these streets were Jewish, and one knew the name of every single family who lived in them, even going further afield to cosmopolitan Old Compton Street, Greek Street and Wardour Street. Everything was within walking distance - shops, schools, and synagogues. A short walk took one to Oxford Street, Regent Street with its elegant shops, Shaftesbury Avenue, and Theatreland, with Piccadilly Circus the focal point, the flower girls with their baskets of multi-coloured flowers sitting on the steps of Eros. Looking back to my childhood, there were few creature comforts, but there was the warmth of family life, and a sense of community in my 'village', emotions perhaps enhanced by the passing of time - but even after many years I am still drawn to my 'roots' in Soho".

"I overheard two women talking and one said, 'How come Becky should marry this fellow Hymie?' 'Why?'. 'What background does he have?' From that day I have always regarded background as important".

"One of the nicest things was that if you were invited to a wedding you had to make a spread on your dining room table, so that your neighbours could come in and have a drink and look at you to see you all dressed up to go to this wedding. You did not have to be related to the bride or the groom, it was enough that you were going to a wedding. You had to lay on a table, wine and whisky and herring and your neighbours came in to have a look at you. 'Marvellous! How well you look!' That was an old custom. It wasn't only the ladies; men went in as well. The men went to have a drink".

"We lived like aristocrats. People were lovely, they were beautiful. They kept themselves refined, even if they were foreign and didn't speak English. There was no snobbery.   Differences, but no snobbery".

"The 'in' word we were brought up with was *mitzvah*; and you always had to do *mitzvahs*".

"Everybody was on a level, none had more than the others and everyone lived in the same sort of climate. Most did not have much money; if they did, they did not stay in the West End.   The people were friendly. There were no street gangs, you just got on with your life. I don't know that there is anything now to compare with it".

"Life was warm and secure and full of activity as I grew up. Mum's magic saucepans could provide the extra dish for the unexpected visitor. It was always a busy household with an ever open door".

"My parents had become anglicised. Dad learned to read and write English, and Mum was learning new words every day from the radio. There had always been music at home; first with our piano [it is astonishing how many families found space for a piano in their crowded accommodation], and many an evening was occupied by Pearl and me pirouetting around. Then there was the hand wind-up gramophone, and I spent many an hour on the floor listening to *Minnie the Moocher* or *Ten Cents a Dance* which always filled me with sadness, although it was years later before I fully understood why, and its connection with the 1920s Depression. Our first radio worked by an accumulator. One was in use while another was being charged in a shop along the street. And of course the one in use always faded during a play, and one of us would run to the shop, pick up the charged battery, and then race home as fast as our legs would carry us."

"We had lovely neighbours, and in our house of six flats, two on each floor, each family had children, so we had lots of playmates".

"We lived in a cocoon, a Jewish one of course".

"I was deliriously happy. It's very difficult trying to explain to people, we lived in rubbish, we lived in filth and crap really, it was a dreadful slum, but I had a blissful time. I was an only child, and I had like 3,000 brothers and sisters. And, of course, there was Regent's Park, that was like a back-garden. I used to spend a couple of hours there every morning and come back feeling better. We didn't have any ready cash, but we had everything else".

"I think the main thing about that district, in those days, was that it wasn't a ghetto, but there was a Jewish community with an infra-structure of some depth".

"I have very fond memories of growing up in the West End; there was a special feeling about the place. My father was a member of Manette Street *shul*; I remember on Rosh Hashonah and Yom Kippur when we all assembled at the Scala Theatre where it was very comfortable and roomy, it was lovely all meeting up together. Then as we all got older the girls went to Lily Montagu's club, and the boys to the Boys' Club. At the weekend we used to go to the Boys Club' for dances, where we had a good time. It was a structured life".

"Everyone knew one another. There were bonds".

"Hooper Struve had a factory in Windmill Street, bottling lemonade. At 7 a.m. you could hear the tramp tramp of the workers in their heavy clogs, passing on their way to work. Then just before 8 o'clock the Bourne and Hollingsworth staff (housed I think in Gower Street) came through Windmill Street on the way to work in Oxford Street. Every hour brought a different sound, and one could tell the time of day by the sound in the street".

"There was a wonderful atmosphere in Broad Street. The doors were never locked. If anyone was ill, women would come and do the cooking and look after the children. If there was a death in the street, the whole street was in mourning".

"The West End was a marvellous place to live in in those days. There was no such thing as waiting for invitations -   there was an open house. If, God forbid, your mother was ill, the neighbours took over right away. Food was supplied, she was looked after, and my mother would do the same if someone else was ill. We could go into each others' houses. Everybody was friendly, and nobody needed to wait for any help, it was always given".

OTHER COMMUNITIES

The West End was very cosmopolitan and contained Englishmen, Italians, Greeks, Germans, French, Swiss and Chinese alongside first- or second-generation Russian and Polish Jews. Books on Soho and the surrounding district almost unanimously emphasise the harmony that existed between the many nationalities. This would appear to be an over-simplification of the situation. Lily Montagu, writing in 1941, recorded the attitude of the members of West Central Jewish Girls' Club to the admission of non-Jewish members:

Although giving a hearty welcome to non-Jewish workers and visitors they recently opposed, when consulted, the unrestricted introduction of non-Jewish members, even in war-time.   They are opposed to encouraging between Jews and non-Jews friendship which might lead to inter-marriage.

After World War II the Inner London Education Authority was minded to end its grant to the Girls' Club because it did not admit non-Jewish members. Bryan Montagu had a difficult time trying to persuade them, eventually successfully, that the grant should continue.

There were a few non-Jewish members of the Boys' Clubs' football and cricket teams, but for the most part non-Jewish members were not encouraged.   As Sidney Bunt says in his book *Jewish Youth Work in Britain*, many Jewish clubs thought that uncertainty about the stranger's intentions made it imprudent to invite him inside the gates, and the apprehension of possible defectors, through proselytising or intermarriage, also led to caution.

It would perhaps be truer to say of community relations in the West End that there was an absence of disharmony. Most groups kept themselves to themselves. Although neighbours would give each other friendly greetings when they met, Jewish shopkeepers pass the time of day with Italian restaurateurs, and Jewish mothers chat with Italian mothers as they did their washing in the communal laundry, really close relationships did not exist on a general scale. The best friends of Jews were Jews, of Chinese other Chinese, of Italians other Italians, with the occasional exceptions of course, and this is confirmed by an analysis of the interviews conducted for this book.

"We did not mix much with the Italians or other local people.   There were a number of Italian restaurants, there were German and French also, but basically the largest numbers were the Jews and the Italians.   I remember the Italian restaurants and the Italian grocery shops.   One big grocery shop was at the bottom of Wardour Street and was called Parmigiani Filio. There were two Italian newspaper shops in Old Compton Street. One is still in existence at the corner of Old Compton Street and Dean Street. There is a shoe shop, who made ballet shoes, very famous, Gamba. Next door was a newsagent and I remember particularly they used to have a poster outside when the Italian newspapers arrived 'I giornali Italiani son arrivati'. When we were in the *Admiral Duncan* in Old Compton Street immediately opposite us was an Italian barber shop and we used to go there for our haircuts and a shampoo occasionally. There were no quarrels between us".

"There were a lot of Jews in Grafton Street - nearly all the houses were taken up with Jews, but there was a little section of Whitfield Street which is round the corner from where I lived, which was all Italian families living there. And in fact during the war, when the war was on, they interned all the men".

"The Second World War had the effect of drawing all the people of the West End a bit closer together. We felt badly about so many of the Italians who were taken away to internment camps as Enemy Aliens, and of course this happened to lots of Jewish German refugees as well.   There was a lovely Italian couple who lived in Saville Street. Mrs Rota was a dressmaker. Her husband was interned, and the next thing we heard was that he went down with hundreds of other Italians on the *Andora Star*, the ship that was taking them to Canada".

"The whole area was very cosmopolitan, with Italians, Greeks, French and the first black people to move in the area. To us, black people were quite a normal event.
Any contact with any non-Jewish families round Whitfield Street?

No - although I suppose there was some. Our school was Jewish and we were brought up in a very Jewish neighbourhood - a very Jewish environment. There were non-Jews but we never played with any that I remember. When we went to Lyulph Stanley there weren't so many Jewish children there, but even then we didn't play with the others. We went to school and we came home and our friends were next door and round the corner".

"I've always made friends easily, but all our social life was in the Club from a very early age. We lived in Tottenham Court Road, and Alfred Place was just across the road. Our whole social life was there, and the school, the junior school, where you really played was all Jewish or practically, and when we went to Lyulph Stanley we didn't really have much time. You went to school, you did your lessons, you came home for lunch, which was two hours. We used to get a 1d return on the tram, and if we wanted to save the ½d we would walk back to Mornington Crescent, quite a walk. So there wasn't a lot of socialising. I don't remember any friends from that school. When I went to work it was a Jewish firm, all the furriers were Jews weren't they? I don't remember any non-Jewish friends".

"We mixed a bit through sport. There was the local football team. Kelly, he was Irish, and he was a carpenter. He used to make the goalposts. We hired a pitch at Regent's Park, but we had to carry the goalposts so we made a small cart on four wheels and he made the goalposts which were collapsible, and we used to wheel it along. Half the team were Gentiles and half Jews. We did not go to each other's houses. We went to one, his parents were German, but only to collect him, we did not stay".

"We got on well with our neighbours. I cannot recall a single fight between a Jew and say a Frenchman or an Italian who lived in great numbers in Soho. There were always relationships, amicable relationships between the Jews on the one hand and the other people on the other. The local English boys were rough, tough, and could be difficult to get on with, but I cannot recall a single incident of a quarrel between Jew and Gentile in the way that one might expect".

Oswald Mosley's Fascists had a recruiting office in Regent Street, and Schmidt's Restaurant in Charlotte Street was one of their meeting places. Speakers' Corner provided a platform, but they were directly challenged there, and there are no records of street fighting in the West End on the scale experienced in the East End both before and after the Second World

War. For a time after the war the anti-fascist 43 Group had offices in Panton Street. Its location in the heart of the West End, with people and traffic passing by most hours of the day and night, made it safe from attack. Its proximity to Piccadilly and Leicester Square tube stations and a host of bus routes enabled its members to reach all points of London quickly should the need arise. Anti-semitism existed in the West End, no doubt, but it was never on a scale to threaten the Jewish West End community.

YIDDISH

For the West End community, particularly those who lived in Soho and Fitzrovia, it was not essential to be able to speak English. There were enough Yiddish-speaking relatives, neighbours and shopkeepers in the 'village' to make it possible to survive on Yiddish alone.

"We all spoke Yiddish. I spoke Yiddish before I went to school. When I went to the grocers and the fruiterer I spoke in Yiddish, and the older generation spoke Yiddish. My father learnt English for gambling, the one o'clock *Star* when they made a bet, and a four o'clock *Star* for the winners. We had a man who lived local who spoke several languages. He taught the Russian children English and did the log-books of the tailors. They used him to write up their books every Friday so that they could get their wages because they could not read or write in English".

"My mother couldn't read or write English and spoke only Yiddish, but she used to travel all over London on the tubes and buses and although she couldn't read the names of the stations or the streets she knew exactly where to get off. She had some method by which she knew, and she was excellent at reckoning".

"They spoke in Yiddish and we used to answer them in English. Eventually, I taught my mother to read the newspaper. She never had any schooling, yet she could read and write Yiddish, and she could *daven* very well".

"My parents spoke Yiddish at home. In school I spoke English, but when I got home I had to speak Yiddish, which I can to this very day".

"My parents spoke Yiddish at home, but they curtailed it because they wanted us to speak English".

"I was born in October 1924. Yiddish was spoken all around me, but I only recall speaking English. However I must have soaked it up like a sponge, for in my twenties I discovered I could hold a conversation in Yiddish".

"It appears to me that the young men I mixed with in the 1920s were anxious to get into the general society and not isolate themselves, anxious not to speak Yiddish as though doing so would set them apart from the influence they wanted to acquire".

"My father was a frequent cinema and theatre goer but he couldn't read or write English other than a few words. He spoke broken English because he was already in his teens when he came here. He had lessons, and he did become naturalised, but he never mastered thc language. He could reckon though; he put his figures down and reckoned in Yiddish so quickly - I could never reckon like that. As a business man he did well".

STREET ACTIVITIES

"We played in the street, there was no traffic and no danger. We had a street lamp outside and that was our wicket for playing cricket and our goal post for football".

"All we worried about was football and cricket. When we played cricket in Poland Street there was a traffic island which we used as a wicket. If the ball was hit straight it would go down the ladies' lavatory and we had to go down and ask for it back. The woman in charge was a tartar, so I hated fielding there".

"There were horses and carts going by in the streets and we had the game of hanging on to the back of the cart to see how far we could go. We made our own scooters, and girls played hop scotch".

"Do any of the children of today with their mechanical toys have the same pleasure we enjoyed? The rope double-tied round a lamp post, sitting in the loop, kicking the post, and swinging round. The joys of 'tibby', hitting with a large piece of wood a small 4" piece tapered to a point at each end and seeing how far we could swing it. Playing rounders, cricket, marbles, bringing out our scrapbooks and exchanging, all this on the pavement and curbs of Windmill Street".

"In the Haymarket, running right through to Coventry Street, was a fun fair, we played on all the different things, we took sixpence or a shilling with us. If you won you got ten Players' cigarettes. We became so skilled at the ball games they stopped us playing".

"In the summer my mum used to get a box from Berwick Street Market and sit outside in the hot evenings with the other women to compare and watch the passers-by. There was a lot going on. Our next door neighbours were tailors and they used to work all night long. People would come up and talk to them while they were working".

"First the cats' meat man came round. You threw him a penny and he hurled a piece of meat into your doorway. Then the muffin man came, then at teatime a Jewish man from the East End with cakes and biscuits in a basket and little sweet bagels on a string. Rag-and-bone carts came round, offering ornaments in exchange for junk. Then there were barrel organs. There was one organ-grinder who dressed up as a gypsy and had a parrot; when you put a penny in his tin the parrot jumped in a box and gave you a folded-up paper fortune. There were musicians, like the blind violinist and his daughter who sang. Another man did magic tricks. The police used to make the pedlars go away, because they were collecting people round them and were a nuisance. They'd move on, but a few minutes later they'd come back. And all the time there would be another one waiting round the corner".

"The self-styled Ras Prince Monolulu with his Indian head-dress paraded the streets selling racing tips, attracting customers with his famous cry, 'I Gotta Horse! I Gotta Horse!'. He was a lovely man who brightened people's lives".

"Ours was a busy street [Wells Street], a mixture of flats, shops and commerce. When business closed for the day, and the large horse-drawn carts left the streets, we children, together with the sparrows and pigeons, would take over. We had simple games which were governed by a mysterious season time clock. Skipping ropes would appear and then at a hidden message would disappear. Ball games would be the in-game, or diabolos, or scooters. Pearl and I owned a small 3-wheeled bicycle, and never seemed to mind sharing, or the limited area to cycle in. There were spinning tops, that with each season we had to learn how to tie the string round the top for a good long spin; yo-yos, hopscotch, with chalk 'borrowed' from my father's workroom; 'feet off the ground', the coal hole covers being the safe ground; and of course 'he', the chasing game that never staled".

OUTINGS

"Our Shabbos afternoons were spent visiting local attractions such as the British Museum, the National Art Gallery and the Tate Gallery. We visited all the parks and particularly enjoyed watching football being played in Regent's Park. What a world of interest the West End of London offered a young boy. I used to walk down Charing Cross Road to look at all the books on display on the shelves there. I used to love looking at these old books, wanting to buy some of them but never having the money.   Father loved walking. We used to walk to Hyde Park, mainly it was St James' Park because he wanted to see the King or Queen come out of Buckingham Palace so that he could make the *brocha* when you see royalty. He knew the corpulent Inspector who stood outside whenever the King or some member of the Royal family was moving in or out. We had a cue, as it were, to the comings and goings of royalty. So there we stood, everybody took off their hats but Lewis, old man Lewis and his family all kept their hats solemnly on, and muttered the appropriate blessing at the sight of royalty. 'Blessed are thou O Lord our God, who distributes his glory to Man.' To see the King was a highlight for my father. The Inspector knew him because father was a very garrulous sort of person who would go up and ask him when the King was coming and the Inspector would say, 'Wait grandpa, wait, be patient'. So there grandpa waited. He called him grandpa because he wore a King George V beard".

"We had a most marvellous life. In the evenings we walked round to the Lyons Corner House and we had a cup of coffee and a pastry for about sixpence. And there were bands on every floor, and entertainment. And the boys came along and sat with you, and at weekends we had egg mayonnaise and a coffee for 1/6d. We were out every night. It was safe".

"Our outings consisted of walks to the lovely parks, taking in the highways and byways of Mayfair and St James, Green Park, St James' Park and Hyde Park, Regent's Park and even as far as the Albert Memorial in Kensington Gardens, at about the age of six! There were visits to the museums and picture galleries, the London Museum, which in those days was in Marlborough House at the side of Green Park, being my favourite. I am very grateful for this introduction to things cultural".

"The excitement when the day of *The Fitzroy Tavern* outing came!   Early in the morning the street began filling up and your ticket referred to the number of the coach   ...   Can anyone imagine the picture?   Coach after coach of happy screaming youngsters - we were on our way, our wonderful day had arrived, and everything we had looked forward to for a year had arrived. I think we went to Brickett's Wood or Eastcote or some such place. There was a fair ground with donkey rides and everything a kid could wish for.   By comparison to what children of today have, it seems very little".

"Where the Dominion Theatre stands, I can still recall the Luna Park, that giant fun fair that conjures up for me a picture of a high diver descending into a small flaming tank".

"On leaving school in 1938 most of my social life was in the West Central Girls' Club, with the cinema and theatres as close runners-up; weekend strolls along Oxford Street to a Corner House for tea, or a milk-bar for a knickerbocker glory".

"As we got older we had the Paramount Dance Hall and the Astoria Dance Hall, and we went to both. We went tea dancing at the Paramount. You had to be a Sunday member to go to the Astoria. It was wonderful, always packed out with Jewish boys and girls. We danced to all the named bands, Ivor Kirchin, Joe Loss. I knew the Jewish musicians well enough to nod to them because I lived near Archer Street, the meeting place for the musicians".

"We used to go to the Savoy, and on Sunday afternoons the Savoy Orpheans played. Five shillings with tea, but in the evenings it was £2 or £3. Society people went then. We were too young and did not have enough money for that. Other tea dances elsewhere were 3/6 to 5/-, so we could afford it on a Sunday. This was where we met boys and had dates. That is how I met my husband. After we were engaged we went to dinner at the Regent Palace Hotel, and for 5/- we had four courses and music and dancing".

"The West End was safe, we could walk anywhere. When we went to Hyde Park on Sunday morning, it was a fashion parade. You wore a hat, gloves, and a mink tie with a head that clipped on".

"My father was very keen on sport, although he didn't have the opportunity to participate himself.   He was particularly interested in football and the year he got married the Chelsea Football Club was founded [1905] and he immediately followed them as it was so easy to get there on a 14 bus from Shaftesbury Avenue which took him direct to the ground for 2d, and from that day he supported Chelsea.   As we got older we too would go to Chelsea, about four miles away.   We would walk half way to save a halfpenny and got in for sixpence.   There could be thousands there, but never once was there a fight".

"On summer days we used to meet our cousins, aunts, and uncles who all lived nearby. We walked to Regent's Park, on the way buying a penny bag of peanuts to feed the birds. We used to take a picnic and had a marvellous tea, the aunts and uncles sitting and talking, and the children playing to their hearts content.   These Sunday afternoons were a wonderful 'get together'. We all gathered at the same spot every good-weather weekend. How is it that the weather always seemed to be good?"

ENTERTAINMENTS

The Jews of the West End were never far away from the world of entertainment, and even the theatre became part of the everyday culture of working-class families.

"There wasn't a show my parents didn't see. My father knew all the seating plans in all the theatres. He wouldn't go to the London Pavilion because there were too many pillars. He couldn't read or write English, but he could understand.   My parents got an awful lot of pleasure from living near the theatres. They had a good and happy life".

"I didn't start going to the theatre until I was 14, and then at that age we used to go to the gallery.   I saw *Tea for Two*, you know, things like that. There was a theatre in Oxford Street, near where Maison Lyons, the Corner House, was in Tottenham Court Road. Lovely reviews were there; the Oxford Theatre I think it was called".

[The Oxford Theatre, one of the best-known music halls, opened on the corner of Tottenham Court Road and Oxford Street in 1861. After two fires it was completely rebuilt in 1892.   Marie Lloyd topped the bill on the first night and sang 'Oh Mr Porter'. In 1917 C B Cochran converted it into a theatre and staged spectacular revues. In 1924 he brought Lilian Baylis's

Shakespearian company from the Old Vic to the West End for the benefit of visitors to the British Empire Exhibition. The theatre was closed and demolished in 1926. A Lyons Corner House was built on the site.]

"On Monday nights a big crowd of us used to go to the Palladium, about 30 or 40 of us; some paid and some forgot to pay.   There was a tobacconist nearby called, I think, Krasnick, and many a star used to go in, like for instance Gracie Fields, and they would talk to all of us locals. We helped to make stars of them".

"My Auntie Ray lived in Meard Court right in the West End. She was a 'First Nighter' and used to mix with all the theatricals. She was wonderful, a character, and she used to take us all to the theatre when we were kids, queue up outside, you known, and take us in the gallery".

"I started going to the Opera, the Old Vic, on Saturday evenings, and for sixpence you could buy the libretto of the opera. When the Old Vic closed down for opera I went to Sadler's Wells, and the Italian season at Covent Garden. I would line up all night".

"We went to the theatre, mostly musicals, at the Palladium, the Coliseum, and the Alhambra.   We used to go to the Old Middlesex - we called it the 'Old Mo' - in Drury Lane. We got in on a Saturday afternoon for fourpence. Mrs Fulberg used to go with a friend with a carrier of food and passed us cakes and bits. They took a whole picnic up in the gallery".

"In about 1915 my father was an impressario.   When I was a little boy he opened a theatre - a Yiddish theatre in Ingestre Place.   I think at one time it was a cinema. My father took it and used it as a theatre. He tried to bring Yiddish theatre from the East End to the West End".

"I clearly remember being taken to the Yiddish theatre in New Cavendish Street in about 1935 or 1936. In a very large room. It may have been a workshop during the day. But they set up a stage and they put on a Yiddish Theatre performance. I can also remember going to the Scala to Yiddish performances, and also to the Garrick Theatre where a famous Yiddish actor, Morris Moscovitch from America, came and performed classical plays, even Shakespeare, in Yiddish. Occasionally they would show Yiddish films at the Scala Theatre as well, on a Sunday. Just one-offs".

"In about 1936, when I was nine, I sold apples and crisps at the Yiddish Theatre which performed in the St James' and Soho Working Men's Club in Greek Street, off Bateman Street. The customers used to pinch my cheeks until they stung. It was not a Jewish club, but there were a few Jewish members, including my father who spent his time there playing dominoes while my mother sat in our freezing shop seven days a week to earn a living. It had a proper stage, with dressing rooms behind, and I think the actors used to hire the hall. There was a stall in a side room where they sold bagels and chopped herring before the performance and during the interval. A play would be put on most weekends, and I can remember Itzkovitch, Meir Tzelniker, Max Goldberg, and Rosa and Harry Gold performing there. The audience participation was intense. They reacted to everything. Each word was believed, and there were constant cries of *Oy veh*. I think the tickets were 6d and 9d".

The West End was full of cinemas, and the children loved them all.

"I loved living in the West End because I loved the cinema, and there were cinemas all over the place. South, north, east and west, and I knew them all. I was a regular punter. There was the Euston cinema in Euston Road, and the Paramount, which was just below Warren Street station, which was quite superb, and two or three others in Tottenham Court Road. There was the Tolmer Cinema, just round the corner. That was awful, that was a flea-pit. But we did not mind in those days, it was all good fun".

"As kids we used to go to the Pix Cinema in Great Windmill Street, opposite the famous Windmill Theatre. It was a flea pit. We used to see Tom Mix, Fatty Arbuckle, Mary Pickford. It was threepence to go in. We used to stand on the seats and wave like anything at all the cowboy films. My mother was an avid cinema goer. I can remember going with her when I was very young, and, as with every Jewish mother, she never went out without taking something to eat. She was peeling an orange and squeezing it, and the juice squirted on to the head of a man sitting behind who cried out 'Blimey, the roof's leaking'.   I remember being told the story by another friend whose mother took her family to the Stoll Opera House, always in the gods. She used to take a couple of bottles of milk and sandwiches. Now in the gods there were very, very, steep stone steps. One of the bottles she had rested on a step fell over, and in the middle of an aria it went bang, bang, bang, all the way to the bottom; and to the horror and embarrassment of my friend everyone in the theatre, including the orchestra, turned and looked up. When the super cinemas were built in the thirties queues would start to form two hours or more before the performance started. But what a performance! A first-rate stage show, the news, the organ, a 'B' film, and then the major film".

"You could go to the Majestic and Carlton in Tottenham Court Road for ninepence, and if you had the extra 3d you could go to the Dominion for a shilling, in the back. Sometimes we would bunk into the emergency doors without paying".

"On Fridays we started at Jews' Free School at 9 in the morning, had lunch from 12-1 instead of to 2, and finished at 2.30. 95 per cent of the school ran up Tottenham Court Road to get into the Tolmer Cinema because before 3 it cost only 3d.   They showed all the old films for which they paid scarcely any rent. Every four or five weeks they would show *Scarface* or *I was a Fugitive from a Chain Gang*, and the dialogue of those films is impregnated in my memory".

"You could never walk quietly in or out of the Carlton or Majestic in Tottenham Court Road, known as 'the flea pit' and 'the bug hole'. You crunched your way along the floor covered with peanut shells and empty crisp bags".

CONCERTS

Living in the West End made it easy to acquire a love of music too.

"There were Sunday concerts at the Albert Hall, 50 people were allowed in free in the gallery to overcome the entertainments law, and I heard many wonderful artists of the day in this way. I remember the first appearance of Yehudi Menuhin as a boy of 12. I lined up all night for one of the Sunday afternoon concerts".

"Theatres, well we couldn't afford them. But I went to concerts at the Queen's Hall on Sundays when there were always a certain number of free tickets given out. My sister Bella, my brother Percy, my brother Leon, me, used to have an early lunch and wait an hour in the queue for people who were going to get in free. And then they led us behind the orchestra. The orchestra was below us, and the audience was far away. We could survey every instrument. Of course, it was very noisy. It wasn't the same as having a seat out in the auditorium, but did we enjoy those concerts. That is where we acquired our love of music".

PROSTITUTION AND PORNOGRAPHY

West End prostitution was most conspicuous in Soho. Before the 1960s, when the Street Offences Act drove most of the girls off the streets and back into their flats, they would parade openly. Many of their 'beats' were in the Jewish areas and they became part of the scene of growing up. Although there was considerable fear in the Jewish community, particularly among clergy and some parents, that prostitutes could be an unhealthy influence, there is no direct evidence that they were. The locals would witness occasional acts of violence between the girls and their pimps, but did not become personally involved.

"My *cheder* was in an area surrounded by prostitutes. I was only 10 or 11, or even younger, and we boys became very friendly with them and had nicknames for them. There was one very nice person we called 'Gifty' because she always gave us sweets and little presents. When I came out of *cheder* I used to go and stand with her in Frith Street, opposite Manette Street. She gave me a squash of the cheek and a peck, and I would stand with her because I liked her. I knew what she was, and she knew that I liked her. If she had a customer, she would say, 'I won't be five minutes, Louis, if you want to wait, wait'. In those days they were quick! She would come down and carry on as if nothing had happened. She never said a wrong word to me, or swore, was always very kind, and when she thought it was time for me to go home she would say, 'Go on Louis, see you tomorrow'. My parents never knew this. My brother knew. He was part of it. It was part of our lives, so much so that when I came out of the army and was walking down Shaftesbury Avenue I went over to her. She thought I was a client, and I said to her 'Gifty!' and she said, 'Is that really Louis?' and she started to cry, and I had a lump in my throat because my youth came before me, and I cuddled her and she called the other girls over and she said, 'Go on, Louis, tell them what a good-looking woman I was', and I said she wasn't just good looking she was handsome. When I went back a few weeks later she had gone, and nobody knew what had happened to her. She had been part of my life. There were Jewish prostitutes but I would rather not speak about that".

"I had my barmitzvah in the West End Talmud Torah in 1907. In my day, Soho was not the strip and porn of today".

"There were lots of prostitutes. From Berwick Street to Tottenham Court Road, we used to have to avoid them walking up and down. My mother gave us rules of how to behave if a man followed us.   A crowd of us, boys and girls, about 8-9 o'clock at night, used to go in a crowd down to Lisle Street and stand looking at the prostitutes. And they would swear at us and ask, 'What are you looking at?' We used to stand there laughing at them. I remember the French girls looking very glamourous with eye make-up. No one wore eye make-up unless she was no good. But the prostitutes were fascinating to look at, and were very smart, not like King's Cross now, dirty and deadbeats".

"It may come as a surprise to know that some Jewish women were members of the oldest profession and were very proud of their religion, having the appellation 'Yiddisher' attached to their names. And whether you believe it or not, they did not work on *Shabbos*".

"I used to talk to all the tarts near Gerrard Street and Manette Street and Greek Street, because we used to go to *shul* through Dean Street and Greek Street, and they used to see us going in our *Shabbos* best.   We were probably lovely looking children, and they were very friendly souls and they used to talk to us and say 'Are you going to the synagogue now?' We sometimes even used to enlist a tart to turn on the lights on the Sabbath or turn them out. They were our *Shabbos Goy*".

"On the corner of Manette Street and Charing Cross Road was Foyles. Between Foyles and the *shul* was a tall house which was a knocking shop. It was said that some of the worshippers would sometimes go up to the knocking shop first before going to *shul*. I believe there was a lot of truth in that".

"There were many prostitutes in our street [Wells Street] but they never bothered us and we never bothered them".

"In Wardour Street where I had my shop there were prostitutes outside. They were nice girls and came in to buy hats. If one had a hat which she thought brought her luck, they would all follow suit. But they never bothered us and we never bothered them. Everyone lived quietly and peacefully with each other. I think I must have been a very nosy child; if I stopped to look at one of them they would give me money to go away."

VI - OCCUPATIONS

The working Jews who settled in the West End in the second half of the 18th century, many of them congregants of the Western Synagogue, were largely employed in servicing the rich, the idle and the fashionable who lived there. They engaged in luxury trades such as high-class tailoring, jewellery, gold-embroidering for military and court uniforms; and in callings such as portrait-painting, engraving, and antique-dealing. Several operated from shops in the Strand. The rate books show they were fairly comfortably off and belonged to the merchant, artisan and shop-keeper classes, a social stratum far removed from the poor Jewish pedlars of the East End.

The members of the Maiden Lane congregation, founded in 1810, had a wider spread of occupations and they included a number of fruit merchants trading in Covent Garden Market, tailors, boot makers, general merchants, brokers, quill-makers, umbrella-makers, corn-cutters, hatters, cab proprietors, furriers, musicians, watch makers, cigar makers, jewellers and engravers.

In the last quarter of the 19th century the moneylenders to the aristocracy, about half of whom were Jewish, congregated around Piccadilly and Old Bond Street. By the turn of the century some staple Jewish trades became less prominent. There were fewer Jewish shoe and boot makers, furriers and cigarette makers, and comparatively few West End Jews engaged in cabinet making, despite the tradition of furniture making in Fitzrovia. Tailoring remained predominant, particularly in Soho and Fitzrovia, and there were more than sufficient West End Jewish shopkeepers - grocers, butchers and restaurateurs - to cater for the Jewish trade - and a surprisingly high number of Jewish publicans.

Situated in the heart of the entertainment industry, West End Jews were well represented in the film industry in Wardour Street, the theatres of Shaftesbury Avenue, including theatrical costumiers, the music publishers in Denmark Street and the musicians who gathered in Archer Street. Several Jewish West End estate agents and developers were involved in the post-World War II property boom.

THE TAILORS

By the beginning of the 20th century, when the majority of West End Jews resided in Soho and Fitzrovia, the employment situation had completely changed. By far the highest percentage was engaged in tailoring, including allied trades such as dressmaking and buttonhole making. (See Rachele Kalman's research notes in Appendix III). Of those who married at the Western Synagogue between 1837 and 1945, 34 per cent were in the tailoring trade. Although the remainder covered a fairly wide spectrum, no other occupation exceeded 5 per cent. In 1914, no less than 90 per cent of the parents of Jewish children at Upper Marylebone Street School described themselves as tailors. The records of Pulteney School covering the period from 1914 to 1977 give the figure of 54 per cent, indicating a gradual overall decline. Many West End Jews owned shops that supplied or fed off the tailoring trade - trimmings shops, dress shops and men's outfitters. Such shops were particularly abundant in Berwick Street, Shaftesbury Avenue and Oxford Street.

The predominance of tailoring applied equally to the East End and the West End, but there was a difference. The *Jewish Chronicle* of 5 May 1872 reported that 'the better class of tailoring is but little effected in the East End, though it is adopted to a considerable extent in the Western or Soho colony of Jews'. The West End tailor handled more of the specialised high-quality work, which was natural given that the centres of up-market trade were Savile Row and the Oxford Street stores. But despite the fact that many craftsmen tailors in the West End serviced the Savile Row establishments, the Jewish tailor in London was predominantly a ladies' man.

Working conditions in the West End also appear to have been superior, and there are no reports comparable to the description of an East End workshop in *The Lancet* in 1884:

In Hanbury Street, we found eighteen workers crowded in a small room measuring eight yards by four and a half yards and not quite eight feet high ... working in the heat of the gas and the stove, warming the pressing irons, surrounded by mounds of dust and chips from the cut cloth, breathing an atmosphere full of woollen particles containing more or less injurious dyes, it is not surprising that so large a proportion of working tailors break down from diseases of the respiratory organs.

Tailoring work in the West End was as hard and seasonal, and the hours just as long as in the East End, and there were some small factories, but for the most part the West End tailor created his own working conditions at home, often in the front parlour of a two-roomed flat where the work-table was also used for family meals or Passover celebrations. In her book *Soho* Judith Summers quotes Michael Klinger:

My father would finish work at 9.30 p m, maybe 10 o'clock, and fall asleep at the table while he was having supper. Then he'd get up again at two o'clock in the morning in order to get the work ready for the tailors to take back and sew the buttons on in the morning. My father had one or two men working for him and they also started work at 2 a.m. They'd start pressing, the fourteen-pound gas-irons would start banging, and they would be talking, and my brother and I slept right through it all on our mattresses under the work-table. And I slept better then than I do now. Hard work is putting it mildly - for as long as I can remember my father was working eighteen or nineteen hours a day. Saturday he would work in the mornings - he hated that, because he was a religious man. But there was nothing he could do about it. If one of my father's workers did not turn up for the early morning shift, I or my brother would be turfed out of our bed underneath the work-table and, still in our pyjamas, go round to the man's house to wake him up.

There was very little organisation in the industry. Jews generally were not natural union members, and only a small minority of Jewish tailoring workers belonged to a trade union. The Amalgamated Society of Tailors and Tailoresses had a branch in Regent Street in 1872, but for many years the foreign-born were not admitted. In 1903, the Society opened a Jewish branch, and within a short time it boasted a membership of 200. However it fell to 140 the following year and shortly afterwards terminated its activities. The West London Jewish Tailors' Union had 67 members in 1908, 100 in 1909, and 98 in 1910, but that too disappeared from view. The Workers' Union founded in 1898 by Tom Mann embraced a wide range of workers, including Jewish tailors, and some Soho tailors became members, but it never secured a firm foothold. There was a strike of West End tailors and tailoresses in 1912, and East End tailors came out in sympathy, but it was soon settled.

The opening of the underground station at Oxford Circus in 1900, and the improved omnibus service to Oxford Street, made the West End stores accessible to a wider section of the general community, and this led to a significant increase in the sale of ladies' clothing. The East End dominated the cheaper end of the blouse and mantle business, but after the First World War small-scale mantle-making factories began to appear both north and south of Oxford Street, and the wholesale manufacturing of dresses, coats and suits really took off. The area around Middlesex Hospital became the headquarters of the ladies' clothing industry, and many leading manufacturers had their showrooms in Great Portland Street and Margaret Street.

"The men's trade used jacket makers, trouser makers and waistcoat makers, each of which was a separate trade. They in turn would use pressers, buttonhole and felling hands, and also visiting journeymen machiners who would come in to do the number of hours necessary. Pressers lived precarious lives and worked terrible unsocial hours. If a garment was finished at 7 p.m. and had to be delivered at 9 a.m. the following day, the pressers would have to work through the night to finish it in time. I remember Shayer Kessler who worked as a presser until well into his 90's. He died at 96 years of age, so the steam and physical strain of pressing with 14lb irons did not do him any harm. Tailors needed trimmings, and within a few streets there were at least nine trimmings shops all of which prospered. Originally Savile Row work was done inside the tailors' workrooms, but with the arrival of the Jewish tailors from Poland and Russia it became viable and more economical to employ them as outworkers. Sometimes the garments were cut inside, taken to first fitting and then given out to outworkers. Or, alternatively, just cut inside and given out. The work had to be taken to shop (it was always called 'shop') three times for fittings and brought back to be worked on and finished. Hence the importance of being close by. Some tailors progressed to owning their own businesses with their own clients. Many wholesale businesses became large concerns and went public".

"I was a dress designer. When we first started dresses it was easy. A straight piece with a hole for arm-holes   Gradually they got more tailored".

Few customers could have had any conception of the conditions in which the coats and suits they purchased from Savile Row or the superior West End stores were made.

"My father had his workshop in the flat in which we lived. I can remember from about the age of three all the greatcoats being made up and piled in the passage and me sleeping on them in the afternoon".

"My father worked for a Savile Row firm on admirals' uniforms. I can remember seeing them hanging up in his workroom with all the epaulettes. He made the garments and sewed on the gold braid. They were sent down from Jenner's in Princes Street, Edinburgh".

Everyone in the family, including the children, helped with the work:

"After school you had your tea, went to *cheder*, came home at about seven, and your father made you go into his workshop and help him for an hour or two before going to bed. I stayed at school until the age of 14. I was interested in painting. I still am, but my father said, 'A painter, you'll never make a living'. So I became a tailor and started with my father. That's what happened in those days. I finished up with my own business in Savile Row".

"My father was a master tailor. He worked very, very, very hard and this must have applied to everybody. He had a workshop in Charlotte Street, and I can still remember as a kid that when we came back from *cheder* my mother would give me a jug of tea and I would run as quickly as I could without spilling anything to Charlotte Street, that is from Broad Street, hoping that the tea would still be warm. He was a Royal Tailor. He never made the trousers. He made the jackets, riding jackets, and overcoats and the lounge suits for the Royal Household".

"Minnie won three scholarships but she still went in the workshop. My father trained her. She did buttonholes, the best buttonholer in London I'd say.   As children we also helped. We used to have to take the coats to the pressers, pull out the bastings, go with the garments to the tailors in Sackville Street and Savile Row and leave them for fittings, and then we had to take the finished garments. Originally my father kept *Shabbos*, but he often had to collect work on Saturdays, and it was only in the slack period that he could go to *shul* regularly".

"My father's workshop was in Broadwick Street, and I came up to him one day as he was making a coat, a beautiful silk coat for the present Queen and I said to him, 'Why are you machining in red cotton?' and he told me off for interfering. Then he looked and noticed it was not quite right. In fact he was colour blind and he had to rip the whole coat and re-do it, and in the end it was fine. All the family were colour blind, and the wrong colour lining often went in the Burberry coats".

Thomas Burberry who was not Jewish but had many Jewish employees, took premises in the Haymarket in 1901. His firm supplied wind-, dust-, cold- and rain-proof coats, motor caps and tie-on hoods for open-air motoring. It also made Burberry-proofed silk dust coats for hot weather, and clothing for the armed forces, polar expeditions and mountaineering.

"My husband was a tailor and he got £5 for a suit and it took him all week".

"My father was a gentlemen's tailor as were all our *landslei*t [persons from the same part of the old country]. We had about fifty cousins, second cousins, third cousins and fourth cousins and nearly everyone was in the trade working for Savile Row. That is why we all lived around Berwick Street and Broadwick Street and D'Arblay Street, and a few on the other side of Oxford Street, because we had to be near to Savile Row".

"My mother wanted to go to Golders Green, even before the First World War, but they couldn't because my father had 'specials' that they used to bring in at 6 o'clock in the evening. The cutter would bring in work for a suit to be prepared for a fitting for a customer who was leaving for India, say, the next day. So in the workshop we had to work in the evening. It was also our drawing room. My aunts all came up for cups of tea and were entertained there, and through all this my father was preparing the suit for the next day's fitting. The customer went away for two months and when he came back the suit had to be altered, his figure had changed".

"I joined my father who was a top-class bespoke tailor making waistcoats, supplying shops like Peter Robinson in Oxford Street, Grieves of Regent Street and Robinson Cleaver in Regent Street".

"Harry and Maurice (Bert) Helman, the sons of an immigrant tailor from Lodz in Poland, started in business together in 1928 in three rooms at 51 Old Compton Street, paying a rent of £100 per annum. They graduated to magnificent showrooms in Bruton Street with the atmosphere of an exclusive London Club.   In the late 1960s when President Nixon was in office, Walter Annenberg, his Ambassador to England, became a customer and, in all, 17 suits were made for him. A unique feature was the making of three dinner suits with the waistband made as a cummerbund attached to the trousers.They also made eight velvet jackets, all in different colours, for him to wear for golfing at his own course in Palm Springs. Walter Annenberg introduced Sir Evelyn de Rothschild, and such was his high regard for them that when Bert had been ill and had recovered sufficiently to return to work, every day, for six weeks, Sir Evelyn sent his car and chauffeur to take him to and from work.   Mohammed Ali became a client when he was in London to fight Henry Cooper. Peter Sellers became a valued client, as did the Fox family of actors and Terence Stamp. To look through the heavy and well-worn order books you could be thumbing through the pages of *Who's Who*. The names of famous men (and their measurements) from all over the world are hand-written there".

Although tailoring was the main occupation of West End Jews, a great many were shopkeepers, market traders, publicans and caterers. The following extracts from interviews are intended to give a flavour of some shops and restaurants in the area and revive a few memories for former West Enders. The spelling of names is as they were given, occasionally two or more spellings for the same person. Sometimes different members of the same family anglicised their names in different ways. Without further extensive time-consuming research there is no way of knowing which is correct, but the context should indicate who is intended. Furthermore, recollections of dates are sometimes inaccurate, wandering from one decade to another without indication that this has occurred, and some inter-·viewees gave no dates at all. In Appendix III are lists extracted from the Post Office Directories of 1900, 1910, 1920, 1930, 1939, and 1950 of some of the businesses in Berwick Street, Broadwick Street, Charlotte Street, Cleveland Street, D'Arblay Street, Saville Street (Hanson Street), Wardour Street, and Windmill Street.

"There were a lot of Jewish businesses in Berwick Street. Fur shops which belonged to the brothers who later had the Houndsditch Warehouse Co., silk shops and lace shops, all Jewish. All good middle-class people. They lived above their shops and then maybe later they moved to Hampstead or Golders Green".

"The dress shops at the Oxford Street end of Berwick Street did not open until just after the First World War, when they started making wholesale dresses and ladies' coats. Before then you had to have private dressmakers. A lot of people went into the trade and became wholesalers in the East End, and they came to the West End and sold in the shops there".

"The dress shops in Berwick Street had *schleppers* [touts] outside. They stopped you at the first, the second and the third shop. They wouldn't let you get away. Once they got you in - there was pressure. It provided a marvellous living, but then they lost it. They ruined it because the customers did not have a chance to go and look. The stores got smarter. At first the stores only had things for older and middle-aged women, ordinary plain dresses. They weren't fashionable, but that changed. When the suburban shops also got more up-to-date, Berwick Street lost a lot of the trade".

"The *shleppers* gave the street such a bad name that they killed the trade. People were afraid to look in the windows".

"Dolly Lewis, the sister of the boxer Kid Lewis, was known as the *Queen of the Schleppers* in Berwick Street".

"Most of the fruit stalls in Berwick Street were non-Jewish, most of the material stalls Jewish".

"During my youth they started all those shops in Berwick Street, the Oxford Street end. The whole street became a dress street. My father bought a drapery shop from Bratters. We sold lingerie and children's clothes. I became a buyer at the age of 15, buying everything. I was given a list and sent to Jeremiah Rotherham's in Shoreditch and they looked at me like mad, you know, I was like a school kid but I knew everything - ladies' knickers, children's clothes, babies' bibs, cotton and all the ranges of drapery and ribbons - you name it, we bought it. It was a very good shop. We called it Franks. We opened a small shop in Shaftesbury Avenue and gradually enlarged it to a 50-foot frontage. It was quite a big business. We opened several other shops in different parts of London".

"Moss Bros, 21 Bedford Street, W.C.2. - Moses Moses started selling second-hand clothes in 1860. His two youngest sons, Alfred and George, opened a little shop in King Street, Covent Garden, later extending it to Bedford Street, and by 1917 had bought up other small shops until the firm occupied the whole corner site. They called themselves Moss Bros. Their famous hire service for weddings and other special occasions including coronations continues undiminished".

"I lived in Howland Street. At the corner were three brothers and Mrs Cohen who had a grocer's shop. I remember the huge barrels of herrings she used to dive in up to her elbows, and I could not bear to look. She was enormous. My father was a very high-class tailor and she used to have a coat made once a year and he had to use two tape measures to go around her, but she was a lovely lady, she was two lovely ladies!"

"Then there was the Iron Cow where we used to go along with our own jug. It was a Welsh dairy in Cleveland Street, you put a penny or two pence into a slot and pulled down a beautiful big brass handle and put the jug into a little opening and milk would come out. It must have been the forerunner of the machines we have today. We always used to wonder what was behind the wall!"

"Our local shops were just round the corner, and we never called them by their names. There was the 'milk shop', the dairy, where they had cows, in Clipstone Street. They dished it out of a churn with a big metal spoon. The owner was Welsh. On the counter was a big round white dish on a pedestal with a ham on it. It used to look so lovely, so pink, and she used to slice it so thin. We used to buy butter there, and she used two wooden things to pat them out. There was the Sweet Shop, of course and what we called the Oil Shop where we went for bits and pieces of ironmongery and for our frying oil. Bought by the pint, and we would take a bottle with us".

"On Sundays a man used to come round with a sack on his back selling tiny water bagels -   'Bagels, bagels, two-a-penny bagels'. There were other Sunday street criers with winkles and cockles and I think chestnuts".

"I thought we had everything in Windmill Street. The grocer at no.8; the dairy at the Tottenham Court Road end; the creamy milk in the huge blue-and-white china container, no lid on, always ready with ladle to scoop up the milk for the customer. The hairdresser, the pastry shop, Rendlick the greengrocer on the corner with Whitfield Street where on summer evenings we took turns to spin on the wheel of the upturned barrow. In Whitfield Street round the corner was a little tobacconist shop where for a halfpenny you could buy a sherbert, a few tiger nuts, all kinds of wonderful things, what a choice for a ha'penny! Once a week we went swimming at the

Whitfield Street Baths. What a joy it was on the way home to pop into the baker shop on the corner of Maple Street and Whitfield Street and buy a penny bag of 'stale cakes' - enormous, and we shared it between us. Nothing tastes like that today."

Mr Lewin was born in 1903. When interviewed he reeled off the following without any hesitation, and could have continued for hours.

"I am about to give you a résumé of all the grocers, restaurants, butchers, fishmongers, fruiterers, vegetable people, and some of the stallholders in Berwick Street market, some from before the First World War. If anyone knows the geography of Soho I will start.

In Green's Court the first shop was a butcher, the name of Davies. He was a very old man, and next to him was a grocer named Sacks. He was an elderly man who always wore a bowler hat, and in my opinion he must have gone to bed in it 'cos he never took it off! There was a fish shop owned by a Mr Lewis who did the fish frying, and the two daughters served. There were two long tables on trestles, and on either side of the table were forms, and on each table were two canisters, one salt, one pepper, and vinegar in a wine bottle with a cork with a hole in it. You could get a portion of chips for a halfpenny. If you asked for a 'penny and a ha'penny' you got a lump of fish and a portion of chips. As youngsters we would ask 'Please Mr Lewis could we have a ha'peth of chips and some crackling'. He would take the scoop with the crackling which was above the frying tray and give us the crackling.

Turning the corner from Green's Court into Peter Street we come across a grocer shop called Brooker. In what was then called Edward Street, which is now called Broadwick Street, was a restaurant run by a man called Kerner. Proceeding along Berwick Street market we come to a butcher called Jacobson. Further up to what is now known as Broadwick Street we turn to the right, there is a grocer shop, name of Levinstat. Continuing along Berwick Street we pass a grocer shop named Taffel, and there was another grocer shop whom we called *Meshugener* Jack Lewis. They all had pet names in those days.

Opposite was another butcher shop run by two brothers, the name of Jacobs. Continuing along Berwick Street, turning into D'Arblay Street was a butcher, the name of Kutock. Opposite this shop was another grocer shop owned by Danny Harris. In all there must have been seven or eight grocers and five butcher shops in a distance of 100 yards. All Jewish, all kosher - it was a ghetto.

Also in D'Arblay Street we had a kosher restaurant called Rose's, who later moved to Tottenham Court Road. In Berwick Street was a restaurant owned by a Mrs Lewis and another one was run by a Mr Silver. Carrying on towards Oxford Street there was Bloom's salt beef bar. Not a restaurant as such, but it catered for quick service. There were long tables with forms, and you could either have a sandwich to take away or sit down and have a plate with a portion of salt beef and a pair of viennas. At the back where they cut the beef was a small tray with constant boiling hot water for the viennas. If a customer ordered a portion of beef and two pair of viennas you would hear the shout 'two pair in' and when they were ready 'two pair out'. Opposite was a restaurant called Goodies.

In St Anne's Court they did not have restaurants as such, just take-away. The Sheakwich people had two sons and they used to send out the meals on a thing with three wheels. It was like a cake stand with three tiers.

Further up in Noel Street there was a first class restaurant called Folman's. Before that it was The Swiss Club. In the basement was a hall for weddings and *barmitzvahs*.

In D'Arblay Street next to Kutock the butcher was a wet fish shop owned by a Mr Fulberg who first started up in Soho not with a shop but by trundling a barrow with fish round the streets. This Mr Fulberg, has a son-in-law by name of Sam Sugarman who took over the shop as a salt beef shop, which later became a restaurant.

I will now give you a résumé of some of the shop and stall holders in Berwick Market. On the corner of Walker's Court was Rosin the baker. Going further along on the corner of Berwick Market there was a vegetable stall owned by a Mr Miller. Then further along there was a stall run by Peter Levine and his mother selling silk lingerie. Next to him a stall run by Mr Lejesky who sold lace, next to him a Mr and Mrs Mitchell who sold stockings.

In Berwick Street there was a man called Jack Bick who sold only eggs. In those days the eggs came in large crates with straw, and there were always a lot of cracked eggs. The people of Soho were very poor, so to make ends meet the *Yiddisher* people used to go to Jack with a jug and for a penny he would throw in 8-10 eggs. The women used to make *lockshen* and cakes from them".

"Adjoining our house was a yard area where there was a dairy which housed a real live cow. From time to time my mother would ask me to get a jug of warm milk, and I would go next door, hand a jug to the dairyman, who would then sit himself on a stool beside the cow and fill the jug".

"We were a big family and mother used to send us for milk, with a jug, and we used to get five pints every day. My mother, clever lady, used to boil the milk. There was no pasteurisation and we used to have that horrible cream on top".

"My mother had a grocery shop in her front room and everybody, but everybody, came in whether they had money or not. But they always brought the money in the end. They were a wonderful crowd".

"In my uncle's shop they used to put the sugar and other commodities in bags, and weigh it down in the cellar. He had a telephone in the back of the shop and a sign 'You may telephone from here'. I don't know who people phoned because nobody had a phone then. He always had a bag in the back yard with milk dripping, to make cream cheese. All the shops made their own cream cheese. They didn't buy it already in little cartons like today. We used to buy broken biscuits. Same with eggs because they came loose.".

Of the almost two hundred licensed kosher butchers listed in the 1898 Jewish Year Book, only seven were in West End:

Mrs J Davis 9 Green's Court, Soho
M Dunn, 26 St Anne's Court, Soho
T Erlinski, 10 Meard's Street, Berwick Street, Soho
H Fiescher, 29 Marshall Street, Soho
A Jacobs, 37 Lexington Street, Soho
M Neuman, 89 Berwick Street,Soho
- Solomon, 18 Baker Street, Marylebone

"My father, Max Raznick, of 37 Charlotte Street, was known as 'the gentlemen's butcher of the West End' because he served the Wolfsons and all the gown and coat people in the area. He retired in the 1950's by which time the trade was mainly business people, not so many local residents by then, though there   were still Jews living in Gordon Mansions and Ridgemont Gardens. There are no kosher butchers in the West End now".

"The butcher shops were like meeting places. Customers sat on chairs waiting for the butcher to perform".

"Mr Raznick stood behind the counter, his red face beaming, almost the same colour as his blood-soaked apron, serving all the local Jewish ladies. In the back were always several men especially employed to pluck the chickens".

"Around the corner was Great Titchfield Street market, and first port of call would be to change our comics two for one. Then over the road to Linchis Jewish grocery shop. Further on to Allsops' sweet shop.   Round the next corner to Foley Street: Eskow's tailoring trimming shop to buy various trimmings for my father's business, carrying on to Jones' Dairy and Marks' delicatessen, into Union Street, passing Cooper's paper shop where we would buy the *Yiddisher Times*. My eldest sister Lily married Harry Cooper so from then on we got the papers free. Next door to this shop was Rumsey's fish and chip shop; all we were allowed was the aroma, but to compensate my mother would immediately on our return from shopping fry up the most delicious fat chips, served not on a plate but in a paper bag. Buying meat was a special excursion to Saville Street, just off Foley Street. Lazarovitch, owned by mother, two sons Lazel and Motgie, two daughters Hunkie and Dunkie, such characters! For fish, yet another special journey across the dividing line of Oxford Street into Berwick Street market, passing on the way Sugarman's kosher restaurant, the Belgian Patisserie, *shleppers* outside the various dress and coat shops, and then to halt at Avrumel's fresh fish stall; further on to Rosin's bakery, and next to that Isow's Jewish restaurant."

"There were a few colourful characters who visited our street on a Sunday morning shouting their wares. The baigel man with a covered basket of hot baigels, the Indian man jingling his bell with his tray of whispy Indian toffee".

"They used to make a cholent for Shabbos. When Rosin the baker in Peter Street had finished baking on a Friday night the Jewish women would come with their basins and their names on it and pay a penny or tuppence and it went into the oven overnight and then it was collected the next day on Shabbos".

"In Berwick Street market about half the stallholders were Jewish. We had kosher butcher shops and kosher salt beef shops and kosher fish and chip shops. Harris was the name of a grocer in Peter Street and Greenberg was the fried fish shop in Green's Court and Kutock was a kosher butcher and Bloom and Sugarman had a salt beef shop and there was a wonderful kosher restaurant, name of Citrons, in Wardour Street".

"Most of the shops had railings round and they were private houses, and they used their ground floor front room as little shops".

"From his tobacconist shop at 29 Rathbone Place my father supplied cigarettes and cigars to the Eiffel Tower restaurant in Percy Street for such clients as the Prince of Wales (the Duke of Windsor) and his brother the Duke of Kent. He built up the business despite opposition from the Librairie Europeanne Newsagent and Tobacconist opposite. The French owners of that were unfriendly in their treatment of customers, and my father was the complete opposite. We had a full clientele of celebrities, as well as passers-by and regulars. The list included Constant Lambert, the composer/conductor, and his wife; Horace de Vere Cole, the famous practical joker; the painter Augustus John, the actor Donald Calthrop who appeared in the film Major Barbara; Nancy Cunard, the rakish daughter of the shipping line family. I served in the shop from the age of three. I also helped with the growing paper-round, with clients such as actor/manager Sir John Forbes-Robertson and actor Sir John Martin Harvey in the Bedford Square area. Some of my father's tenants were well known, such as Leslie Starke, the celebrated Punch cartoonist and his wife; Gomer Williams, Welsh poet and private schoolmaster and his wife, who taught King Farouk, when Farouk was still a slim Prince".

"There was a shop in New Compton Street called Harris which sold stage make-up. They were Jewish. So were Berman & Nathans and Morris Angel, the theatrical costumiers".

"Further along in Panton Street was Mrs Brand's grocery shop. It had all the smells of a grocery shop at the time - coffee and spices of all kinds. They had open counters with compartments in which various commodities were kept, just in front of the counter sometimes, and then large trays behind the counter. Nothing was prepacked in those days, in the early twenties".

At one of the gatherings of the West Enders they were asked to list the shops they remembered circa 1928. The following are a few not mentioned above:

Carnaby Street
Zughaft - cobblers
Kosky - barber
Josephs - rag merchant
Koss - publican

West St [now Newberg Street]
Kloss - pub
Fireman - cobblers

Berwick Street (North)
Blanks - soft drinks, ice cream
Maison Nettie - fashions
Kopelwitz - lace
Weintaub - shoes
Parnes - dresses
Shaer - dresses
Rosette Kingsley - milliner
M.King - trimming shop
Taffels - grocers

Berwick Street [south - market]
Hilda - separates [Weinberg]
Cherns - linens
Kriechewski - fabrics
Falbers - fabrics
Borovick - fabrics
Florrie Streer - hardware
Milbour - dresses

Mendleman - stockings and gloves
Poushnoff - haberdashery

Ganton Street
Sharps - tobacco
Eifer - grocery
Flinder - barber
Rubin - tailor

Broad Street [North]
Singer - trimming shop
Rees - grocers
Finkel - confectionery
Feldman - shoes
Yugin - shopfitters
Krassny - news, confectionery
Lieberman - trimming shop

Broad Street
Weiners - trimming shop
Rubin's - hardware
Helders - fish and chips
Tanowitz - photographic equipment
Myer - poultry, fruit, vegetables
Brummer - tobacconist

Walker's Court
Rosen - bakers
Gold - milliner

Schwartz - hats
Burstin - furs

Charlotte Street
Zeiderman - grocers
Levene - tobacconist/confectioner

Windmill Street
Massin - haberdashery
Alf Fegan - barber
Moshe Magar - barber

Cleveland Street
Weiner - tobacconist
Bancroft - trimming shop
Solly's - fish and chips
Hersken - butcher
Rosenkrantz - hairdresser
Freedman - tobacconist

New Cavendish Street
Jack Davies - butcher
Gilberts - barber

Hanson Street
Epstein - grocers
Cohen - boxes

Poland Street
Nygates - cloth merchants

Livonia Street
Bacrac - fishmonger

Peter Street
Alec Brooker - grocers
Joelson - grocers

Soho Street
Cohen's - tobacconist

Wardour Street
Taffel - delicattessen
Green - shoes
Goides - bakers
Betty Paquin - dresses
Esther Spiegel - hats

St Anne's Court
Savitt - furniture

Shaftesbury Ave
Diana de Paris - gowns
Denvaux - gowns
Emma - gowns
Ninette - gowns
Weiss - lingerie
John Jacobus - shoes

Dean Street
Becks - haberdashery
Cohen - tailor

RESTAURANTS AND CATERERS

Catering and hotels were among the most important Jewish contributions to the West End. J Lyons & Co, owned by the Salmon and Gluckstein families, opened their first tea shop in Piccadilly in the 1890s. The same company also established their much-loved (and much-missed) Corner Houses in Coventry Street in 1907, the Strand in 1912, and Oxford Street in 1923. It also built a chain of hotels, offering good service at reasonable prices, in Sherwood Street (Regent Palace) in 1912, the Strand Palace in 1925, and at Marble Arch (Cumberland) in 1933. The Coventry Street premises could seat 4,500 customers and the Strand and Oxford Street premises could each cater for 2,500. The firm was also famous for its tea shops which eventually numbered 260. Its waitresses were popularly known as 'Nippies'.

"At one time my parents [Biedak] had a restaurant in Archer Street opposite the Musicians' Club, 99 per cent of whose members were Jewish. They used to congregate daily in the street looking for work. Wardour Street was the cinema centre which had a large Jewish content. They used to meet at our restaurant and brought with them many theatrical and cinema celebrities to dine every day and enjoy my mother's cooking. I also remember a great number of Damon Runyan characters, some a little unsavoury, members of the boxing and racing fraternities, many of whom were Jewish and who lived or congregated in the West End."

"My grandfather started a kosher restaurant with Ross. They were Goodie and Ross in Tottenham Court Road. But by the time I was born my parents had a kosher restaurant in Berwick Street. It consisted of a basement where there was a kitchen where my mother and grandmother were, and the ground and first floor was the restaurant, and we lived above. A lot of very famous people came in, a lot of cinema and recording people were there. There was one table at the top of the restaurant that was always kept for the cinema people. My grandfather decided to build the first Jewish kosher hotel in the country and chose a site in Noel Street near the Great Marlborough Street end. It had 26 bedrooms and he named it Goodie's Kosher Hotel. The family lived on the first floor and the rest was let to guests. In the basement was a ballroom where many very *frum* people got married. There was one section where a *chuppa* could be erected, and the ceremony would be performed there before they went into dinner. It held 150/200 people. We also used to have a communal seder in the restaurant in the thirties".

"We moved to the West End, to no4 Charlotte Street, and my father opened a restaurant there and we lived on the top floor. Opposite was Raznick the butcher from whom my father bought his meat, and next to Raznick's shop on the same side was a dairy with the Iron Cow. Next door to my father's shop there was a very good Italian restaurant called Vanani's. Very high class. Mr Vanani and my father were great friends. Just across the road, in Percy Street, was a restaurant then called the Eiffel Tower which was visited by very distinguished people, including royalty. One day a man came into my father's shop and asked for a salt beef sandwich. My father, who usually served while smoking a cigarette, cut this man a salt beef sandwich. The man asked how much it cost, and my father said it was fourpence. He put some mustard on. The man gave my father half a crown and my father bent down to put the money in the till to get this man his change, but the man had disappeared. A few minutes later the doorman who stood outside the Eiffel Tower with a top hat with gold on it came over to my father and said 'Do you know who just came into your shop and had a salt beef sandwich?' My father said, 'No', and he said 'That was the Prince of Wales'. My father thought he ought to get the Royal Warrant".

"We moved to 15 Moor Street and had a small shop with a salt beef bar and a few tables. A lot of personalities would come in, including one day Charlie Chaplin and his secretary. I asked his secretary if I could get an autographed picture of him and I received a wonderful large photo. We moved to Denman Street, opposite the Regent Palace Hotel. It was quite a large restaurant. We ran this until 1950. My father died in 1942 and my mother ran it with my sisters, but they eventually gave it up. It was quite well known, but I think the emergence of the Nosh Bar round the corner became the thing of the day, not to have waiters with black ties serving you. The nosh bars took over from the kosher restaurants including Feld's and another restaurant in Berwick Street. Opposite my father's restaurant was another restaurant called Bedax in Sherwood Street, later carried on by the son, Nat Bedax. There was also the famous Jack Isow's whom my father knew well. It was always crowded".

"All the boxing fraternity came into Isow's Restaurant -   Jack Solomons and others.   All the celebrities, all the film actors and actresses - it was known world wide.   Lindy's in New York used to send food over during the war, and after the war used to recommend it to visiting Americans. Howard Hughes came in, and wouldn't have anyone else in the restaurant at the same time.   Danny Kaye, Betty Hutton, Frank Sinatra and Walt Disney were all customers - and the chairs had celebrity names on them".

Some of the catering was on a grand scale:

"We had Stern's Hotel in Aldgate and outside catering. We sold the hotel in 1952, and I joined with my cousin, and we used to cater at the Café Royal and then went on to the Royal Garden. Dad catered about 6,000 weddings which is quite a record. I don't think anyone else had done so many. We created the idea of Silver Dish Service and taught all the other caterers who followed. It was a different world before the Second World War, more civilised. What amazed me was how people had the stamina. Functions used to go on till two in the morning, and people still went to work the next day. Sometimes we would do three functions a week and get back at 6 a.m. by the time it was all finished, and then we would go to a different part of London to cater again.

We used to do a lot at the Portman Rooms, a huge place where the headquarters of Marks & Spencers is now. The Princes Galleries in Piccadilly was more 'high class' at the time. The Portman Rooms was a fantastic place to hold functions, but   there were 60 concrete stairs at the back and no lift, and all the equipment, all the plates, food, and a hundred and one things had to be transported by an army of people up those 60 steps; and down again. We were not allowed to take the plant away till 6 o'clock in the morning because of the local residents. We used to spend the odd two or three hours in the all-night Lyons Corner House, and then all the stuff had to come down by hand.

It was a day-long eating. We even sent waiters round to the bride's home and served food to her neighbours and relatives before she left for the synagogue. They would come to the hall from the synagogue, usually about noon. The guests would have snacks and tea, then they would sit down to a light lunch, chopped liver, giblet pie, *lockshen* pudding, that was a light lunch! Then they would go home to change and come back, and tea was always available, some of them used to play cards. And then about 9 o'clock they would sit down to giant dinners, with seven or eight or even nine courses. Then there was dancing, during which we served pineapple and cream, and chocolates were always on the table. Then they would sit down for tea again, and sandwiches and cakes, and they they would go on dancing until about 2 a.m.. When we first started, the caterer and the cook would sit at the door, and as the guests went out they used to tip them. My dad was the first one to stop that practice.

I could tell stories! We operated from a private house in the East End before we bought the hotel, and all the cooks would have to prepare the food and put it on to a giant pantechnicon drawn by about four horses, and sometimes in the winter you had to get off to help turn the wheels. It was a vast experience. I think people who have either been in the catering, or public house business, have a thoroughly all round experience that no other business gives you. You learned to deal with staff who were different people from those working in a shirt or dress shop. The hours were not the usual 9 to 6. We went to people's homes to make the arrangements and met such a variety of people. The ordinary person does not get that opportunity. Dad had a marvellous reputation, was very strict and prompt about payment of bills he owed, which was imbued in us, and he was very well liked by all the customers".

Many of the wedding ceremonies took place in the banqueting hall:

"I married into the Mintz family when I was 22 and my husband was one of five Mintz brothers, and my father-in-law, Hyman Mintz, was very well known in the West End in the catering. Those living around the Berwick Street area gave their *barmitzvahs* and weddings to him. He had five sons, three of them became musicians and played at the functions, and two were with him in the catering. He did most of his work in the Northumberland Rooms.   There were the Westminster Palace Rooms, and the Princes Galleries in Piccadilly, and a set of rooms in the Queen's Hall which was in the top part of Regent Street. And the Portman Rooms where my wedding was celebrated. The *chuppa* was in the hall. It was quite common for people to be married at home or in a hall. Dean Street *shul* provided the minister, and the warden and the *shammas* would come with all the necessary paraphernalia".

THE PUBLICANS

There appear to have been more Jewish publicans and Jewish customers than has generally been thought. Mayhew, writing in the 1840s of the area immediately around Duke's Place in the East End, noted that 'even the public houses are of the Hebrew faith'.

A Jewish firm was the first to start a chain of public houses, the well-known 'Chef & Brewer' group. Its founder was Isaac Levy, a travelling salesman who was first a bookmaker and then a publican because, it is said, he 'noticed that so many punters who backed horses and had money to spare were in fact publicans. He decided to join them'. His idea was to alter the image of public houses from being gin palaces to places where food was available, particularly at lunchtime. They had several branches, first in the East End and then in the West End.

"My father took me to a pub in Berwick Street, The *Blue Posts* I think. Pickled herring, *schmaltz* herring, and anchovies were available. All day, all the time, and you helped yourself".

"*The Blue Posts* in Berwick Street sold food with a very *heimisher* flavour, and I still meet people who remember the stuffed *miltz* and other wonderful specialities they used to serve. At Pesech the upstairs bar was turned into a *Pesachdik* bar so that the Jewish clients could still come".

"My grandparents had a public house on the corner of Dean Street and Hands Court , called *The Rose and Crown*. They later had *The Blue Posts* in Berwick Street and lived over the pubs".

"Jack Bloomfield, the ex-boxer, had a pub in Cranbourne Street off Leicester Square".

"My mother and father were the licensees of a public house called *The Earl of Aberdeen* in Hoxton. They begged for a transfer and were later allowed to take over *The Black Horse* at no.19 Tottenham Court Road a few doors away from the corner of Oxford Street".

As customers, Jews were not particularly heavy drinkers. Records of the London Hospital show a comparative absence of alcholism and associated problems among working-class Jews in the 1880-1939 period. Deaths caused by a drunken mother lying on a baby, or serious injuries following drunken fights, were extremely rare among Jews. And yet there were a high number of Jewish publicans in the West End. The correlation between the two is not clear, but perhaps it was the apparent profitability of public houses, and the poor working conditions of tailors, that led many West End Jews to become publicans.

"My paternal grandfather was Joseph Moore, known by his friends as Kleine Jossele. His elder sister, Sarah, was the first one in the family to have a pub. She and her husband, previously a tailor, bought a pub on the corner of Old Compton Street and Dean Street which is no longer in existence, called *The Two Ships*. My dad was also a tailor, and he had a workshop at 3 Frith Street where we lived. He gave up tailoring and became a publican, as did all his brothers and sisters. Being a publican was a hard life, but he thought it was easier than tailoring. The first pub my dad had was the *Golden Lion* in Dean Street. It would have been been during World War I. We had quite a number of Jewish customers. They mixed with everybody. There were a number of other Jewish publicans and we all knew each other. My father's youngest brother Joe had *The Coffee House* in Beak Street; Sarah had *The Two Ships* and *The Blue Posts* in Newman Street (no longer called by that name); Sam had *The Shaftesbury Tavern* at the corner of Shaftesbury Avenue and Frith Street; Dolly Less had *The Yorkshire Grey* in Charlotte Street. There was a man called Dave Laholt in Charlotte Street, and he and Phillip Lee had the place just by Charing Cross Hospital when it was down the Strand.   I helped when I was a boy, but it wasn't something I wanted to do; it was much too tied down a life; it was very hard".

Public houses were also a centre for the West End's bohemian life.

"My parents, Annie and Charlie Allchild, and my mother's father Judah Kleinfeld before them, ran *The Fitzroy Tavern* in Charlotte Street, on the corner with Windmill Street, between 1919 and 1956. My grandparents, Judah Morris and Jane Kleinfeld, came from Szydlowiec near Lodz. Judah was a veteran of the Russian Imperial Guard. Having been naturalised in 1904, he was eligible to take over a public house. In 1919, he found *The Fitzroy* but needed his daughter's (my mother's) help. She was only 14, under the legal age for even being in a pub. She had been educated at the Westminster Jews' Free School where she had been an excellent student, and had gained a scholarship to further her studies at the Burlington School. However permission was granted for her to leave school to work in the pub.

Nina Hamnett, the artist, lived in rooms above the Etoile Restaurant in Charlotte Street. She was the first of the bohemians to discover *The Fitzroy* with its new landlord and charming daughter. She told her friends Tommy Earp and Augustus John, and the pub was soon transformed from being near derelict into a rendezvous for writers, artists, actors, politicians, and businessmen, people from all walks of life, trades and religions, and from all over the world. They loved the friendly atmosphere, and soon gave my grandfather the nickname 'Pop' which stuck to him for the rest of his life. As one ex-neighbour, and now renowned West Ender, Henry Morris (Itsbitsky) put it 'Long before the term 'community relations' came into the language *The Fitzroy Tavern* was the centre for social activity for miles around.'

Many Jews took over pubs after World War I. My grandfather set his three sons up in them after they finished serving in the forces. One had a pub in D'Arblay Street. *The Fitzroy* was renowned for its charity work. The ceiling money box, or 'Pennies from Heaven', as it became known, was my grandfather's brainchild. People threw money wrapped in silver paper which had a dart in it which then stuck in the ceiling. They were removed once a year and the collection funded an annual outing to the country for the local children. Annie made a ruling right from the start that these were for children of every race and creed, and 500 were taken annually. When I was born in 1936, I was taken on the outing at the tender age of 12 weeks. I have been told that because of the excitement that after all those years Annie at last was to take a daughter of her own on the trip, all the children in the coaches lined up in Windmill Street, which had been shut off to traffic, and were all told to sing *Sally, Sally*, the Gracie Fields' song, as a surprise for Annie and Charlie. The whole street vibrated with the deafening sound of almost a thousand voices, and I did not even wake up!

On Rosh Hashonah and Yom Kippur *The Fitzroy* closed, much to the delight of the other publicans in the area. On those day the Kleinfelds became part of a band of Jews marching towards Tottenham Court Road, down Charing Cross Road, and into Manette Street to listen to the sermons of Rabbi Ferber at the West End Talmud Torah and Bikur Holim.

In the 1930s, the tailors got paid on Sunday mornings. They put on their high hats and came and had a whisky and smoked the free cigars handed out by my grandfather. Rachele Kalman told me that her grandfather said, 'I remember drinking with Augustus John in *The Fitzroy*'. Rachele was staggered, because she had never seen him drink anything stronger than a lemon tea".

Annie Allchild recounted memories of her father trying to become a publican with no prior experience.

"When my father first applied to have an interview with the brewers about taking over *The Fitzroy*, he was not granted one because they thought he was a German.   He kept on writing and I was later told by one of the managers there, 'We got so fed up with receiving these letters from your father that we eventually decided to grant him an interview. Once we spoke to him, that was it. He had a terrific personality.' He did not know the first thing about running a pub. I loved school. I won the Eveline de Rothschild Prize there and my name went up on the board. I hated the pub at first, but I would not disobey my father because we were very close and I knew he had nobody else to help him. My mother did not get involved in running the pub, she kept the home. Originally, there was purely a local clientèle. Once Nina Hamnett became a customer she attracted a lot of bohemian people to the pub. Through the bohemian crowd we got the theatrical people, and the clientèle just grew and grew. Augustus John wrote in his autobiography 'some day, at some time, everybody comes to *The Fitzroy Tavern*'. He also wrote, 'If I knew the Yiddish for gentleman, that's what I would use to describe Mr Kleinfeld'.

One contributor recalls her grandfather's success in making the transition from Polish tailor to West End publican.

"My grandparents were born in Poland where they married and had the first of their ten children, all daughters, of whom six survived. On arrival in England, my grandfather went to live with *mishpocha* in the East End where he was greeted with the cry 'Here comes another greener'. By the time my grandmother had followed him to England he had moved to Old Montague Street where he set up as a tailor. Tragedy struck when the oldest daughter fell down the stairs and died after fracturing her skull. When he looked at his remaining five daughters, he realised they were growing up into womanhood and, he hoped, marriage, and he knew he could not make enough money from tailoring to pay for five weddings, but it was the only trade he knew.

One day a *landsman* suggested that he should try to take over a public house. My grandfather was shocked at the idea. He had never been in a pub in his life, and any drinking he wanted was done with a few friends and a glass or two of schnapps. The idea of making a livelihood in a pub was abhorrent to him, and anyway he could hardly speak English. He was a little man, barely five feet tall, and a circumference to match. Hardly the idea of an English 'Mine Host'. However, his friend persuaded him to get in touch with the brewers, an interview was arranged, and before he knew it he was the licensee of the *Hercules Pillars* in Greek Street. A sign outside the door proclaimed 'Harris Rothstein, Licensed to sell beer, wines, spirits and tobacco.' What he knew about the trade could have been put in a thimble and still left room for the finger, but the brewers had faith in him, showed him the cellar work which is a vital part in running a pub, put staff in until he found his feet, which wasn't very long, as he realised what a wonderful opportunity this was, as not only did he have a trade but living accommodation he would never have dreamed about in Old Montague Street.

It was a very large pub on the corner of Greek Street and Manette Street. There was a Tap Room where the local yokels used to play dominoes, skittles, shove-'alfpenny, and darts, never letting go of their tankards of beer. The next bar was the *Bottle and Jug* where the wives used to come in each evening for a pint of beer to save their lords and masters from having to exert themselves too much by having to come into the pub. Next there was the Public Bar, and this was one step higher in the hierarchy; even if they did come in in their shirtsleeves, at least they were wearing shirts. Then there was the Lounge or Private Bar. This was very posh. Only spirits were drunk, and nobody spoke over a whisper. Bar staff were often invited to have a drink, and it was all 'tewwibly tewwibly Bwitish', with my little Polish Jewish Grandpa trying to take an interest in cricket matches, horse racing, or football, depending on which bar he was serving in.

There were huge cellars which ran underneath the building, and it was a wonderful place to play hide-and-seek when the grandchildren arrived. The brewers decided that the pub was rather too large and a part of it was divided off into separate living quarters in Manette Street, and when my mother married she and my father moved into it, and that is where I was born, a Sohoite if there ever was one. My grandparents stayed in that pub from before the First World War until the early 1930s. All their daughters were married from that pub, and all lived in the area. But only one daughter and her husband went into the trade. Just before the Second World War the brewers decided to pull it down and remodernise it".

Rachele Kalman has compiled a list of some of the Jewish publicans in the West End in the mid-1930s:

Admiral Duncan	Morry Moore	Old Compton Street
Black Horse	Rose Abrahams	19 Tottenham Court Road
Blue Posts	Hannah Barnett	6 Tottenham Court Road
Blue Posts	Lewis Canter	81 Newman Street
Bricklayers' Arms	Chas. Kleinfeld	7 Edward Street
Bromley Arms	Leslie Harris	84 Cleveland Street
Burlington Arms	Percy Freeman	21 Old Burlington Street
City of London	Leon Molen	104 Berwick Street
Coach & Horses	Ray Koss	43 Carnaby Street
Coach & Horses	Saul Lyons	5 Hill Street
Cock Tavern	C. Arbogart	134 Shaftesbury Avenue
Coffee House	Joe Moore	Beak Street
Crown Hotel (and others)		
	Levy & Franks	43 Charing Cross Road
Duke of York	Hyman Kleinfeld	45 Hanway Street
Fitzroy Arms	Lewis Hart	21 Clipstone Street
The George	Nathan Kaufman	151 Cleveland Street
The Globe	Sydney Cohen	15 Maple Street
Golden Lion	Mrs S Canter	61 Dean Street
Holyrood	Frederick Frank	77 Well Street
Horse and Groom	George Barnett	128 Great Portland Street
Shaftesbury Tavern	Jack Metliss	93 Shaftesbury Avenue
Sun Tavern	Solomon Jesky	21 Drury Lane
White Hart	Harry Myers	39 High Holborn

THE MUSICIANS

From the 1920s onwards Archer Street was the home of the musicians, a kind of outdoor labour exchange, and Denmark Street housed the music publishers. Jews were well represented in both professions. In the 1930s, and post war, several of the leading dance band leaders were Jewish, including Geraldo, Joe Loss, Harry Roy, Oscar Rabin, Lou Praeger, Lew Stone, Ambrose, Sidney Lipton, Roy Fox and Maurice Winnick.

"My father was a musician. When he was in the army in World War I, he met the American bandsmen and was very impressed with the way they played the saxophone and clarinet, so when he came out he taught himself to play. In the 1920s he played in night-clubs in the West End, but he gradually dropped out in the early thirties because he wasn't a very good reader of music and the music profession changed. The dance bands were more organised, and it was required that you read. My father was a street-wise Cockney who wanted me to be an artist and I wouldn't have been one if it were not for him. In a gesture of sublime generosity he gave me his instruments when I was 13. I used to play in a little room at the West Central Club and then when I got to a certain standard, this would be when I was about 17, he said he was going to get me a proper teacher. In 1944/5 one of his old friends, Harry Hayes, gave me lessons for two years, for nothing. He wasn't Jewish. When I met him, he was the lead, the star saxophone player in Geraldo's orchestra. I remember him saying to me, he was ten years younger than my father, 'Your father taught me the ways of the world, so I might as well teach you the ways of the saxophone'".

"I was bought a set of drums by my brother. A character called Jack Grey taught me and I played in clubs in the West End, with Ambrose, with Joe Loss at the Astoria, and with other Jewish band leaders who worked in the West End, Geraldo, Maurice Winnick and Oscar Rabin. I used to go to Archer Street to get jobs. You used to socialise there as well as look for work. Between the wars we would be paid £1 an hour for a wedding, 6 p.m. to 2 a.m.".

THE BARBERS

"Our shop was in Windmill Street, facing Whitfield Street. We had what we called weekly, fortnightly or monthly customers, according to the frequency with which they paid their account. All these customers had their own cups, shaving mugs, shaving brushes, and all the gear that goes with it. Mr Kleinfeld was a monthly customer. I always remember his little box in which was a little mug, shaving brush, hair cream, face cream and friction. He used to come in twice a day, at about 11 a.m., on the way to or from the bank, and he used to have hot towels and hand massage, face massage, have his moustache waxed, and friction and cream on his hair, and he would also come in about 5 o'clock in the evening when he had a shave followed by the same performance as he had in the morning".

"My mother acted as lather-girl in my father's barber shop in Carburton Street.   She got ½d for every face she lathered and Dad received 2d for a shave and 4d for a haircut".

THE SCRIBE

"My mother used to write letters in Yiddish to make a living, and she sent parcels, mainly to Poland. She charged sixpence, or a shilling if they were wealthy. Kitty and I used to write the addresses in English. My mother also used to cut *lockshen* for a restaurant to earn a little money".

VII - POVERTY AND CHARITY

In the 1840s poverty amongst the West End Jews was worst in Newport Market and Seven Dials where the Jewish quarter plumbed the depths of indigence. Nowhere else matched such dire conditions, either before or subsequently. In 1875, George Ellis, son of the founder of the Western Jewish Philanthropic Society, gave the results of his personal observations and investigations of the local poor.

> It is thought by some that the condition of the poor is better than it was. I doubt it. We have among our resident poor those who for many years have been recipients of your bounty, but who long since have been crushed by misfortune through ... increasing old age.

What particularly worried him was what he perceived to be an increase in the number of *schnorrers*, professional beggars. While there had been an expansion of the number of charities dealing with poverty, there had grown up concurrently a tendency to exploit these charities and to turn poverty into a profession.

> They look upon each new institution as a newly found friend, with a general invitation of which they are not slow to take advantage. The professional poor are always on the look-out for gifts of benevolence, and, like the rest of mankind, try to get as much as they can. And until some well-defined system of communication shall be established with the existing charities, there will be no check to the imposition practised by those who beg at every door that is open to them.

Rev J.H.Cardwell of St Anne's Church said 'Prosperity is usually written on the faces of West End Jews'. This was certainly not true of the majority of them during the 19th century. Nor was it true in 1904, a mere seven years before the Rev Cardwell made this remark. At that time, there were still pockets of extreme poverty amongst Soho's Jews. This is clear from contemporary correspondence in the *Jewish Chronicle*, but just how widespread it was is a matter requiring further research.   A letter was published on 18 January 1904 under the heading 'Poverty in Soho and the West Central Ladies' Society'.

Sir,

Never before have I taken up my pen to address you and to appeal to the Jewish public under such painful circumstances as I do now. Soho, which as far as I know, has given the least trouble to the Jewish Board of Guardians or to any other charitable institution in the way of applying for relief, *is now in a state of actual poverty.* The Jewish population in Soho, over 10,000 in number [this would appear to be a considerable exaggeration], no matter how much the poorer class - which are the majority - suffered from want of support, has always kept their misery within them, without letting it go outside their own doors. But now that they have 'come into deep waters' where the floods of hunger overflow them, the heartrending vociferation 'give us bread, lest we die' is being loudly heard in hundreds of Jewish homes there.

Since the West Central Ladies' Society was formed some seven weeks ago, the Committee at all their meetings have had to deal with several applications for immediate relief. During the last few weeks, the Society, though the funds are closed, helped no less than a dozen women in distress. *But the poverty in Soho is growing day to day, and is now beyond description.* At the last meeting, the Committee had more than twenty urgent cases to deal with, and although the Society, owing to the state of its funds which at present are very small, cannot do much for these poor women, the Committee appointed investigators to visit and help the poor applicants as far as possible. But, alas, what a poverty! At one place the poor woman was found in bed seriously ill, her husband suffering with consumption, the children (four in number) without boots or clothes, and the room - for the poor family occupy only a small back room - without fire or light.

In another case, the poor woman, a widow with six young children, was holding her two youngest children in her lap just to warm them a little. The rest were cases of similar character. The Society, of course, helps several of these poor women, but this help, compared with the urgency of the cases, is only like a drop of water in the ocean. There are cases in which, if not attended to immediately, a whole family, I tremble to imagine, will be found dead due to hunger and cold.

I thus appeal to the wealthier ladies and gentlemen of the Jewish community for help. Ye kind hearted mothers! Imagine a mother to have to tell her fondling to go to bed without food! Imagine a child, looking at its mother in a kindly manner, asking her why she makes no fire in the morning, and the mother replies in a trembling voice, 'I have no money to buy any coal, my dear.' How dreadful! As no deserving appeal in your esteemed columns has ever been made in vain, I trust that this appeal will reach the hearts of those generous ladies and gentlemen who can and will do something in this matter. Donations, which will be acknowledged in the Jewish Chronicle, will be gratefully received by the treasurer, Mrs.L. Berg, 151 Wardour Street, W.1; by the Honorary Secretary Mrs Pyser, 29 Tolmers Square, Hampstead Road; and by

Yours obediently,

H Jerevitch
9 Cambridge Gardens, North Kensington.

The essence of what she said was challenged in a reply the following week from Samuel Rapaport:

Sir,

I was amazed at the inaccuracies contained in the letter published in your journal signed 'H Jerevitch'. The writer, who I presume is a member of the seven-weeks' old West Central Ladies' Society, seems to have found out, in this short space of time, more than I am aware of, after visiting and working among the poor of Soho for more than seven years, during which period my visits averaged 46 a year, and the families visited about 12 each visit.

It would be interesting to know what, in nautical language, would be called 'the bearings' or the geographical position of Soho, according to the writer, when such extravagant assertions are made that there are 10,000 Jews in Soho, that the majority of them are poor - tacitly indigent poor - and that there are hundreds of families without food or fire. The majority of the Jewish inhabitants of Soho are tailors, generally speaking, gaining a livelihood by the work of their hands, who try to tide over slack times by having recourse to the well-known kind 'uncle' rather than accept charity; most of them would, in fact, resent any offer of charity. There are, of course, some indigent poor families in Soho as anywhere else, but I challenge contradiction when I say that there are not 40 families in the whole of Soho who can be called indigent poor.

A case such as is described by H Jerevitch has not come to my knowledge during the seven years I have visited the district. The worst case I have met with was three weeks ago; yet while the family, the head of which was a barber who had been out of work for some months, was in a state of abject poverty, there was a fire in the grate and a loaf in the cupboard. I am very glad to say that, through the great kindness of some friends, I was able to afford assistance in this case, as well as in some other cases, in the shape of a supply of coals, provisions, and some money.

I am afraid H Jerovitch has failed to learn, but it is never too late to learn, to take statements *cum grano salis*.

Samuel Rapaport.

H Jerevitch responded. She said she was the originator of the Society, had spent more than seven years in the neighbourhood, and quoted two further cases to support her allegations. One was a family in Broad Street. The mother was seriously ill, the husband out of work, and the poor family, four of whom were young children, were in a state of starvation. 'There is the doctor's bill to be paid, and there is not a shilling in the house, save the few shillings the woman received from the West Central Ladies' Society.' The second case was of a woman in Wardour Street with six young children. Two of the children had been taken to hospital suffering from consumption. A committee member hired a room for the family and was making collections for the rent. She said she knew of the case that Rapaport had quoted, but that family were once again without food or heat - and it was for such cases that the Society existed.

The principal institution for the relief of London's Jewish poor was the Jewish Board of Guardians, founded in 1859. Though East End based, its facilities were available to West Enders, and many took advantage of the benefits it provided. However, even prior to the founding of the Guardians, the West End had made its own arrangements, and there were a number of philanthropic organisations which assisted the sick and the needy. Most were synagogue based, and all the West End synagogues contributed to the welfare of the poor.

Records of the Western Synagogue show that in the 1770s frequent gifts were made to the poor, *'Mattan Baseter'* implying that these alms were given in secret so that the recipient should be spared any embarrassment. Over the next 50 years, typical payments were for kosher food to be sent to poor prisoners (probably in the Fleet Prison); a guinea for some un-named emigrant from America; and a £10 dowry for a poor girl. While Westminster may have been the resort of 'the idle and the rich' for some, the Western Congregation had a considerable number of regular poor pensioners whom it supported very liberally over long periods.

The first West End charitable organisation appears to have been the West-ern Synagogue's Westminster Benevolent Institution, founded in 1822 with the object of providing clothes for poor youngsters. It was reorganised in 1827 under the title Western Jewish Philanthropic Society 'for the relief of the poor, and to grant loans to tradesmen without interest'. Samuel Ellis was President of the Society 1827-61, succeeded by J W Solomon 1862-63, Rev Professor D W Marks 1863-95, Rev Isidore Harris 1895-1911, David Angel 1911-28, and his son Edward 1928-40 when activities were temporarily suspended until after the war. The Society continued its work until just a few years ago, and application has recently been made to the Charity Commissioners for its funds to be passed to the Western Charita-ble Foundation of the Western Marble Arch Synagogue.

Although the Western Jewish Philanthropic Society never attained any really sizable dimensions, it nevertheless performed a desirable and es-sential function. It began by granting loans not exceeding £5 and gifts not exceeding £2, and before the approach of the Jewish festivals distributed monies to the 'deserving poor' to enable them to observe the Holy Days with a few extra comforts. In its first 20 years the Society helped 1,000 cases, and in accordance with Jewish teaching emphasis was placed on assisting the recipients to become self-supporting. Throughout its long history, there was an almost 100 per cent record of repayment of loans.

The Society acquired an independent status and its subscribers, supporters and committee members included members of other synagogues. Rev Arthur Barnett was minister of the Western Synagogue for 30 years from 1924. He said he knew that he could always call upon the Society to come to the aid of those in particular need, and no genuine application would ever be turned down. This was particularly so during the Depression when there was much unemployment and hardship in the district. Through the good offices of the Society, many congregants were enabled to tide over periods of illness and other disabilities, and ultimately to find their feet again. There were many occasions when a timely loan from the Society prevented a respectable artisan or shopkeeper from falling by the way.

Barnett said the synagogue vestibule presented a pathetic sight before the Holy Days. A long queue of obviously penurious people assembled there, waiting to be interviewed by the committee, and hoping to receive some assistance. He said there may well have been a number of imposters among them, but he could not recall any instance where they went away empty-handed, the committee preferring to trust their hearts rather than their heads. 'This may have been an injudicious policy, but it was good Jewish *rachmones*'.

With the advent of the Second World War, there was a complete change in the social conditions of the district. Many West End residents, particularly on the Soho side, left London for rural districts. The Society's activities were suspended for the duration, but with peace came the Welfare State that made the original purpose of the Society somewhat obsolete. On Barnett's instigation a new scheme was devised for applying funds on a broader basis. Greater funds were obtained, and within a short time income was in thousands rather than hundreds. It was ultimately decided that the resources should be allocated in more or less equal proportions to the needs of home charities and those of Israel.

Help for the poor also came from other quarters. As late as 1910, the Westminster Jews' Free School distributed a hundred pairs of shoes to its poorest students. Indeed, at that time the work of selecting children for its various benefits was too overwhelming for its ordinary Care Committee, and the school paid a visiting social worker to do the job. In 1915, the West End Talmud Torah found it necessary to set up a fund to provide clothing and footwear for the Jewish poor in the district, and during and just after the Second World War the West End Great, as it had then become, still handed out tickets for coal and food to the poor.

The National Insurance Act of 1911 provided limited medical aid, sickness benefit, disablement benefit, and maternity benefit. In addition there was undoubtedly a high degree of mutual aid in the community. Friends and relatives could be relied upon to a greater extent, it would seem, than is the case today. Many shopkeepers, particularly grocers, gave extended credit and, often to their own detriment, allowed customers to pay as and when they could afford it. There were local philanthropists such as Max Rosin, who spread much needed help on an informal interest-free basis.

'We didn't suffer poverty' was a frequently repeated phrase in the interviews. 'We didn't want for food or clothes.'

"The Jewish people in the West End were all fighting for a living. Although they all did reasonably well, they were living carefully, I would say".

"We didn't starve and we didn't go hungry. We were what you would call respectable poor in Soho. Most people were careful to keep their pride. All the men worked hard, and our mothers supported them. *But at the end of the week you were no better off than you had been at the beginning.* Conditions were hard. You were working to live. The question of a holiday or better living conditions was very remote".

"When we were kids there was a Green Line coach station at the corner of Lexington Street and Broad[wick] Street. The coaches went up Poland Street to Oxford Street. We used to go to Oxford Street to look for people who wanted their cases carried to the bus station, and they paid us a penny or two".

"My brother and I used to stand in the street and ask passers-by if they could change a penny for two halfpennies. Most gave us the halfpennies and didn't take our pennies".

"We were in theatre land and the restaurant area, and if Lex Garage was full up, and to earn extra pennies, we used to wait and jump on the side running board of the car and say 'Sir or Madam, Can we take you to a garage?' 'Yes, please. How far?', and we used to take them to the Poland Street Garage they did not know about. The garage paid us twopence a car. You went home and gave your mum some of the money because money was hard to come by. You never took it for granted, your never asked 'I want this or can I have that?' because you had a sixth sense to know it was not there".

"There were poor families living all round the West End. It wasn't all rich Jews there. Plenty of poor people at all times between the wars and during and after the Second World War. I used to run functions from Dean Street and Great Portland Street *shuls* once or twice a year, and with the proceeds we clothed children at Rosh Hashonah".

"My father went back to Poland and never returned. He sent my mother a *get* [religious divorce]. We had it very hard. We lived in one room which I can't bear to think about now.   But if people from the *shul* got Pesach parcels, they were very supportive. The Jewish families were very kind to us.   One particular family called Bacrac were fishmongers. They were a very big family and very *frum*. On a Friday evening Mr Bacrac used to look for people who were down and out and make them clean out the barrels and give them a meal and a little money, but he'd make them work for it. On the Sabbath he would visit people in hospital. He was a very kind man".

"On the corner of Walker's Court was Rosin the baker. He was a very benevolent man and his wife and daughter served in the shop. He gave orders that if any beggars came in and asked for an 'offer' they were to be given a loaf of bread and twopence for a cup of tea".

VIII - FRIENDLY SOCIETIES

[The following section is largely based on material kindly supplied by Raymond Kalman]

The West End had several active friendly societies which fitted in well with Anglo-Jewry's philosophy of self-help. Their very nature - combining mutual self-help, social activity, grandiose titles, elaborate regalia and ritual - appealed to the Jewish community. Some fathers made it a condition of giving their daughter's hand in marriage that the prospective son-in-law should become a member of at least one friendly society. Petty tradesmen, shopkeepers, skilled and unskilled workers enrolled, though not the very poorest who could not afford the subscriptions. Other institutions provided for the poor.

Friendly societies were, perhaps, the most important adult social institutions after the synagogues. They were not only the means by which a group of men could provide for mutual assistance in times of sickness and for the benefit of widows and orphans. Many operated more like savings clubs that periodically paid out, usually at Pesach and Rosh Hashonah. Equally important, all the societies had a social aspect - hence the word 'friendly' in their title. They were institutions where friends met. Each filled a small world of its own, furnishing members with a sense of belonging and participation in affairs. Each required a president, a vice-president, trustees, a secretary, and a large committee. Their proceedings, often a byword for contentiousness, gave scope for debate and civic activity, and schism was a dependable source for new societies.

Jewish involvement in the friendly society movement dates back at least to the mid-18th century when the first specifically 'Jewish' society, the *Rodphe Shalom* (Pursuers of Peace) was established in the City of London. From that time on, West Enders too played a significant role as members of specifically Jewish or general societies. It is likely that West Enders were originally members of East End Jewish societies, but the community gradually established its own or set up local branches of the large Orders.

Public houses or synagogue premises were the most common meeting places. The early Reports of the Registrar of Friendly Societies list the West London Hebrew Loyal United Brethren, formed in 1894, which met at 95 Dean Street; the West Central Hebrew Tontine & Benefit Society formed in 1898, which met at *The Red Lion & Ball* in Red Lion Street; the Hebrew New Year Benefit & Divisional Society, founded in 1899, which met at 158 Great Portland Street; the West End Radom Hebrew Tontine & Benefit Society of 1903, which met at 49 Brewer Street; and the West London Hebrew Benefit & Divisional Society formed in 1904, which met at *The Newcastle-on-Tyne* in Broad Street. The West London Hebrew Benefit & Divisional Society was probably fairly typical. In 1915/16, it had 149 members. Notices of its proceedings were published both in English and Yiddish, and its members were 'earnestly requested to introduce young and healthy candidates'. During the year, it paid out for sick pay, *shiva* benefit, relief grants, wife's death allowance, and funeral and tombstone expenses.

For the Society's forthcoming elections at an Annual General Meeting to be held at the *Newcastle-on-Tyne* on 8 April, 1916, candidates for the the main offices were unopposed:

For President:	J M Kleinfeld
For Vice President:	E Kleiman
For Treasurer:	S Levy
Trustees:	J M Kleinfeld, J Stone & M Needleman.

There were no less than 14 candidates for the Committee: S Schneider, I.Figov, S Stone, M Galkin, S Somers, S Kohn, L P Gilblatt, S Noble, L Simons, T Goldberg, H Somers, I Silver, M Naselsky, M Isbitsky.

The medical officer for non-insured members and examination was Dr Grant. Dr Sidney Yale succeeded him.

The Orders had a central office, and expanded through branches or lodges, which gave greater financial strength and viability, and enabled more professional 'head office' staff to be employed. The Registrar's Report for 1907 shows that the Order of Achei Brith (Brethren of the Covenant), founded in the East End in 1890, had two West End lodges, the Lord Rothschild Lodge (1898), which met at *The Roebuck* in Broad Street and the Sir George Jessel Lodge (1899), which met at 206 Kensington Park

Road, Notting Hill. The Grand Order of Israel, founded in Hackney in 1897, had the Duke of Edinburgh Lodge (1899), which met at the *Bath House Tavern* in Dean Street, while the Order Achei Ameth (Brethren of Truth) founded in Commercial Road (1897), had the Baron Ferdinand de Rothschild Lodge (1900), whose meeting place was at 3 Broad Street. By 1900, the West London Hebrew Loyal United Brethren had moved to the *Cecil Tavern*, Noel Street.

The largest Order was the Order of Achei Brith and Shield of Abraham, and five of its 43 lodges were in the West End. The Grand Order Sons of Jacob had a lodge which met in Manette Street (the West Central Dr.Moses Gaster Zionist Lodge No.15). The Order Achei Ameth included The Brothers of Ozorkow, The Samuel Montagu, and the Hebrew Roumanian, all of which had West End addresses. Similarly, The Grand Order of Israel and Shield of David listed The Diamond Jubilee, The Prince of Wales, The Duke of Cambridge and The Fulham & Kensington, all Western London lodges.

By 1939, Jewish involvement in the friendly society movement was extensive, with a total national membership, (some belonged to more than one lodge) estimated at 90,000, nearly 400 lodges of Orders, and between 30 and 40 independent societies. Given that the total Jewish population of the country was some 330,000, Jewish membership was really remarkable. Since the establishment of the Welfare State the Jewish friendly society movement has become all but extinct.

IX - HEALTH, HOSPITALS, DOCTORS AND MISSIONARIES

The West End was as well supplied with medical care as any district in London. Almost within walking distance of every part were the two great voluntary hospitals, the Middlesex and University College - teaching hospitals of the highest reputation. Between 1900 and 1939 people used out-patient departments of hospitals for problems that today would not go beyond the local G.P.

"In those days you went to the hospital even for a sore throat. We had a doctor of course, but it meant paying him each time, so we used to go to the Middlesex to have our minor ailments attended to".

There was no shortage of good doctors in the 1920s and 1930s. They usually charged 2/- to 3/6 a visit. and most dispensed their own medicines at the surgery.

"We went to Dr Taff in Broadwick Street in those days [the 1920s]. He wasn't Jewish. If he came to you it was 5/- and if you went to him it was 2/6. He was very good, and when he came to the house he always looked at both of us. If there was anything serious grandma *schlepped* us to the Middlesex. It wasn't because you didn't have to pay there, but for anything she thought was serious".

"Our first doctor was Dr Cowan who charged 2/- or 2/6d. Then we had Dr Yale who was the very essence of what a family doctor should be because he had the total interest of the patient at heart. He treated us not only as individuals but as families too, and that is how he stood out from doctors of today. He knew every one of us, all our problems, and had a caring, almost loving, interest in each of us. He came originally from somewhere near my mother's village in Russia. He had a lifetime interest in the family and even visited me when he came to America. I had a letter from him during my mother's final illness".

"My father got pneumonia but was so hard up, and in those days I think it cost a shilling to see the doctor, and to see a better doctor cost 2/6d. Mother found a doctor who charged 6d".

For the better off, the benefits of Harley Street and private clinics were available. There was also an excellent dental clinic for children in Gerrard Street and there were free dispensaries, rather like the group clinics of today. The German Hospital in Dalston opened a branch called the Western Dispensary in Great Portland Street, and in 1907 an official was reported in the *Jewish Chronicle* as saying that 'about 75 per cent of the outpatients belong to your community. They come to us because being a German hospital there is no language difficulty'. Most Jewish friendly societies provided sickness benefit, the services of a doctor and even convalescence. They helped workers survive bouts of illness without having to deprive their families of necessities.

"My father belonged to a benevolent society, The Order Shield of David. Our doctor was Dr Sidney Yale, second to none, par excellence. His practice was in Euston Road opposite Warren Street. The Middlesex was our local hospital. In fact my brother Hymie with a group of youngsters was instrumental in installing a kosher kitchen. They raised money when they were in their teens. I fell over and I broke a finger and I had to go in and stayed just one night, but I was very worried and upset. I said 'I cannot eat here. It's *Pesach*. I need *matzo*.' They found *matzo* for me".

For at least fifty years, the Montagu sisters, ever out and about on their visits, referred residents with medical problems to the appropriate centres for treatment and ensured that any illness they encountered did not go untreated.

"The Misses Montagu were always walking around, and if anyone was ill they would find a convalescent home to send him to".

Christian missionaries had a medical mission off Lisle Street at which treatment was given, either free or for a small charge, but only after the patient had listened to a short sermon or read Christian literature, sometimes in Yiddish. The Christian mission had minimal influence as far as conversion was concerned. In the East End, it was reported that women put cotton wool in their ears so that they would not hear the name of Christ. Doubtless there were similar practices in the West End.

"Off Lisle Street was a mission to induce Jews to take up Christianity, and they had a very good doctor there, so, the cynical women would all go to the 'missionaire' as they called it. No one was converted. There would be some preaching, but they didn't listen to what was being preached. Years later Mother could really see the funny side of it and laugh and talk to me about it".

Though few Jews were converted by the missionaries, their activities were feared, particularly by the clergy. The West Central Institute opened a Free Dispensary at 15 Greek Street in February 1912 to counter the influence of the Christian missionaries. About 400 patients were treated within two months of opening, including several children sent on to convalescent homes. Many doctors provided their services gratuitously, prominent among them being Dr Bernard Goitein, Dr M M Goldfoot, Dr Julius Landman, the Jewish specialist for chest and lungs (a malady then prevalent among Jewish residents of Soho), and surgical dentists Dr Goldfoot and Mr Isidore Spero.

Jewish Chronicle 9 February 1912.

"West End Central Jewish Institute opening of free dispensary and adult classes. It is hoped that the new dispensary, which will be ready to administer to the needs of the poor within a week or so, will cripple conversionist activity and put a stop to the pernicious system of bribing carried on at present to a large extent by the missionaries.

The Rev C Voysey of the Theistic Church, Swallow Street and the Rev Charles Roper of the Unitarian Church in Quex Road, Kilburn each sent letters of goodwill addressed to Dr Lazarowich which were read.

Mr Voysey said:

I wish you would tell your dear people for me how I hate and detest the methods of those Christian conversionists whom you are now endeavouring to frustrate. We do not blame anyone for trying to persuade others to think and believe as he does; but we do blame, with our untmost indignation, the wicked endeavour to bribe by gifts and alms anyone to give up the faith of his fathers.

Mr Roper states that:

The splendid way in which the Jews look after the needs of their less fortunate co-religionists, and also the way in which they so readily respond to appeals made on behalf of Christian sick and poor have for many years won my admiration. There is a further feature of this new effort of yours with which I sincerely sympathise. You are establishing this institutional work in a distinctly Jewish quarter where hitherto, I am given to understand, Christian philanthropy has been carried on from a mixed motive. An attempt has been made while rendering brotherly help, to proselytise in the interests of Trinitarian Christianity.   This is altogether at variance with the fundamental principles of Christianity and alien to the higher ethics.

Dr I.Lazarowich spoke at great length on the aims and objects of the institution and made a passionate appeal to all to give the conversionists a wide berth, and said that no Jew or Jewess in the district would now have occasion to attend the missionaries for material or any other comforts, seeing that all would be provided for them by their co-religionists."

Many West End Jews developed ailments connected with their strenuous occupations in the tailoring trade.

"My father died at 54. A tailor had to lift a heavy gas-iron and the machines you had to work by your feet. He developed a double hernia and then a twisted hernia, and that killed him".

1   The Western Synagogue, the first in the West End (1761), was at St Albans Place, Haymarket from 1826 - 1914. It was rebuilt and reconsecrated on 13 April 1851.

2   Central Synagogue, Great Portland Street (1870). "A *shul* for the Rothschilds and the great of the land".

3   University College, Gower Street (1826). As the first English
    college with no religious requirement for its students, it played
    an important part in Jewish education.

4   Beth Hasepher, Soho Square. Founded in 1910 in Berwick Street
    as the West Central National Institute, it provided an educational
    centre, Hebrew classes and synagogue which were frequented
    particularly by those with Zionist leanings.

Soho Clarion

5   Rabbi Zvi Hirsch Ferber. A scholar in Soho. Beloved and revered by the congregation he served at the West End Talmud Torah and Bikkur Cholim in Manette Street (later the West End Great Synagogue).

Jacob Ferber

6   The earliest Jewish arrivals in the West End were upper and middle class families. The Waley family at home at 22 Devonshire Place in 1898, where they had lived since 1840.

Evelyn Waley

7   Members of the Spielman family leaving the Reform Synagogue in Upper Berkeley Street c 1932.

Evelyn Waley

8   A composite photograph of the Dembinsky family c 1890. Note the elaborate clothing worn for the studio photograph.

Rachele Kalman

9   Tailor's workshop at Ramillies Place c 1902, owned by Isaac Woolf. The West End workshops were generally less crowded than those in the East End.

Constance Cowan

10   Pulteney Street Board School in Peter Street averaged more than 80 per cent Jewish pupils. A girls' class in the mid-1920's. 27 of the girls in the photograph are Jewish.

Ettie Gontarsky

11   A boys' class at Pulteney Street School, 1930. "The school provides the essentials of a good education in a stimulating atmosphere created by sympathetic and educated teachers". LCC School Inspectors' Report, 1933.

Louis Feldman

12   Miss Lily Montagu (1873-1963), leader of the West Central Jewish Girls'
      Club for half a century, aged 18. Her strength of purpose can be seen in
      her eyes.

Rose and Jeffrey Segal

X - THE YEAR 1930

The year 1930 - midway between the two World Wars - has been selected at random to give a more detailed flavour of some facets of life experienced by Jews who lived in the West End. The following are extracts from the *Jewish Chronicle* of that year.

Films shown at West End cinemas in 1930:

Mr George Arliss in *Disraeli* (all talking) opened at Marble Arch Pavilion and became the longest running film of the year

Dolores del Rio in *The Bad One*, 'a love drama of the seven seas'

Clara Bow in *The Saturday Night Kid*

Clive Brook in *The Return of Sherlock Holmes*

Emil Jennings and Marlene Dietrich in *The Blue Angel*

The film of the *Kid Berg and Kid Chocolate Fight*

Loretta Young and Douglas Fairbanks Jnr in *Loose Ankles* (and on the stage Billy Cotton and his Band)

All Quiet on the Western Front

John Barrymore in *General Crack*

Eddie Cantor in *Whoopee*!

Greta Garbo and Lewis Stone in *Romance*

Harold Lloyd (talking for the first time) in *Welcome Danger*

Ronald Colman in *Raffles*

Maurice Chevalier in *The Love Parade*

Constance Bennett and Lew Ayres in *Common Clay*

Bebe Daniels in *Rio Rita*

Herbert Marshall in Alfred Hitchcock's *Murder*

Gary Cooper in *The Virginian*

Ronald Coleman in *Condemned*

Greta Garbo in *Anna Christie*

Anna May Wong in *The Flame of Love*

Paul Whiteman in *King of Jazz*

Theatre:

Evelyn Laye in *Bitter Sweet* (His Majesty's)

Anne Croft in *Maid of the Mountains* (Hippodrome)

Gladys Cooper and Gerald du Maurier in *Cynara* (Playhouse)

Nigel Playfair and Diana Wynyard in *Petticoat Influence* (St Martin's)

Carl Rosa Opera Company in *Carmen* (Strand)

Yvonne Arnaud and Ronald Squires in *The Command to Love* (Savoy)

Denis King in *The Three Musketeers* (Drury Lane)

Balliol Holloway in *Richard III* (New)

Sophie Tucker and Jack Hulbert in *Follow a Star* (Winter Garden)

Noel Coward and Gertrude Lawrence, supported by Lawrence (sic) Olivier in *Private Lives* (Phoenix) [the *Jewish Chronicle* critic was not impressed]

Frank Lawton and Nora Swinburne in *Lucky Dip* (Comedy)

Binnie Hale in *Nippy* (Prince Edward)

Martin Harvey in *The Devil's Disciple* (Savoy)

Charles B. Cochran's *1930 Revue* (London Pavilion)

Franz Lehar's *Frederica* (Palace)

Paul Robeson in *Othello* (Savoy)

Music at **Queen's Hall** (the Proms, 2/- to 7/6d)) and **Wigmore Hall** was provided by Mischa Elman, Sir Henry J Wood and the B.B.C. Symphony Orchestra, Constance Lambert, Harriet Cohen, Solomon, Marion Anderson ['a great new contralto'], Myra Hess, Moisewitsch, Leon Goossens, Adrian Boult, Arthur Schnabel, Sir Thomas Beecham, British Women's Symphony Orchestra, Elizabeth Schumann, Bela Bartok and the Hallé Orchestra.

Music Hall Artists who appeared during the year at **The Palladium, Holborn Empire** and **London Coliseum** included:

Nellie Wallace; Randolph Sutton; Sandy Powell; Jimmy Jewel; Clapham and Dwyer; Jack Smith ('the whispering baritone'); Gracie Fields; Will Hay; George Robey; Teddy Brown; Sybil Thorndike; Julian Rose; Nervo and Knox; Robb Wilton; Eddy Gray; Billy Bennett; G.H.Elliott; Max Wall; Naunton and Wayne; Nat Mills and Bobbie; The Houston Sisters; Layton and Johnstone; Richard Henderson; Gillie Potter; Billy Caryll and Hilda

Mundy; Jack Payne and his BBC Band; Will Fyfe; Max Miller (third on the bill at the Holborn Empire); Bennett and Williams; Gertie Gitana; Jeanne de Casalis; Florrie Forde; Burns and Allen; Hetty King; Beatrice Lillie; Tallulah Bankhead; and Kid Berg, junior welter-weight champion of the world, in 'Exhibition Bouts'.

Jan 17   Double- fronted shop, corner of Edgware Road and Oxford Street.   £400 per annum.   Reasonable premium.
 In the heart of the West End - 6 bedrooms, 2 receptions, lounge, hall, bathroom, c.h., continuous hot water - £425 p.a.   Long lease, small premium, agents Harris & Gillow of 80 Wardour Street.

Jan 24   Abrahamson's Kosher Restaurant 178/180 Wardour Street. 'The Only Kosher Restaurant in the West End of London holding the licence under the Commission for Kashruth.'

Astoria Cinema - admission 1/3 to 3/6

Tea Dance at Astoria Dance Salon 3-6, 2/6d; evenings 8-12, 3/6d

At the Carlton Danse Salon in Tottenham Court Road 2/- in afternoons and 2/6 in evenings.

Feb 2   Goide's restaurant advertised - Head Office 54, High Street, Whitechapel, branch at 124/126 Wardour Street.

A Weingarten & Co of 72/73 Margaret Street holding Mannequin Parade for 'Trade Only' of Afternoon and Evening Gowns, Coats, Costumes and Sportswear - 14/11d to 5½ guineas.

Jewish Agency for Palestine, West and West Central London Committees put on showing of a film 'New Life in Palestine' at Regal Cinema, Marble Arch.

Feb 14   Burberry's Half Price Sale.

The Burberry - The World's Best Waterproof - 73/6d

Men's overcoats   84/- (previously 8 to 10 guineas)

Tweed lounge suites   84/- (previously 8 and 9 guineas)

Ladies' overcoats 63/-

Astoria Dance Salon had a Sunday Club.   On Wednesday an open waltz competition adjudicated by Victor Sylvester.

Feb 21   Westminster Jews' Free School annual meeting.   Claude Montefiore presided. He reported that there was no improvement on the numbers on the roll, but there had been a halt in the rapid decrease of the previous few years.   As at 31 December 1929, they had 110 boys and 79 girls. The halt was partly attributed to the admission of children under the age of 5 which had been made possible by various alterations in the building.

Feb 28   200 delegates of British Lodges of the Independent Order of B'nai B'rith met at Princes Galleries, Piccadilly, ending their conference with a banquet for 400.

Z Salinson (S Weinstein) gentlemen's tailor of 2a Portman Street (established 20 years at same address) offered suits from 7 guineas.

West Central Jewish Lads' Club took part in Second Annual Display of Junior Clubs of Association for Jewish Youth at New Scala Theatre - gave P T display.

Mar 14   Heart of West End Textile Trade: four entire buildings, each communicating and having 3 floors. To let as whole £650 per annum. No premium. Agents Millard Bros of 231 Oxford Street.

Selfridges announced opening of a Kosher Department for Passover - Under Beth Din (London).   Orders of £1 and over delivered free to any part of England and Wales; plus free copy of the *Haggadah*.

English Zionist Federation, 75 Great Russell Street, celebrated 30 years of its establishment with the publication of *Zionism in England* by Paul Goodman.

West Central Zionist Society held a *M'Lave Malkeh* at the Beth HaSepher. Mr H Vetchinsky presided. Decided to apply for affiliation to English Zionist Federation. Agreed to create a fund to send one member a year to Palestine.

Mar 21   Warwickshire Motors Ltd of 118-122 Great Portland Street offered showroom-soiled £1075 Daimler Limousine de Luxe for £775.

Federation of Jewish Relief Organisations of 33 Soho Square (President Chief Rabbi Dr.J.H.Hertz) appealed for funds for Russian, Polish, Roumanian and Lithuanian Jews.

B.Danzig & Co of 66a Berwick Street - 'It will cost you less at Danzig's' - offered Palestine Wine (Port Style) at 2/3d per bottle; Cherry Brandy (made of the finest cherries) at 10/- and Fine Old Palestine Brandy at 13/6d.

Disraeli with George Arliss entering its third month at London Pavilion.

Mar 28   Auteuil Hat Co 'The Well-Known Milliners' acquired 82 Oxford Street (next door to Dolcis, opposite Dean Street) and announced opening on 1 April with display of Genuine Paris Models. Large range of hats from 2/11d upwards. 'HATS at prices that will ASTONISH you'.

A new theatre, Prince Edward, opening in Old Compton Street on April 3, with a musical play 'Rio Rita'.

Beth Din gave list of traders under its supervision for Pesach goods. Of the 95, only 3 in West End - Selfridges for groceries, Express Dairies of 26 Tavistock Place, and Goide's for cakes and chocolates.

Another *M'Lave Malkeh* at West Central Zionist Society at the Beth HaSepher and Federation Synagogue.

Throughout the year many East End Societies held their annual functions in West End venues.

Apr 4   Some of Selfridges' Pesach prices:

Bonn's American Motzas 10d a lb

Bonn's Tea Motzas   1/3d a lb

Manischewitz's special motzas 1/- a lb

Motza meal, fine or medium   9d

Farful   11d

Lump sugar   4d

Granulated   3d

Worsht with garlic   2/4d

Smoked brisket   3/-

English eggs	2/- per dozen
Dutch eggs	1/9d per dozen

Opening for *Pesach*. On April 12. Goody's Hotel and Kosher Restaurant, Noel Street. 'Telephones and constant hot water in all bedrooms. Lift to all floors. Night porter. Visitors are invited to inspect the entire premises, kitchen included. The most beautifully appointed kosher Hotel and Restaurant in Europe. The choicest food cooked and served under ideal conditions'.

Holborn Restaurant, corner of Kingsway, available for weddings and *barmitzvahs*. 20 luxuriously equipped large and small halls.

Disraeli to continue indefinitely at Marble Arch Pavilion

Medical Aid and Relief Society to hold a ball at Royal Hotel, Woburn Place on Saturday April 5. *The positive appearance of the Delfont Boys direct from their recent Continental successes.* Tickets 5/-. Dress optional.

Apr 4   Last *M'Lave Malkeh* of season at Beth HaSepher. Rabbi Ferber and Revs J K Goldbloom and B Fertleman and Mr M Rosin gave addresses. Chairman H Vetchinsky.

Goody's Hotel can accommodate 150 in the ballroom.

Advert, under heading in Hebrew *Mah Nishtana?*

First question: Where is there a kosher restaurant in the centre of West End Theatreland?

Secondly: Where can the best food be found?

Thirdly: Where can be found prompt service, courtesy, and comfort, and a restaurant that is open until 2 a m.?

Finally: Which good restaurant is not raising its prices for Passover?

Answer: Kahn's Kosher Restaurant. 15 Moor Street (by the Palace Theatre), Charing Cross Road.

West Central Jewish Girls' Club annual sale of work at 31 Alfred Place. Library open every night. It had 66 workers and teachers. Employment bureau run by Miss Lewis catered as far as possible in these difficult times for needs of the girls. 291 girls had gone away on holidays through the Club. New effort, Mothers' Week, started. 29 mothers went on holiday through the club.

Apr 11   The social side of West Central Jewish Girls' Club is not neglected. There are excellent concerts held about twice a month attended by large number of parents, members and friends. Once a month there is a dance for senior members over 19 and once a month for juniors over 15. On Saturdays there are mixed socials, girls' socials, and games evenings held and organised by members themselves. About 175 members and friends attended the last dance of the season on Sunday.

Apr 18   Of the three West End bankruptcies reported this week, two were manufacturing costumiers in Wells Street and Berner Street respectively; and the third a mantle manufacturer in Newman Street.

Apr 25   West End Talmud Torah, Bikkur Holim Synagogue and Chesed v'Emeth in Manette Street. Opposition Party meeting. Internal dissension in the congregation which numbers well over 1,000 members. Opposition alleged incompetence and formed a Protest Committee that called a meeting at Poland Street Rehearsal Rooms for the purpose of nominating candidates at next week's elections. They complained they were still without a proper *shul* despite spending thousands of pounds, and what was there to show for it?

April 25   Beth HaSepher Synagogue. Annual meeting. Elected:

President	Haham Dr M Gaster
Vice President	L Schalit
Chairman	S Goldenberg
Vice Chairman	L Apple and A Bieda
Treasurer	Z Kopelovitch
Trustees	D Stear and S Stern

and a committee of ten.

May 2   **Report of election meeting of West End Talmud Torah.**

SCENES AT A MEETING
'THAT IS WHY YOU LOST YOUR TEMPLE!'

Remarkable scenes were witnessed at the 37th annual meeting of the West End Talmud Torah, Bikkur Holim Synagogue and Kindred Institutions which was held on Sunday afternoon at the West End Central Jewish Girls' Club, 31 Alfred Place, Tottenham Court Road, W.1.

As stated in last week's issue of the *Jewish Chronicle*, the Institution is divided into two camps - the 'Ministerialists' in power and an 'Opposition' which has formed itself into a Protest Committee and which alleges that the Management has been guilty of incompetence.

Chaos and confusion reigned supreme almost thoughout the entire proceedings on Sunday. Many of the members shouted themselves hoarse, the most uncomplimentary epithets were indulged in, people rushed about excitedly all over the Hall, and the noise was so loud that it was quite impossible for the President, Mrs Wenter, who was in the chair, to conduct the proceedings with even a semblance of order.

When our representative arrived he was given a seat on the platform, and one of the speakers declared: 'We have got the representative of the *Jewish Chronicle* here now, and I would like this meeting to go off quietly.

The balance sheet was presented, and the Secretary, Mrs Levene, read the certificate of the Chartered Accountant that the balance sheet was correct and in accordance with the books and documents and information supplied to them.

'Where are the books?' demanded someone.

When Mr Shankleman rose to second the adoption of the balance-sheet, he was greeted with uproarious opposition from a section of the hall. On a show of hands the Chairman declared the balance sheet carried. The report had been previously adopted.

Election broken up

When the Chairman announced that the meeting would proceed with the election of officers, the storm, which had slightly subsided, broke out anew and with increased fury - so much so that two of the members had to be separated because they were on the point of coming to blows.

It was impossible at this stage to hear precisely what members were saying, but it was decided to allow three speakers to address the meeting for the Management and the same number for the opposition.

M S Goldstine appealed to the meeting to work together for the common good. They were, after all, he said, out for the benefit of the Institution. His words had no effect and the meeting became more wild and ungovernable as time went on.

M L Weinstein, who had seceded from the Committee, alleged in his speech that six people were ruling the Institution, and he spoke of them as 'The House of Lords'. Nothing was being done by the present management, he added. As a straightforward man he could not agree to be on the Committee. Mr Weinstein was on his feet for half an hour facing a veritable fusillade of interruptions mingled with applause. People from all parts of the Hall shouted to him impatiently to give the other speakers an opportunity to speak as time was short. Mr Weinstein persisted in proceeding, and he alleged that the Balance Sheet was not a proper one to put before a meeting. 'We are given everything in a lump' he said 'and are expected to swallow it'.

During the rest of the meeting - it was now four o'clock - no speaker was able to make himself heard because of the booing, hissing and shouting that was going on.

It was obvious that it was impossible for the Chairman to control the gathering, and he was urged by some of his own supporters to close the meeting. Mr Wenter continued, however, and when he made a reference to a conversation which he had had with Rabbi Ferber, someone shouted out 'liar', and again a number of people nearly came to blows.

Angry and worn after his fruitless attempts to keep order, the Chairman declared, 'This is just the reason why you lost your Temple!'

Councillor Bolsom, who represents the St Marlboro Ward on the Westminster City Council, made a strenuous but unsuccessful effort to restore order by taking the Chair when it was decided to proceed with the election of officers.

Nominations were asked for the office of President, and Mr Wenter was nominated by the 'Ministerialists' and Mr J M Kleinfeld by the 'Opposition'.

Five minutes remained, and it became obvious that it would be impossible to proceed with the election as there was no semblance of order. Ultimately the meeting broke up in chaos and confusion.

May 16   Elections at Central Synagogue.

Wardens	Joseph H Jacobs and Desmond A Tuck
Board of Management	Sir Robert Waley Cohen KBE Leon Engel, Harry Franks, G Gabriel, Henry Jacobs, Hyman Lewis, Edmund A Phillips, Anthony de Rothschild, Charles Stone, H Strauss

The Board donated £200 to the West Central Jewish Lads' Club. A call was made for younger people to join in the work of the Synagogue.

May 23 West Central Ladies' Guild working under the auspices of the West End Talmud Torah distributed over 1,000 lbs of Matzot etc prior to Passover besides £70 in cash to the poor of the West Central District. The West End Relief Institution distributed boots and clothes among the poor children attending the Talmud Torah.

On Wednesday next, prizes to be given at the Astoria Dance Salon included 'the most novel Tennis, Boating, and Golf attire'.

May 30   Western Synagogue elections:

President	Joseph Ullmann

Senior Warden	Lewis Phillips
Junior Warden	Max Rosin
Treasurer	John Shackman
Hon Solicitor	Samuel Moore
Hon Auditors	Charles C Lyon & Lewis Edwards
Board of Management	M Goldberg, W Herrmann, H Harris, E Konskier, Lewis Edward, C C Lyon, H M Marx, H Nelson, L Rose, S Rosenbloom, D L Moss

Jun 6   *Othello* at Savoy Theatre with Paul Robeson, Sybil Thorndike, Maurice Brown, and Peggy Ashcroft.

Jun 20   *All Quiet on the Western Front* at Regal, Marble Arch and Alhambra, Leicester Square.

Jul 11   Letter from Mr M Eisenstadt (secretary for Tarbut) 75 Great Russell Street.

Permit me to bring to the notice of the readers of the Jewish Chronicle that the Tarbut Association has opened a Hebrew Lending Library at the premises of the Beth HaSepher, 26a Soho Square.   The library, which contains works of fiction (original and translated), books of reference etc. is open on weekdays (Monday to Friday) from 11 a.m. to 7 p.m. The library has been opened to meet a long-felt need for easier facilities to obtain Hebrew books in London.

25th annual athletic meeting of the Association for Jewish Youth at King's Oak Sports Ground, Epping Forest.   West Central came second to Cambridge and Bethnal Green out of nine in the Boys' Section. The Old Girls' came third out of five, and the Girls third out of eight. [Complete list of winners and runners-up in *Jewish World* of 10.7.30]

The adjourned annual meeting of the West End Talmud Torah will be resumed on Sunday at Poland Street Rehearsal Rooms when it is hoped to proceed with the election of officers.   Mr Elsley Zeitlyn, who has consented to act as arbitrator in certain disputes which have arisen between groups of members, will preside.

Jul 18   Adjourned AGM of West End Talmud Torah:

Since the last meeting in May, which ended in chaotic disorder, Mr Elsley Zeitlyn has acted as arbitrator between the two disputing factions and has succeeded in securing agreement so that last Sunday's meeting passed off perfectly satisfactorily.

Officers were elected and a new constitution, as drawn up by Mr Zeitlyn for the Talmud Torah and its kindred institutions, was adopted.

Mr Zeitlyn, who presided, urged the members to forget the past and to subordinate every consideration to that of the Institution. He expressed the hope that unity and harmony would now characterise their activities and that they would all combine to continue the good work that had been accomplished in the past. The *Jewish Chronicle,* said Mr Zeitlyn, had a representative present that afternoon. It was a journal which was in every English-speaking Jewish home. As the conduct of the meeting would be closely scrutinised it was very important that their demeanour should be in consonance with the great objects for which their Institution existed.

Elected:

Elder	S Wenter
President	E Zeitlyn
Vice President	J M Kleinfeld
Treasurer	H Liberman
Wardens	David Cohen and J Raphael
Trustee (President of the Protest Committee)	S Fisher
Trustee	J Handel
Auditors	S Goldstein, M Goldberg, G Lyons

and a committee of 25[!].

36th Annual Report of West Central Jewish Girls' Club. 52 educational classes with 39 teachers provided by the London County Council. 13 voluntary teachers and 10 members who act as voluntary teachers. Average evening attendance of 170 and a total membership of classes of 790. A feature of the Club is that the work is self-supporting, the members taking responsibility for its upkeep.

'More and more', says the Report, 'we become a Central rather than a West Central Club, serving a wider radius and extending our influence in many directions.   Increasingly, our members are our helpers, workers, and leaders, and we take some satisfaction in the knowledge that many have, through Club influence and training, gone forth into the life of the City as workers and leaders in communal and civic affairs, imbued with the Club ideals and with a strong attachment to Judaism and the belief in it as the foundation of all work.

Total membership of club 964 - actual members 908 (350 over age of 21), associate girl members 18, associate men members 38.

In the report of the Jewish Day Settlement (of which Mrs L B Schlesinger is President) mention is made of the fact that it caters for the families of West Central Club members.   It also concerns itself primarily with local needs, and offers facilities for medical help for adults and children, has an employment bureau for girls, gives legal aid for its associates, and provides educational and recreational opportunities for married women and children.   The Misses Montagu, through the help of Miss Lazarus, are in touch with 800 homes which are not directly connected with the Club.

Jul 25   Central Synagogue Religious Classes.   On Sunday last the children attending the classes were entertained by Mr and Mrs Joseph H Jacobs at their country estate 'Woodlands', Chesham Bois, Bucks.   During the day, sports were held and the winners were awarded with prizes presented by Mr and Mrs Leon Engel.

West End and West Central Talmud Torah had their annual outing to Eastcote on Monday.   Each child was presented with a sixpence and prizes for sports were distributed.   M L Isenberg presented the prizes and gave each child a box of chocolates.   Gifts were also presented by Mr J M Kleinfeld.

Astoria Dance Salon announced the very latest in new dance floors had just been laid down.

Aug 8   Social and Personal. Jeanetta Lady Tuck will return to 29 Park Crescent on 22 August from Harrogate. Lord and Lady Jessel have left 24 South Street for the country.

Sep 19   Social and Personal. Lady Rothschild will return to 148 Piccadilly at the end of the month from Yorkshire.

Full page appeal for funds by the Federation of Jewish Relief Organisations, 33 Soho Square, on behalf of 'suffering brethren in Eastern Europe'.   Federation in its 11th year.   'Harried in Poland; Famishing in Russia; Tormented in Roumania; Starving in Lithuania'.

George Topper advertised opening of new salons for men and women - 'distinctive modern hairdressing' at 237 Oxford Street over Oxford Circus Station. Entrance in Argyll Street.

Golders Green Orphan Aid Society held their 8th Annual Ball in the New Ball Room at the Trocadero in Shaftesbury Avenue. Tickets one guinea. Catering by J Lyons and Co. Dancing to Ambrose and his Famous Dance Band. A Ball for the Brady Associated Clubs was to be held at the Savoy.

Sep 26   Letter from Mr W Warshansky and others:

May we bring to the notice of Old Boys of the Westminster Jews' Free School that Mr L E Israel, their old friend and schoolmaster, is leaving after 36 years service. Knowing the regard and esteem in which he was held we feel sure there are hundreds of Old Boys who would like to join in presenting Mr Israel with a suitable momento on his retirement. A committee for this purpose has been formed and we would be glad to receive remittances from all those who would care to associate themselves with this presentation, which should be sent to the joint treasurers at 191-3 Oxford Street on or before October 20 next.

At Association for Jewish Youth 21st Annual Swimming Competition West Central came equal last of eight clubs.

Sep 26   Murray's Club, Beak Street, advertised open for all functions, including weddings and *barmitzvahs*, April to September, on Sundays only. Catering by M Stern & Sons. 'Only a few Sundays left'.

Of approximately 500 personal and trade greetings for *Rosh Hashonah*, only seven from West End addresses:

> Mr and Mrs M Kutock and son, 31 D'Arblay Street, Soho

Rev and Mrs A Kezelman, the Western Synagogue, Alfred Place

Mr and Mrs C Kleinfeld, the Fitzroy Tavern

Mr and Mrs J.M Kleinfeld and daughter, 43 Windmill Street

Mr and Mrs Harris Savitt, sons and daughters, 138 Windmill Street

Mr and Mrs Isaac Woolfson, 66 Portland Court

Mr and Mrs S Jay and family, 32 Charlotte Street

Oct 24   Double-fronted shop in Oxford Street, with basement, advertised at £650 p.a. by Rosswick, estate agents of 245 Oxford Street.

Dec 19   Abrahamson's Restaurant in Wardour Street under new management. Introduced a special *Table D'Hôte* Luncheon for 2/9d from Monday December 22. Specimen menu: chopped liver or herring; lockshen or pea soup; roast or boiled beef and two vegetables; fruit compote; tea or coffee. Only restaurant in West End under Commission for Kashruth.

XI - THE SYNAGOGUES

The immigrant quarters of large towns often included a proliferation of *shtiebls*. They generally occupied small houses or shops, and had services marked by their passion, length and noise. Their congregants were determined to ensure that their religion endured and their children carried on the work. To a large extent, such *shtiebls* existed in the East End, but it was not quite the same in the West End. There were one or two examples of that genre, but they were not widespread.

For the most part, the original Jewish settlers in the West End were not fleeing from persecution or economic hardship. Rather, they were the well-established, better-off section of the community who, by the 1880s, when the main influx into Soho and Fitzrovia began, had already established synagogues to satisfy a wide spectrum of religious preference - from 'cathedral' synagogue to vociferous *shtiebl*. There was no representative of extreme orthodoxy, but the choice was wide. The principal synagogues, in order of foundation were:

Western [1761], independent, a maverick of synagogues. A secessionist group formed **Maiden Lane Synagogue** [1821]

West London Synagogue of British Jews [1842], Reform

Central [1855] originally a branch of the Great Synagogue and subsequently a founder member of the United Synagogue

West End Great [1880] started as the **West End Talmud Torah,** merged with the **Bikkur Cholim** [in 1910], and moved from its original premises in Green's Court to Brewer Street, then to Manette Street, and finally to Dean Street. It now incorporates the **Beth HaSepher** [1910] with which it merged in 1948, and is an independent synagogue affiliated to the Federation of Synagogues.

West Central Liberal Synagogue [1928] which arose out of the Jewish Religious Union [1902].

Marble Arch [1961] which amalgamated [1991] with the Western at Great Cumberland Place under the title **Western Marble Arch.**

Only Marble Arch remains on its original site. The buildings of three of the Synagogues - the Western, the Central and the West Central Liberal, were destroyed by bombing in 1941.

There were other comparatively minor or short-lived synagogues. The Sephardi community opened a branch of **Bevis Marks** at 4/5 Wigmore Street in 1853, which moved to Bryanston Street in 1861. Neither attracted good attendances and in 1896 the congregation moved on to Lauderdale Road in Maida Vale.

Bloomsbury Synagogue was established at 40 Lamb's Conduit Street in about 1912 and the **West London Hebrew Congregation** at 119 New Cavendish Street in 1943. By 1950 the two congregations had amalgamated at Lamb's Conduit Street under the title **West London and Bloomsbury Synagogue.**

There were a few small synagogues that came and went, more *minyans* of friends meeting in a room for prayers rather than established synagogues. Some synagogues, outside the boundaries that we have set, would doubtless consider themselves to be - or to have been - West End Synagogues. The **New West End** [1879], the **Bayswater Synagogue** [1863, but no longer in existence], and **St John's Wood** [1876], could lay claim to be so included, but the line had to be drawn somewhere.

THE WESTERN SYNAGOGUE AND THE MAIDEN LANE SECESSIONISTS

The Western Synagogue started its life in or about 1761 in the house of Wolf Liepman in Great Pulteney Street. Liepman was born in Germany in 1698 of a distinguished family. He came to England, via Vienna and St Petersburg, and established himself as a prosperous merchant. A philanthropist, he was a generous patron of learning and culture. In the mid-18th century, there were several Jewish families in and around Rupert Street, Broadwick Street, Berwick Street, Carnaby Street, Great Windmill Street, Leicester Square, Strand, Pulteney Street, Panton Street and Orange Street - enough Jews to justify holding regular services, for which Wolf Liepman supplied the premises.

Thus was the *Hebra Kaddisha Shel Gemilluth Hassadim, Westminster* established. It became a combination of synagogue and burial society, with some features of a friendly society out of which the Westminster congregation gradually evolved. The minyan moved to a hired room in Back Alley, Denmark Court, Strand, on the site of the present Strand Palace Hotel. In 1797, it removed to Dibdin's Theatre, *Sans Souci,* also in Denmark Court. The building had previously been occupied as a picture gallery by the Royal Academy, and had a hall of some 50 feet by 36 feet, as well as two rooms for vestry and office purposes. The Strand, and certain other streets nearby, were infamous for their houses of ill repute, but by the synagogue's rules any person keeping a disorderly house was debarred from all religious privileges.

The Parish Overseer annotated the rate-books in the following terms:

"Denmark Court - as respectable as most of the courts in this ward. Here the Christian and the Jew associate in apparent harmony, an instructive example to the rest of the community."

There never came a time when it needed to be said that this harmony no longer prevailed. Overt anti-semitism reared its head in the West End comparatively infrequently.

The synagogue was strict in preserving the dignity of its officials and the services. Anyone leaving a meeting without the permission of the President was fined. Anybody bringing a *mitzvah* into contempt paid 18/-. No youth under the age of 18 was allowed to join in the processional circuits of *lulav*-bearers on Succoth. One unexpected rule was that 'No flunkey in livery' *[meshoret in sein leevra-malbushim]* could have either an *aliyah* or a *mitzvah*. There were Jewish coachmen and footmen, butlers and valets, waiting upon their blue-blooded masters in the Sephardi community as well as on non-Jewish nobility and gentry. They were not necessarily frowned upon as inferior; they were allowed entry to the synagogue, but silken breeches and golden hose were not regarded as an enhancement of the dignity of a house of worship.

In 1810, the almost inevitable occurred: there was an internal squabble the cause of which, as is so often the case, is obscure. A secessionist movement, calling itself *Amude Yesharim,* 'The Pillars of Uprightness', established a rival congregation. Its leaders hired a room for services first, probably, in Dean Street, a little later in Brewer Street, and finally in larger premises in Maiden Lane, Covent Garden. It became known as the **Maiden Lane Synagogue** and purchased its own burial ground in Bancroft Road, Mile End. It did not rejoin the main congregation until almost a hundred years later, in 1907.

The Western's next move was to St Alban's Place, Haymarket in 1826. It accommodated 500, and on High Festivals the number could be increased. For the first time it was officially named the Western Synagogue. Long after it left this site, it was still known to many West Enders not as 'The Western' but as 'The Haymarket Synagogue'.

By 1840, there was a distinct change in the general composition and outlook of the congregation. It was not being fed by newcomer immigrants and was becoming increasingly anglicised. The more successful denizens of the City, who included people with a fair standard of secular education and English culture, had been rapidly migrating westward. They no longer 'lived above the business' in the City, but were socially rising in status and motivated by the desire to equate their Jewish life with their English background. They rejected Chief Rabbi Herschell's excommunication imposed on the West London Synagogue of British Jews in 1842, and refused to allow it to be read out in the synagogue. Subsequently, a number of prominent families joined the Western.

When the Central Synagogue opened in 1855 some feared that the Western would lose members to it. Undoubtedly, it did. The Haymarket was ceasing to be residential and was becoming geographically obsolete as a synagogue site. The number of vacant seats was increasing, so Chief Rabbi Nathan Marcus Adler was consulted to see whether some terms could be negotiated to prevent further erosion of their numbers. The Western's toleration of the Reform Congregation could not have helped their cause, nor the fact that they had voted against Adler's election to his office. The Central, which also had a large number of vacant seats, made it plain they would not co-operate. The approach was rejected.

In 1870, three events occurred, making the Western Synagogue's future in the Haymarket even more precarious. The Central moved to its fine new building in Great Portland Street; the Reform Congregation erected its magnificent edifice in Upper Berkeley Street; and the United Synagogue, founded by statute that year, became a powerful influence in the Anglo-Jewish community. The prestige of the Western's antiquity did not compensate for its diminishing support.

Nonetheless the Western Synagogue survived. It had some notable members, including Lily Montagu's father, Sir Samuel Montagu MP, Mr (later Sir) Stuart M.Samuel MP, Viscount Stern, Lady Battersea, Leopold Neumegen (who kept the well-known Jewish school at Kew), Sidney Woolf QC, and Hannah de Rothschild (who, despite marrying out of the fold to the future prime minister Lord Rosebery, often attended on Sabbaths and Festivals, made gifts of £25 on Yom Kippur, gave 200 guineas to the building fund, visited St Alban's Place after the birth of each of her children to render thanks for recovery from childbirth, and remained a member until her death in 1890).

The Western's position was strengthened when it added to its Brompton cemetery by opening another burial ground, at Edmonton, with the first interment in 1886. Further, some fences were mended when Hermann Adler succeeded his father as Chief Rabbi. However, given the mobility of the Jewish population in the West End its site was becoming increasingly untenable. In 1897, at a celebration at the synagogue at which Dr Moses Gaster, the Haham, and Professor D W Marks of the Reform, were also present, Adler said although the Western had outlived its usefulness in an area which was rapidly diminishing in its Jewish population, there was a spot within half a mile or so which was crying out for spiritual ministrations and influences. He was referring to Soho, where the new Jewish migrants, he said, had the reputation of being generally irreligious and over-zealous in their search for excitement and amusements. He compared the blank monotony of the toil of the East End worker with the lives of the young people in Soho who, he said, had abandoned the traditional Jewish love of home life, and were wont to spend the evenings walking abroad in the crowded streets where snares and pitfalls were found at every step. They were even known 'to frequent places of entertainment which had too often proved entrances to the Chamber of Death!' He emphasised that living in the Soho district demanded 'extreme vigilance and circumspection' and gave rise to 'the gravest apprehensions for the future of Jewish youths and maidens'. He appealed to the Western's congregation not to be contented to remain just an empty shadow of its former self but to 'seize the opportunity of becoming a new centre radiating spiritual, moral and social betterment'. He begged them to take advantage of the opportunities that now existed of union with the metropolitan community.

The *Jewish Chronicle* approved of the Chief Rabbi's speech, and said that although union with the United Synagogue might prove difficult, because the Western would not want to give up its independence, it hoped that means might be found of amalgamating St Alban's Place with the Maiden Lane Synagogue and the West End Talmud Torah which had been established in the very heart of Soho 17 years earlier. An entirely new synagogue, it urged, could be erected in place of the three existing structures, which were all inadequate to the needs of the locality. This did not happen, although Maiden Lane did later return to its mother synagogue.

In 1903, the Western Synagogue received a large bequest from a Sephardi called Judah Varicas. He had been a member of the Spanish and Portuguese congregation but fell out, first with them and then with the Central over seating arrangements. He joined the Western, and left it close upon £12,000. In 1905, Sir Stuart Samuel, the President, said that although the financial position was satisfactory, and although the synagogue was supplying a need, he could not urge its continuance on its present site. Quite apart from the adverse flow of population, the property upon which the synagogue then stood was shortly to come on to the market, so the ultimate future of the congregation would have to be decided. He pointed out that the synagogue was already carrying on good work in Soho, where their ministers were continually doing their utmost to elevate the social status and improve the religious education of the Jewish population in that district. Their classes had been reorganised and had over 100 pupils, and one of the ministers, Gerald Friedlander, voluntarily undertook regular tuition to the Jewish children attending St Anne's Church Schools in Soho, numbering upwards of 120. Although the synagogue was in the midst of a neighbourhood of very large hotels and proved very useful to temporary visitors from all parts of the country, and indeed from every continent, he said that he believed that in view of the expiry of the lease, due in 1914, it would be unwise to spend any more money on the present structure.

In May 1914, it was resolved to erect a new building in Alfred Place, close by Tottenham Court Road, and in the meantime temporary accommodation was found in Whitfield Street. The foundation stone of the new building was laid on 7 June 1915, and due tribute was paid to Judah Varicas whose legacy had made it possible. Chief Rabbi Hertz said, 'This Western congregation has been a lighthouse of Judaism to many that otherwise might have been swallowed up by the waters of assimilation.'

The new building adjoined the Emily Harris Home and the West Central Jewish Girls' Club, with whom it had good relations. Lily Montagu, one of the leading figures in the Liberal Jewish movement, had many hundreds of orthodox young women at her Club, and on Sabbath she held divine services at which she acted as the Lay Minister. There could easily have arisen causes for conflict between the two organisations whose religious views were widely divergent. Happily, however, there was only co-operation. It was one of Miss Montagu's principles never to interfere with the religious views of her protégées so long as she knew that they were following a religious life. Rev Arthur Barnett, Minister of the Western for 30 years from 1924, could not recall a single instance where there was any attempt at seducing girls from orthodox homes into the Liberal movement.

The building was fully completed in 1924. Its architect was Claude W Ferrier, and it was beautiful in design with the furniture all of rich oak. However, despite its attractive appearance and seating capacity for 650 people, the building lacked adequate offices, a board room or a meeting hall of any kind. Even more importantly, it lacked suitable classroom space. Barnett said that the paucity of numbers at the normal Sabbath services was quite heartbreaking to those who ministered within its precincts, and in spite of repeated efforts to improve the situation very little progress was achieved. Most unfortunate of all, the building had again been sited in the wrong place. It had not been foreseen, and perhaps could not have been foreseen, that within a very short time the residential character of the Western Synagogue's new neighbourhood would undergo a complete change. Residences in Bloomsbury Square and other squares, then occupied by fairly well-circumstanced households, were being transformed into commercial and office properties, while Soho was inhabited mainly by poorer artisans and shopkeepers who could not easily maintain expensive buildings that eventually cost more than £45,000. Moreover, they were already being served by the West End Talmud Torah Synagogue, which was rapidly expanding and, through its Burial Society and Religion schools, was proving most attractive to the Soho population. It was only on the festivals, and particularly the high holydays, that one could experience any warmth in the services at the Western. Nevertheless, many members who had moved away from the area still supported the Western Synagogue, and the soul of the congregation survived.

Rachele Kalman has carried out most interesting research into the marriage registers of the West End synagogues where one or both parties lived in the area at the date of the marriage [See Appendix II]. Her results and conclusions will be referred to throughout this and following chapters. The Western's Marriage Registers show that in the period between 1870 and 1910 38 per cent of its members lived in Soho, 22 per cent in Bloomsbury, 13 per cent in Fitzrovia, 10 per cent in Marylebone, and 5 per cent in Mayfair. The percentages remained more or less constant in Soho and Bloomsbury until 1945, but in the latter part of the period Fitzrovia became increasingly important, and the numbers there increased to 23 per cent at the expense of Covent Garden, Mayfair and Marylebone.

By 1927, the congregation was compelled to recognise that if it wished to serve the poorer population in the district and compete with the West End Talmud Torah, it had to set up its own burial society. A Western Synagogue Burial Society was duly established, and it did lead to an increase of membership.

Though many were worthy of praise, Arthur Barnett made particular comment on two men who contributed greatly to the work and the funds of the Synagogue during the 1920s and 1930s. Max Rosin, who became Warden in 1926, was described as:

... a man of large heart and keen mind who understood the needs of Soho probably better than any other member of the Board of Management. Max Rosin never tired of relating with pride how he had begun life in Poland as a *Yeshiva-Bachur* [seminary student] and came to this country with exactly 12/- in his pocket. By the time he had become Warden of the Western he was the owner of a chain of continuously expanding bakeries and shops which had turned him into a man of considerable wealth. The headquarters of his extensive business were in the heart of Soho and he understood its needs. He never forgot his origins, indeed he was proud of them. Although his greatest love, apart from his family, was his business, he had a warm corner in his heart for many other things. He was naturally at home with Yiddish literature, and read avidly not only his Shalom Aleichem and his Sholem Asch, but equally his Tolstoi and his Talmud. An avid zionist, he gave lavishly to that cause as well as to numerous other needs both at home and abroad.

It was through his beneficence that when the troubles in Germany broke out in the 1930's the Congregation became the channel of a gift of a mobile synagogue to the Magen David Adom organisation working in Europe. Barnett describes him as a tower of strength to the congregation during one of its most difficult periods.

Another man who contributed enormously to the Western Synagogue was Alfred Tannenbaum, for many years its Treasurer. He came from Poland, and entered the provision market in the City, and was for some time a very highly esteemed Chairman of the Provision Brokers' Association. He rejoiced in helping deserving cases secretly, and very few knew of the extent of his philanthropic activities. He shunned publicity of any kind and 'did good by stealth and blushed to find it fame'. In 1946, the Western received £7,000, one seventh of his residuary estate.

In 1939, the synagogue opened a hostel to house and maintain a small number of refugees from Nazi Europe. This was made possible by the generosity of the firm of Covent Garden merchants, Messrs. Manuel, that placed the upper part of their business premises in Goodge Street at the disposal of the congregation. The Ladies' Guild renovated and furnished the rooms and obtained sufficient subscribers to guarantee a weekly subsistence allowance for the residents, while Messrs. Manuel daily provided such fruit and vegetables as they cared to choose.

Services continued after the Second World War started, but to a diminishing congregation. Then, on the night of 16/17 April 1941, the building was destroyed by bombing. Twenty-seven people sheltering in the basement of the adjoining club were killed.

"There is one aspect of this tragic scene, however, which inspired a comforting thought.   Mounted above the entrance-gates, which had withstood the force of the bomb, was a massive piece of masonry in the form of the 'Two Tablets of Stone' inscribed with the Decalogue. It stood miraculously, phantastically, gaunt and desolate against the sky, as if suspended in mid air. And it seemed to deliver a message of triumph, as though defiantly to declare: 'Many are the devices in the heart of man; but the plan of the Lord, *it shall stand'* ".

Barnett's opinion was that the Alfred Place synagogue could justifiably be termed a magnificent failure, and that when eventually it met with catastrophe, terrible and tragic though it was, out of the dust and ashes there arose a new hope.

The congregation was offered facilities by the Central, but that too was destroyed by bombing six months later. Both congregations transferred to Woburn House where joint services were held. Despite pressure, they did not succumb to suggestions that the two should amalgamate; the Western wished to maintain its independence.

In 1943, the congregation re-established itself in the Grotrian Hall, Wigmore Street, at a rental of £400 per annum. Within six months, this building was destroyed by an incendiary raid, and the congregation was on the move again. Worship continued in an adjoining shop, which was named the Max Rosin Hall. Here, they welcomed servicemen and played host to the Jewish Historical Society of England, whose building had also been bombed. In 1946, a new home was found in Carton Street, Marylebone - the congregation's eighth consecration. The building was the former 'Royal Chapel of the French Exiles', originally built in 1789, and it was consecrated on 4 June 1947. Membership increased to 400 within a year.

The search for a permanent site continued, and in 1957 the congregation moved to Crawford Place, Marylebone, just a few yards from Edgware Road. This building was previously a nonconformist, non-sectarian chapel, founded in 1846 by the Rev Ridley Haim Herschell, a renegade Jew born in Prussian Poland of two Jewish parents. (His son became Lord Herschell, the Lord Chancellor). The congregation thus vacated a church, once the home of French refugees, for another church founded by a converted Jew! The new building had accommodation for 800, adequate offices and classrooms, a library, a museum and a large meeting-cum-banqueting hall.

The exterior was modern and rather severe, but the interior had dignity and warmth. Numerous stained-glass windows added to the colour and pleasing aspect of the interior.

The Western's traditional tolerance was exemplified in its policy on the use of its cemeteries in Edmonton and, from 1951, in Southgate. The cemeteries served as a burial ground for many congregations of widely divergent Jewish views - synagogues of the Federation, other synagogues in north and south-east London, and, in more recent times, communities as different as the Adath-Israel and the Bernhard Baron Settlement. Through its cemeteries, the Western offered 'an acre of peace' and helped to reconcile Jews whose views kept them apart in life.

However, West End Jews continued to move out of the area and the Western became less and less viable. In May 1991, it was amalgamated with the Marble Arch Synagogue in Great Cumberland Place under the title Western Marble Arch - still independent but associated with the United Synagogue.

In his foreword to Arthur Barnett's book, Cecil Roth said of the Western:

> From the beginning it had its own physiognomy, expressing its intermediate geographical - and by the same token 'political' - position. It lay between the City and the West End, and hence reflected to some extent the atmosphere of both. It maintained cordial relations with the various London communities and organisations, but was not subservient to them and refused to be swallowed up by them. At all times of communal strife it persisted in observing a benevolent neutrality between the warring communal organisations, whether East or West, 'Right' or 'Left' of it, without however surrendering or imperilling its own conservative independence.

WEST LONDON SYNAGOGUE OF BRITISH JEWS

After a long period of gestation, the Reform movement in England was established on 15 April 1840. The declaration that heralded its arrival was signed by 24 gentlemen, nineteen Sephardim and five Ashkenazim, at a meeting at the Bedford Hotel in Russell Square. The founders sought:

> ... the establishment of a synagogue *in the western part of the metropolis* where a revised service may be performed at hours more suited to our habits, and in a manner more calculated to inspire feelings of devotion,

where religious instruction may be afforded by competent persons, and where to effect these purposes, Jews generally may form a United Congregation under the denomination of British Jews.

Nearly all the founders were members of 'the Cousinhood', the significant omission being the Rothschilds. Nine were Mocattas. There were Montefiores, Henriques, a Lousada and a de Castro - all old established Sephardi families with broad economic and secular interests covering the spectrum of law, commerce and banking. Of the five Ashkenazim three were members of the Goldsmid family.

The declaration had followed many criticisms made over a period of years against the City synagogues. The complainants considered the services were too long, held at inconvenient hours, and observed in an unimpressive manner. They objected to the order of the services and to the absence of religious instruction. Many disliked the inattentiveness of worshippers, the sale of special prayers *(misheberach),* and congregational behaviour which they considered were 'more suited to the coffee house or exchange'. Most importantly, from a West End viewpoint, they wanted synagogues nearer their West End residences. Sir Moses Montefiore, who lived in Park Lane, and a few others, were content to make the 4½-mile journey on foot, but they were a very small minority. Some stayed away from the synagogue, and others withdrew completely from both the community and religion. There was an attempt in the 1820s to hold services elsewhere, but under threat of *herem* (excommunication) the offenders recanted.

Appeals for change made to the elders and clergy of Bevis Marks and the Great were largely ignored. No positive response was forthcoming to the request for West End branches. The older synagogues feared losing direct control of the community; they feared that giving a little might lead to sacrificing a lot. Their basic response was to do nothing and hope that somehow the clamour would die down. It was an impossible position to maintain because the tide of fashion and wealth was flowing westwards. The new West Enders were articulate and wealthy. Their actions were the beginning of the move of the centre of control of the London Jewish community from the East End to the West End.

Following the declaration of 1840, the reformers proposed the writing of a new prayer book, a revised order of service, and the inclusion of a sermon in English. All suggestions were considered heretical, and served only to increase the distrust and consternation of the East End elders. In September 1841, Chief Rabbi Solomon Hirschell - with the backing, and indeed at the instigation of Bevis Marks - issued a *herem* against the new community, and it was publicly read out by the respective secretaries in the Great and other Jewish places of worship in London (except at the Western which in keeping with its independent position refused to do so).

The resolve of the reformers remained undiminished and the new prayer book was completed. A minister, Rev Professor David Woolf Marks of Liverpool was appointed, and a synagogue in Burton Street, Bloomsbury (situated between Upper Woburn Place and Cartwright Gardens) was consecrated on 27 January 1842. The new congregation called itself The West London Synagogue of British Jews.

The *herem* created problems with regard to marriages and burials. The Registration Act of 1836 made special provision for Jews. They were allowed to maintain their own practices after giving notice to the Registrar and obtaining the appropriate certificate. The stumbling point was that they first needed confirmation from the Board of Deputies that they were a recognised place of worship. Sir Moses Montefiore, who was President of the Board, opposed the new synagogue and refused to grant it recognition. As a result, members had to have civil marriages before a Registrar. Later in the day, they stood under the *chuppa* in the synagogue.

The *herem* also barred the congregation from the existing burial grounds, and temporary arrangements were made with Maiden Lane Synagogue. In 1843, the West London opened its own burial grounds in Balls Pond Road, Islington. Long since closed for interments, it contains the graves of many of the leading lights of the early days of the Movement.

The congregation soon outgrew the Burton Street building and in June 1849 it moved into a new synagogue at 50 Margaret Street that had seating for 400 - 250 downstairs and 150 in the Ladies' Gallery. Shortly before the new building's consecration the *herem* was removed by the Ecclesiastical Authorities of the Spanish and Portuguese synagogue. The problem of marriages was overcome when in 1856 the West London obtained a Marriage Act of its own, making it independent of the Board of Deputies.

The congregation continued to grow, and a search began for larger and more permanent premises. In 1866, they acquired a site in Upper Berkeley Street, and sufficient funds to appoint the architects, Davis and Emanuel, to design the building. The new synagogue was consecrated in September 1870.

Of the Jews who lived in the West End district and married at the West London Synagogue in the 103 years between 1842 and 1945, only 6 per cent came from the Soho area. Thirty-eight per cent lived in the Bloomsbury/Holborn district, thirty-eight per cent in Marylebone, and 13 per cent in Mayfair. Few were tailors; the largest single occupation of the bridegrooms was 'merchant', followed by stockbrokers, jobbers and professional men. In 1900, the 32 members of the Council included five Henriques, three Mocattas, three Montefiores and two Waleys.

The magnificent interior of the present building reflects its origins. The strong Moorish influence in the great arches of the interior and cupola above the Ark are eloquent reminders of the Sephardic background of the founding fathers of the synagogue.

The West London, one of the most beautiful of the Victorian synagogues, continues to flourish with a membership of more than 2,000, but only 6 per cent live in the West End!

CENTRAL SYNAGOGUE

A full story of the events leading to the consecration of the Central Synagogue in Great Portland Street can be found in Cecil Roth's *History of the Great Synagogue*. As previously indicated, the Great was slow to react to the opening of the Reform Synagogue in Burton Street. When, at last, there were no excuses for further procrastination, it took the lease of a warehouse in Portland Street and adapted it for synagogue use. On 29 March 1855 (six and a half years after the proposal had first been approved) the new place of worship was inaugurated in the presence of a large and distinguished congregation. The inordinate delay had, of course, given the West London synagogue valuable time in which to consolidate itself in the community in general, and in the West End in particular.

To make the position of the new synagogue crystal clear, a proclamation was made from the *bima*:

> Notice is hereby given that this building now about to be consecrated is a *branch* of the Great Synagogue, situate in Duke's Place, in the parish of St James's Aldgate, in the City of London.

Originally, the Central Synagogue was not permitted to have its own honorary officers, save those appointed on its behalf by the parent congregation; it could not solemnise marriages; and its financial affairs were strictly managed by the Great. Control of this West End synagogue was firmly in the grip of the East End.

Central's first reader was Aaron Levy Green, and one of his successors, Michael Adler, said the Synagogue owed its prominence in the community as much to his remarkable personality as to the social status of its worshippers. Green was born in London in 1821 and was already taking part in services at the Great Synagogue at the age of fourteen. He became such an eloquent and witty preacher that it was said of him:

> He was certainly *the* minister who established the Jewish pulpit in England, and made it a necessary adjunct of the Synagogue. There had been preachers before him, but when one heard some of them, one felt inclined to say 'Thank God we have no Jewish pulpit' ...'.

His nephew, A A Green claimed that his uncle 'more than any other man created the position of the Jewish minister in this country'.

The reference to the social status of the Central's members gives a clue to the position it held. It was initially a synagogue for the wealthy and influential in Jewish society. The Building Committee included Sir Anthony Rothschild, Lionel L Cohen, Jacob Waley, Hyam L Beddington, Edward H Beddington, Alfred H Beddington, Ephraim Alex, Samuel Montagu, Alderman Sir B S Phillips, and Henry B Worms. In 1870, of the eight Jewish MP's five, including three Rothschilds, were members of the Central Synagogue. The other three were members of the Reform Congregation.

The Portland Street building was superseded in 1870 by another in Great Portland Street, whose consecration was very much a grand Anglo-Jewish occasion. Erected to the designs of N S Joseph it had a traditional layout with a central bimah, was 'Moorish in detail, Gothic in feeling (with a soaring vaulted nave) and employed cast iron columns to carry the galleries and roof'. It was England's largest synagogue and seated 860, almost equally divided between men and women. The reporter of the *Jewish Chronicle* who attended the ceremony said, 'As far as can be judged by a non-professional eye, the whole building represents an appearance of great solidity, of strength, and it seems to be such a structure as would yet be in its prime when our great grandchildren will be old men.' It became one of the great cathedral synagogues of Anglo-Jewry, and remained so until the fatal day of 10 May 1941 when it was destroyed by enemy action.

Its 396 male seatholders in 1875 compared with 449 at the Great in the East End. In 1913, the figures were 400 and 434 respectively, and during the intervening period were mostly within this range. The average financial contribution to the United Synagogue from 1875 to 1894 was higher at the Central than at the Great. Sir Anthony de Rothschild was one of its first wardens, and Leopold de Rothschild married Mademoiselle Maria Perugia there in January 1881 during one of the worst blizzards of the century. The Prince of Wales and Lord Rosebery were among the guests, and they sat with Alfred and Nathaniel in the Warden's Box.

Others associated with the Central in the 1880s were S J Phillips of 113 New Bond Street, Leopold de Rothschild, the Beyfus family of Russell Square and Bedford Square, Ellis Franklin, Isaac Franklin, Alfred de Rothschild, Sir Nathaniel de Rothschild, Baron F de Rothschild, Simon Montefiore Waley of Wimpole Street, the Wertheimer family of New Bond Street, Baron G de Worms of Park Crescent and Baron H de Worms (later Lord Pirbright) of Old Burlington Street.

The Central continued to be one of the larger and wealthier synagogues in London, but as the century progressed it was surpassed by the New West End, Bayswater and Hampstead synagogues.

The 1898 *Jewish Year Book* notes that seatholders included Nathanial L Cohen of 3 Devonshire Place, D L Alexander QC of 11 York Gate, Regent's Park, several Beddingtons, B A Fersht of 151 Wardour Street, Ellis A Franklin and Sir Samuel Montagu,

Between 1920 and 1939, members included Mark Bonn of Gordon Mansions (Bonn's Matzos), Samuel Samuel MP, Sir Stuart Samuel MP, Alderman Percy Simmons (LCC), Louis Sterling, Albert Whelan, Isaac Wolfson, Cecil Bernstein, Charles Clore and S Gestetner.

Rachele's research reveals the residences of those who lived in the West End at the time of their marriage in Great Portland Street Synagogue. Not all those who married at the synagogue were members, nonetheless the figures provide a good indication of the changing nature of the congregation. Between 1871 and 1900 13 per cent were drawn from Soho, 54 per cent from Bloomsbury, 5 per cent from Covent Garden, 3 per cent from Mayfair, 16 per cent from Marylebone, and 9 per cent from Fitzrovia. Between 1900 and 1945 Soho reached a peak of 28 per cent and then fell to 6 per cent. Bloomsbury declined from 54 per cent to 16 per cent between 1921 and 1935, and Fitzrovia grew from 9 per cent to 35 per cent between 1921 and 1945. Marylebone jumped from 13 per cent between 1901 and 1920 to 34 per cent between 1936 and 1945. In the 1920s and 1930s the synagogue could still boast amongst its seatholders the Rt. Hon Viscount Bearstead, Lt Col Charles Waley Cohen, Sir Robert Waley Cohen, Anthony de Rothschild, and the Rt Hon The Lord Rothschild, and many members lived in Piccadilly, Park Lane, Berkeley Square, Mount Street, Devonshire Street, Weymouth Street, Portland Place, North Audley Street and Park Lane. However seatholders could also be found in working- or lower-middle class Little Titchfield Street, Howland Street, Cleveland Street, Great Titchfield Street, Grafton Street, Bedford Court Mansions, Foley Street, Dean Street, Goodge Street, Berwick Street, Charlotte Street, Rathbone Place, Bolsover Street, Broad(wick) Street, Whitfield Street, Saville Street, Wardour Street and Margaret Street.

A thriving religious school was instituted in 1880. Numbers hovered between 70 and 100 until the end of the 1920s, but after the Second World War neither the Central or the West End Great could sustain classes alone, and they joined forces for this purpose.

After the bombing in May 1941, the congregation held services at the Academy of Music in Marylebone Road, and then at Woburn House. It played host to Jewish servicemen from every community in Great Britain and to many from overseas. In the post-war years, it supplied kosher lunches for pupils at Marylebone Grammar School, and doubtless at other local schools.   It also supported refugees who had found a home in the West End.

With generous financial support from the Wolfson family and others, the new Central took two years to build and was completed in 1958.   There were more than 500 seats on the ground floor and 400 in the ladies' gallery.   It was consecrated in March 1958. Until the end of the 1960s, it retained much of its influence, but since then membership has declined and 83 per cent of its existing membership now live outside the area.

"When we were young most old Jewish families lived between Gloucester Square and Portland Place and they all went to synagogue on Saturday - either Upper Berkeley Street or Great Portland Street.   Everyone walked there and everyone dressed in black, and the men wore top hats ..."

"The magnificent and prestigious Central Synagogue was considered either as 'too posh' or 'too liberal' for many Sohoites. Despite that, it is surprising how many Jews who lived in this area chose Great Portland Street as the venue for their weddings."

"Slightly to the north-west was the beautiful cathedral synagogue in Great Portland Street, alas destroyed by fire in the blitz and now replaced by a simile of the Cumberland Hotel. Understandably a subjective view, but I consider the earlier synagogue to be the most beautiful and awesome I have ever known.   In company with Bayswater, Hampstead and the New West End, it was a temple for Anglo-Jewish ladies and gentlemen. The building itself was lofty and faced with glowing stained glass - the circular top windows were of a peculiarly beautiful violet/blue hue. The tall mahogany doors of the Ark were ceremoniously opened and closed by the top-hatted and frock-coated wardens, one of whom was Sir Raphael Tuck. The minister, whose delivery was in Oxford English, was the Rev Michael Adler DSO.   The *chazan* was the Rev Stoutzker, whose rather lamentable voice did not blend with the most magnificent choir I have ever heard in any synagogue. Mixed, of course, and perfectly acceptable to the Chief Rabbi of the day. At Succoth the *Succah* was a veritable Kew Gardens of fruit and flowers. The children were given sweets, a sixpence and - I shall always remember this - a large round biscuit smelling strongly of spices".

"Great Portland Street was a *shul* for the Rothschilds and the great ones of the land - my father used to call them the *Englischer Yehudim*. He disapproved of that synagogue because it had a mixed choir and that was contrary to his high standard of religious practice. He did not care for the minister, Rev Michael Adler, because he wore a dog-collar, and that was aping the *goyim*. Despite this, I was barmitzvah at the greatest, the noblest, the most exclusive synagogue of the West End, where Sir Adolph Tuck and Desmond Tuck and other noble families of that period used to *daven*. I was barmitzvah there because my father had quarrelled with the other three, and he had no option but to place me, as it were, in the midst of those *Englischer Yehudim* of whom he disapproved ... I remember the day. I think I read the whole *sidra* and the minister was very proud. When he gave his sermon he addressed the barmitzvah boy and praised me for my knowledge and my love of Hebrew. I felt very proud of myself. It was a great day, but at the end of the service my father said he doubted the strength of the minister's blessing. 'It will carry no weight in heaven'.

I was treated well there, although we were not members, and we were able to enjoy all its facilities. There was no *kiddush* in the *shul*, in those days. My father went home and he invited a few of his little *chevra* to come and have a glass of whisky at home at 76 Berwick Street. No presents. My father gave me a *chumash*. I looked upon Great Portland Street as my *shul* although I never became a member of it. Adler was a fine scholar. Later, when I made progress in my studies, I remember reading his books on Anglo-Jewish history, and I discovered Rev Adler was a man of considerable learning who had done a great deal of research on early medieval history. I also used his Hebrew Grammar. It was a standard book we had at the time for learning classical Hebrew. He was a man of considerable ability, considerable knowledge, and so later on I didn't share my father's contempt for the minister of Great Portland Street".

"I remember the West End Talmud Torah. ... it had more soul in it, more than Great Portland Street with all its marble".

WEST END GREAT AND RABBI ZVI FERBER

By 1880, the West End offered its residents a choice of synagogues - the Central, the Western and the West London, but none was attractive for many of the newly arrived, orthodox immigrants from villages and small towns in Russia and Poland who preferred the steamy, heady, intimate atmosphere of a *shteibl.* For these immigrants the Reform was out of the question. The Central was perceived to be for the wealthy, ('the Rothschilds and the great of the land'), and its service was in any event too English and its ambiance too church-like. The Western, only a little better, was at an inconvenient distance. Moreover, all were probably beyond the means of most immigrants. It was natural for the newly arrived immigrants not only to seek out their relations and *landsleit,* but also to set up a meeting place for worship that was more conducive to their desires, where they would feel more at ease with their God and with themselves. In such a place, they could recreate the social and religious life they had left behind.

Beatrice Potter, the social investigator, observed that most such *shteibls* were to be found in courts and alleyways, and so it was in the West End. Green's Court is a short, narrow uninviting alleyway, not more than ten feet wide which -   long before the era of strip and porn - was in a respectable if lively working-class area with a large Jewish residential population. It runs from Brewer Street, where Marks and Spencer had one of its first 'penny bazaars', to Peter Street, best known for the Pulteney School.

It was there, at number 10, that a small group banded together and formed a *minyan* in 1880. They met on the first floor above a shop where they remained for 30 years. For some years, they could not afford a rabbi and a member, Mr P Cohen, conducted the services.

In November 1892, they founded the West End Hebrew and Religious Classes which were held in Pulteney School. They soon had more than 100 children attending which caused some conflict with Westminster Jews' Free School which thought it placed too great a burden on their own pupils who were already taught Hebrew and religion at school. The differences festered for some years. The honorary president of the classes was Sir Samuel Montagu, Joseph Victor its president, and Mr O Kleinfeld its treasurer.

In 1897, the Rev S Fyne from Southampton was appointed minister, teacher and secretary at the princely salary of £75 a year. It was the first synagogue outside the East End to become a member of the Federation of Synagogues, and in 1898 was eighth in size of its membership.

Already looking to expand, a building fund was started in 1897. At the 1897 prize distribution, the Chairman J Trimmer said that efforts of the Jewish community were being directed to the East End to the detriment of the West End. It seemed strange to him that while so much was being done for the East End by the noble President of the United Synagogue (Rothschild), by South African millionaires, by philanthropists and many others, yet no steps were being taken to develop the various classes in the West End. This was the reverse of the complaint made after the Second World War that West End Jewry neglected East End Jewry. Trimmer said there were more than 500 children who did not go to either Westminster Jews' Free School or the Talmud Torah and for whom no provision could be made for lack of funds.

In 1897, the Synagogue's President was Mr J Davis and there were 148 members. The officers and committee members included J Victor, S Trenner, B Astman, D Adler, L Herman, M Goldwater, B Cohen, P Cohen, J L Meek, S Klovonsky and H Lieberman. On 25 December 1897, Davis was deposed and J Victor elected President. Whether by coincidence or not, at the same time it was discovered that money was owing to the Federation for burial funds that had been collected but not passed over. Davis later returned to the fold, and the deficit was paid to the Federation over a number of years.

The new president, Joseph Victor, was an immigrant tailor from Minsk, lived in Bloomsbury and worked in Shaftesbury Avenue. He was a good example of the many immigrants who served the local community well. He specialised in military uniforms, and in his workshop had a life-size imitation horse for his clients to sit upon so that he could make sure their trousers fitted properly.   In addition to his work for the synagogue, he became a member of the Jewish Religious Education Board, was on the Visitation Committee of the United Synagogue, the Executive Committee of the Federation of Synagogues, a Founder and President of the West London Hebrew Loyal United Brethren, and a Grand Trustee of the Order

Achei B'rith. He was chairman of the West Central Ladies' Society and one time President of the West Central Philanthropic Society and of the West Central Naturalisation Society. His obituary in 1916 recorded:

> There are philanthropists whose vision does not extend beyond the borders of their cheque books; but there are philanthropists whose vision embraces the whole field of communal suffering and neglect, and who dedicate themselves to the noble task of spurring on those with whom they come into contact to a higher sense of their obligations to the community. Joseph Victor was one of the latter school ...

He sacrificed his leisure and material interests to help others, and made life better for those among whom he came to live, Jews and non-Jews alike.

In May 1980, David Pela, another notable West Ender who, amongst other things was Managing Editor of the *Jewish Chronicle,* wrote an article in that newspaper in honour of the synagogue's centenary. He received a letter from John Rubens, one-time president of the Jewish Welfare Board, vice-president of the J I A, chairman of the Maccabi Foundation, and president of Brady Maccabi Club, who said, 'I was born in Soho, and many of my relatives lived in Green's Court. In quite an extraordinary manner, I have an absolutely vivid recollection of the *shteibl* (not a synagogue). It was busy all day long, as a *shteibl* was in Eastern Europe, with a curtain at the rear to separate the men from the women.' There was also a small room which was used as an office. A great uncle of his was the *shammas* and collector before he emigrated to Australia. His grandson became Sir Zelman Cowan, the Governor-General of Australia.

Another letter arrived from Morris Sherman, who was living in Philadelphia. He wrote:

'My *barmitzvah* took place at the West End Talmud Torah in 1907, and I attended the *cheder* for several years. I remember Mr Heiser and Mr Napper who taught there. Green's Court stands out vividly, and was sharply brought back to me when, on a brief visit to London this past summer, I pointed out to my 21-year-old grandson who accompanied me the house where I was born, the school I attended (Pulteney) and, last but not least, Green's Court where I had my barmitzvah. Any who lived in Soho at that time must remember Sack the grocer, Lewis the fish and chip shop, and

Davis the kosher butcher - all in Green's Court. The Jewish population was closely knit and the majority came from Poland. The few Litvaks for some reason or other were looked down upon with disdain. I distinctly remember Mr Victor who was president of the Talmud Torah. He bore a striking resemblance to King Edward VII.'

In spite of the limited space and facilities, members had a great pride in their synagogue, and throughout most of the year Victor attended in a grey morning suit and a silk high hat, exchanging that in winter for a black suit.

For a number of years, St Andrew's Hall in Newman Street was hired for the High Holyday services. Seats were 6/-, 4/- and 2/6d for men, and 5/-, 4/- and 2/6 for women - quite expensive for the time but presumably the congregation could afford it, or saved up for it, and thought the expenditure worthwhile. By 1903, membership had increased to 283. In 1910 there was a merger with the West London and Bikkur Cholim Burial Society which had a synagogue at 41 Brewer Street The merged body, under the title of The West End Talmud Torah and Bikkur Cholim, used that synagogue but retained the Green's Court premises for use as offices. [Contemporary documents refer to the congregation by variations of Bikkur/Bikur/Bikor and Holim/Cholim]. Victor remained president of the joint congregation.

The earlier minutes are generously littered with reports of quarrels, 'animated' discussions, personal abuse, calls for apologies (only reluctantly given), walk-outs, resignations and frequent bickering with the collectors whose figures never seemed to tally with those of the treasurers. Nonetheless, above all, there shines through a burning love of the Jewish religion and a determination to ensure their children were properly prepared for a life of devotion and Jewish upbringing.

By 1912, the congregation had left the Federation in a dispute over burial rights, with threats of writs passing in each direction, and it took two important steps that were radically to change the community's future. The search for larger premises and independent burial grounds were intensified, and in 1913 Rabbi Zvi Hirsch Ferber was appointed their leader, at £2 per week.

The premises eventually decided upon were at 14 Manette Street, a short street running between Charing Cross Road and Greek Street, between the two sides of the site where Foyle's bookshop now is. [The building remains, and has recently been refurbished]. Previous occupiers had been a Church of England School; the House of Charity, which later moved to 1 Greek Street; a Baptist Mission House; and a church home for working boys. The congregation moved there in 1916, and registered both as a place of worship and as an institution authorised to solemnise weddings. The first marriage ceremony took place in 1917 at a cost to the parties of £1.17.6d. The happy couple were presented with silver candlesticks to mark the occasion. The marriage registers indicate that in the early years, 50 per cent of the members lived in Soho; 36 per cent in Fitzrovia; 10 per cent in Bloomsbury; and 4 per cent in Marylebone. From 1917 to 1944, the majority of its members came almost equally from Soho and Fitzrovia, each accounting for more than 40 per cent. Just under 10 per cent lived in Bloomsbury, and only a handful in Marylebone and Mayfair. Almost 60 per cent were in the tailoring trade; no other occupation could muster as much as 10 per cent.

The interior of the new building was simple, and the synagogue itself was on the first floor, with ladies in the balcony a further floor up. According to the *Jewish Year Book* there was a *mikvah* attached to the premises.

"The synagogue was nothing to look at. It was hollowed out of two floors of an old rambling house said to have belonged to Dr Manette of Dickens' *A Tale of Two Cities*. The floors were bare of carpet, the walls a sweat of peeling cream paint, and the hard wooden benches a treacle-coloured stain that seemed to be completely at one with the sallow faces peering out of them".

"The main centre of West End Judaism lay in this tiny synagogue. This may be disputed by others whose loyalties lay elsewhere. However, all my contempories attended the *cheder* in the Manette Street Synagogue (not then named the West End Great - in contradiction of its present size and influence). Our respective *barmitzvahs* took place, one after the other, on the small *bimah* in the miniscule *shul*, flanked by the elegant top-hatted wardens, Mr Cohen and Mr Raphael, and facing the saintly Rabbi Ferber whose gentle high-pitched voice I can hear in my mind today. Almonds and raisins were showered on our heads from the ladies' gallery above at the termination of our *maftir* and *haftorah*.   The paradox was that this tiny synagogue and its Burial Society constituted, at that time, one of the largest congregations in the British Empire".

"The West End was a thriving community in those days [post First World War] with several *shuls*.   The *shul* we went to was Manette Street.   It had hundreds, literally hundreds of Jewish boys and girls who went to *cheder* from both sides of the border line, Oxford Street.   We went four days - Monday to Thursday.   We finished school at half past four and went home to let our parents know, and then on to *cheder*.   On Sunday classes were from 11 to 1. There was a *barmitzvah* almost every week. The lovely thing about it was that in those days they gave you a year to learn it.   All the women upstairs used to throw down rice and *mandleman*. Sometimes there was a *kiddush* downstairs. Parents were just working people, so most people would have party at home and all the family came and had salt beef and tongue".

"I used to walk round the streets, play in the streets singing my *barmitzvah*. I knew it by heart. We lived opposite Dufours Place where they had the vestry where the dustmen came and went, and they used to hear me singing it, and eventually one day one of them was walking along singing part of my *barmitzvah*. Perhaps he thought it was the latest tune of the day!"

"On the *yom tovim* my dear grandfather, Solomon Tucker, would dress himself as if going to a *simcha* - a top hat was a must. I was so proud that his name was on the Board of Founders at the entrance to the *shul*".

"I remember that Talmud Torah.   It was a little building,   I will tell you what it was like.   Did you see the film *The Jolson Story?* Well, it was like the *shul* in that. It was dingy. There was a ladies' gallery. What I remember was the *yom tovim* at the Scala Theatre. When Rabbi Ferber delivered his sermon all the women used to cry ... He used to tell people off".

A burial site was purchased at Streatham in 1915, the *Chesed v'Emeth*, and this proved to be an important member-winning asset. The plaque, now in the synagogue premises in Dean Street, lists the founders:

H Cole, J East, S Goldstein, P Kerner, E Kleiman, J M Kleinfeld, S Levy, A Lipman, H Lipitch, H Lupinsky, J Nadler, M Needleman, B Rosen, D Sherman, S Symons, M Taper, L Weinblatt, S Wenter and M Zains.

Its presidents were S Wenter, 1915-42, L Wainstain, 1942-6, and they were succeeded after the war by S I Diamond. By 1918, the Talmud Torah's membership had reached 600. Relationships with Ferber were not always sweeetness and light. He complained about the Warden's attitude to him, and the Warden said the problem was caused by Ferber's inconsistency, that made it impossible to work with him in harmony. The committee thought the difficulty was caused by the Rabbi's 'untactfulness'.

David Pela's centenary article commented that the synagogue survived largely because of its dead, lying in the Streatham cemetery. The site is now full except for reserved plots, and new burial grounds, shared with the Western Synagogue, are at Cheshunt. Streatham was let out for burial purposes to a dozen East End synagogues and organisations and this was the synagogue's main financial prop. After the Second World War, there was a wholesale exodus of Soho Jews, largely to the north-west suburbs but also to Ilford and Romford. Nevertheless, despite this the West End Great's paper membership - in its heyday probably around 1,200 - was still a healthy 700 in 1980. However, this was largely a nostalgic membership with 'many of us living elsewhere, but anxious to retain the spirit which our parents forged.'

An increase in the Talmud Torah's activities was noticeable after Rev Alexander Amias commenced his duties as *Chazan* in 1921. In 1923 a Yeshiva was formed within the existing Hebrew classes. The synagogue was affiliated to the English Zionist Federation, and was the focal point for many communal activities including the Burial Society; the Relief Fund which had been set up to give aid to the poor, sick and elderly; the hiring of rooms to other Jewish organisations; and lectures by eminent Jewish intellectuals. In addition the synagogue supported the London Jewish Hospital, the Deborah Wenter Jewish Girls' Club, the Home for Aged Jews, Norwood Orphanage, and the Jewish Board of Guardians. It prided itself that no appeal for charity fell on deaf ears. During the 1920s and 1930s, it was specially active in promoting meetings to protest on behalf of persecuted Jews in Germany.

The community's continuing success led its leaders to look for still larger premises. In 1941, they purchased the site at 21 Dean Street, which had previously housed St Anne's Church School, for £11,000. Sydney Diamond became President in 1946. He had opposed the purchase because he feared that part of Soho was too seedy, surrounded by night clubs and prostitutes, and there were insufficient local Jews for a congregation. He suggested the purchase of a church in Fitzroy Square, but his views were not accepted and although his name is on the foundation stone he claims that it is there wrongly. Unfortunately, extensive bomb damage caused a delay in their use of the premises, and temporary accommodation was found.

In 1948, the West End Talmud Torah fully amalgamated with the Beth HaSepher of Soho Square (a plan which had been mooted for more than 30 years). The combined membership rose to 800, and the name West End Great Synagogue was adopted. The following year the Central Synagogue merged its religious school with that of the West End Great.

Temporary work on the building was completed in 1950, and the community operated from there until 1960 when a complete rebuilding was undertaken, premises in nearby Berner Street being used while the work was done. The members of the Building Committee were:

B Abrahams, C Allchild, B Apple, S Barnett, A Cohen, D Cohen, S I Diamond, G Dinerstein, H Hanri, A Harris, M King, M Klinger, H Langsman, L Lyons, S London, R Massin, H Samuels, S Segenfield, J Weisberg, J Wishings, J Zaidem.

It was not until 1964 that the synagogue was re-opened and consecrated by Chief Rabbi Israel Brodie. Rabbi M Lew was inducted as Rabbi.

As they marked their centenary in 1980, the honorary officers - Messrs S Barnett [president], S Witzenfeld, S Lukover, J Herman, M Spiro and J Stephens - faced the difficult task of somehow preserving an ageing, dwindling and once-proud congregation that had little hope of receiving a big injection of new blood. Today, the West End Great is part of a complex of Jewish social, cultural and political activities. The synagogue occupies the first two floors and there is a large banqueting hall and a smaller hall for meetings. On the top floor, the well-known Ben Uri Art Gallery exhibits paintings by Jewish artists and holds recitals and lectures. On another floor are the offices of the Labour Friends of Israel, the British Na'amat and the Boys' Town Jerusalem, a charitable organisation for orphans.

The West End Great still has a scattered membership of about 600, many of whom keep up their membership more for burial rights than for the religious or social activities the synagogue offers in this life. Only 25-30 of its current membership live locally and the probability is that its days on this site are numbered.

RABBI ZVI HIRSCH FERBER

Chaim Lewis, a son-in-law of Rabbi Ferber and author of *A Soho Address*, was interviewed by Debbie Seedburgh, and the following is an extract of their conversation:

"For much of its earlier period the spiritual leader of the congregation was Rabbi Hirsch Ferber, a venerable figure and great scholar. My father loved to listen to his sermons and attend his *shiurim* and the lessons in Talmud that he conducted at home or in his study nearly every night.

The Rabbi and his family lived in an annexe behind the *shul*. So when the rabbi went to *shul* all he had to do was go down a flight of stairs and walk through a passageway.   The house overlooked the nunnery. There was a lovely private garden that linked it to St Anne's Priory.

His main interest was in his commentaries on the books of the bible, commentaries on the Talmud. He wrote a commentary on the *Haggadah*, on the siddur, and on the Five Books of Moses. He has become so beloved by the religious circles in Golders Green that they recently sought out his books, found they were out of print, and some benefactors decided to reprint all his publications. He was one of the great scholars of Anglo-Jewry. I rate him among the top ten rabbis that have ever graced the Anglo-Jewish community, going back to the early 17th and 18th centuries.

He came from Kovno, Lithuania, a great city of learning, and studied at Slabodka Yeshiva near Kovno. He came to England as a rabbi, as a young man. His wife was a descendant of one of the outstanding rabbis of the 19th century - Rabbi Yisroel Salanta. Rabbi Ferber was a friend of the Chief Rabbi of Israel, Rabbi Kook, and they used to correspond regularly. They were close friends because when Rabbi Kook was the rabbi of Machzike Hadath in the East End Ferber and he used to discuss and learn together regularly.

He was a rabbi of the old school, a master of Jewish learning. He taught, but he always had young people to run the class at the *shul*. He used to inspect them, but left it to teachers of his own choosing. He would give a private Talmud *shiur* for people like me, or grown ups.

He did not attend every funeral, only the funerals of those he admired for their observance, for their righteousness, or their goodness. Otherwise the *Chazan*, Alexander Amias, attended to the pastoral duties. He undertook what I would call the educational work of the Rabbi. Run lectures, *shiurim*, give *droshas*, lessons in Talmud, address public gatherings, public meetings. Only Jewish audiences, and in Yiddish. He spoke English but haltingly. He understood English, but more than he spoke.

He wasn't the kind of modern rabbi who wants to get the best synagogue and a higher salary. Today's rabbis are career minded, but he wasn't that kind of man. For him if he could spend 8 or 9 hours in study that was the acme of his aspirations. [The minutes of the synagogue show that Rev Ferber was not quite so reticent about seeking increases in his salary as this passage suggests.]

"Do you know why he went to the West End?"

"Crazy! He was crazy really. He was such a giant of a scholar, he needed to have the company of scholars, the fellowship of scholars. There he was lodging among tradesmen, tailors, people who were not necessarily observant, and there he was lost among them. The British Museum and its Oriental Room just five minutes away must have been the attraction for him. Ferber had a large study with thousands of books, valuable books, and he spent all his days and nights in study. He wrote 22 books himself, and visited the Oriental Room every day. He knew more about the collection of oriental Hebrew books than the custodian himself, and very often the custodian would consult him on the location or authorship of this or that book. He was a mine of knowledge, a mine of information. The Oriental Room has wonderful collections of Hebrew books going back centuries, including books by Rabbis who lived in little places, in remote places, and somehow their works managed to find their way or their home in the British Museum Library. He was particularly intrigued by this.

He used to correspond with all the great scholars in the world. Every morning piles of letters arrived, scholars consulting him on various aspects of Jewish law. That was his world. The Soho world was an irrelevance for him. He made no demand on life, if he had a roof over his head, his books by him, and he had time to study, he was quite content.

He was a remarkable orator and a great wit, he could keep you roaring with laughter, with the jokes he used to muster, any time of the day. He had a wonderful sense of the absurd, and a sense of fun, which his looks rather belied.

Seeing him poring over some tome, what caught your eye first was the homely black *yarmulka* perched on the crown of his shapely head, and it served as a foil to the lustrous intelligence of his deep-set eyes and the delicate, translucent features of his face. It had a radiance and fragile grace that Rembrandt, I imagine, would have delighted to paint".

Other interviewees have vivid memories of Rabbi Ferber.

"My late father was treasurer and subsequently vice president of that *shul* and sat, on the *yom tovim*, at the side of Rabbi Ferber and I, as his son, sat beside him.   I cannot think of two nobler people to be my companions - in this life or the next".

"Rabbi Ferber was a poor man, and if you tried to give him a fiver he would accept it, send you a receipt, and give it to some charity or Yeshiva".

"Anything that went wrong, my grandmother would go to Rabbi Ferber. She used to think he was God, and any money she could collect she would pass on to him to give to the poor".

"Ferber always made the women cry. He loved it, he thrived on it, and you would hear all this sobbing from the balcony, particularly when he spoke of the plight of co-religionists still oppressed in Poland or Russia".

"I can still see the tiny figure of Rabbi Ferber standing alone on the vast stage giving his *drosha* in Yiddish to his packed and silent congregation. When he entered or left the synagogue, everyone stood in spontaneous respect".

"I had my barmitzvah at the Manette Street Talmud Torah. I remember it very well ... Rabbi Ferber spoke mostly in Yiddish, and although I knew some Yiddish I could not understand all that he said. At the end it was the custom for the women to throw down nuts and sweets. My Auntie Ethel who lived in D'Arblay Street was a very autocratic and forthright lady.

Little nuts were not good enough for her. They had to be walnuts or brazil nuts. One hit Rabbi Ferber in the eye, and I can remember him shaking his fist at her".

Rev Saul Amias says that his father Alexander Amias who was the *chazan* at Manette Street was originally a capmaker, simply because when his family arrived they lived among *landsleit,* in Christian Street, in what was called the Garden Suburb of Shoreditch, and they were all capmakers, so they made him one. He became *chazan* for a *shul* in Artillery Lane where he stayed for a few years, and there he became known as the Rev Alexander Amias.

"After a short time at a *shul* in Hackney he got a position in Manette Street. We moved to Colosseum Terrace in Albany Street, Regent's Park. Dad was smart; he wore a neat beard and had flowing hair; he wore a wide-brimmed black hat, and was known as the Bishop of the West End and was very popular. I conducted the choir at the Scala although I was quite a young boy. I used to *layn* and my father used to *daven,* so it was an Amias family show. Eventually Manette Street had 1,100 members, which in those times was most unusual".

"Every year, at the High Holydays, the Scala Theatre [used for overflow services from 1926] in Charlotte Street (still in my memory as the most beautiful theatre in London, and long since gone) was filled to capacity, and the atmosphere remains with me today. The awe and wonder of the services led by the autocratic and handsome Alexander Amias and the choir conducted by his son, Saul, are as fresh in my mind as it was fifty-odd years ago. Compared with the other West End synagogues the West End Great had more families of foreign origin".

"Rabbi Alexander Amias always had little poems for the women. He would always put a smile on people's faces."

WEST CENTRAL JEWISH NATIONAL INSTITUTE, SOHO
THE BETH SEPHER LE'OMEE

The West Central Institute and Beth Sopher Le'omee, later Beth HaSepher, was founded toward the end of 1910 by a small group of workers, mainly tailors, under the chairmanship of Mr Vishinsky, a fishmonger. It was commonly referred to by the local community as the Beth Sepher.

The founders hoped that the institution would become a powerful educational centre and a focal point for Jewish life. A principal promotor, Dr Isaac Lazarowich, outlined their aims:

> To provide a free medical dispensary as a counter to the missionary medical centre in Bateman Street [this is dealt with separately in the chapter on Health]

> To provide lectures and classes for adults on subjects of Jewish interest and culture, including the teaching of English to immigrants 'who wished to accomplish their duty as citizens in the country where they had found a happy haven and refuge'

> To provide a library and reading room 'where the weary and worn workers might find rest and intellectual solace from their dingy surroundings in a well-lit and cheerful hall'

> To teach the young to read and speak Hebrew, and train youths to conduct divine services on Sabbaths and Festivals.

In a letter to the *Jewish Chronicle* in May of the following year, Dr Lazarowich, who had a lyrical turn of phrase, called upon the community to provide financial assistance:

> The work cannot entirely be left to these tailors, machiners and pressers who while at work at the machines, amidst the bustle and clatter of the workshop, and with drops of perspiration on their brows ... dream dreams of their children's progress and see visions of a sun-flooded future.

Their whole outlook was dominated by Zionism. Mrs Deby Freeman, daughter of one of the teachers at the Institute, Mr Harris Teacher said their main object was to prepare graduates to settle in Palestine. The Institute became a centre for Jewish national and Zionist work and one of the later headmasters, Lewis Bakstansky, became General Secretary of the Zionist Federation of Great Britain and Ireland. Zionist organisations were allowed the use of its hall for gatherings, for lectures of Jewish interest and for other Zionist activities. West Central *Zeirei Zion,* a group of West Central young Zionists, were particularly active there.

Classes for the young in Hebrew and religion were held at 81 Berwick Street. The *Ivrit B'Ivrit* method of teaching Hebrew in Hebrew was adopted. From the outset, the selected teachers were Hebraists capable of imparting both colloquial Hebrew and religious education, and over the years they included S M Pearlman, Dr S M Melamed, Dr Lazarowich, Leon Simon, Woolfe Miller and Asher Perlzweig. Mr A Shershevsky was the first headmaster, and the classes were an immediate success. Within a few months, there were 100 children, 90 boys and 10 girls, receiving instruction, and the parents of another 120 were clamouring for their children's admission.

In March 1911, a public meeting was held at the Cavendish Rooms in Mortimer Street to rally support for the Institute. It attracted an audience of more than 700. S M Pearlman presided. Lazarowich emphasised the importance of Hebrew as a living language, like French, German or any other language, and proclaimed that it was not a waste of time studying it. In his view, the Judaism of the modern Jew seemed to consist of three things: eating fried fish, reading the *Jewish Chronicle* and getting married in Duke's Place *shul*. He was delighted to note that now the *Jewish Chronicle,* 'this leading Jewish newspaper in the world', was promoting a fourth by advocating the study of Hebrew by the *Ivrit B'Ivrit* method, and he spoke of remarkable strides already made under headmastership of Mr Shereshevsky.

Joseph Trenner complained that the United Synagogue did not have enough regard for teaching Hebrew and teaching the children. He pointed out that there was no Hebrew school for middle-class children in the neighbourhood, and he hoped they would attend the Institute's classes. Others who spoke in support included Drs J M Salkind, S M Melamed and I Kopelowich, Rev J K Goldbloom, Rabbis Schneiderman and B Balzac, and Messrs Henry Snowman and Leon Simon. On the night of the meeting 60 pupils enrolled.

Classes were moved to premises at 15 Greek Street, which had a large hall and which, after a few structural alterations, afforded reasonably commodious and airy classrooms. It became, effectively, a Talmud Torah, with heavy emphasis on attachment to the land of Palestine. Classes were held on weekdays from 5 to 7 and on Sundays from 10 to 1. Contributions were sixpence a week, but children of the poor were admitted free of charge. Services were held on the premises.

Some concern was expressed by the West End Talmud Torah, then still at Green's Court, fearing unnecessary competition with its own classes which had been operating successfully since 1892. It would lead, they argued, to wasteful duplication and an additional drain on the limited communal funds. Correspondence followed in the *Jewish Chronicle,* and the viewpoint of the Beth Sepher was put by one of its committee members, Mr Snowman, who said they appreciated the other efforts being made, but the available tuition in Soho was unsatisfactory:

> ... an antiquated, obsolete and exploded method of teaching our sacred tongue. That system may satisfy some so-called ministers and ministerial aspirants of the former standard, but will not satisfy modern scholars and students of Hebrew. The West End Talmud Torah states that they are preparing 16 *barmitzvahs* yearly. This is just the thing which we so greatly deplore, this system of perfunctory preparation! ... We hope that one of our children who has attended the Beth Sepher for a number of years, say from 7 to 12, should then be able thoroughly to understand the Pentateuch and *Haftorahs,* and not require any further preperation, but rather be so well equipped even before he reaches his religous majority.

Many of the teachers came via Jerusalem, often originating in Poland or Russia. Typical was Zvia Ben-Horin's father, Jack Wolf Weintroub [1887-1955] who was born in Poland. His family emigrated to Jerusalem where his father was a Rav, but although educated at *Yeshivat Totat Haim* in the Old City he did not follow in his father's footsteps. He left for England in 1910 because of the political and economic situation in Jerusalem, and could not return during Turkish occupation. He worked here first as Hebrew teacher at the North London Talmud Torah in Canonbury, and then at the Institute in Soho as teacher and superintendent. He was one of Gaster's secretaries, assisting him from time to time with his Hebrew correspondence. In 1915, when The National Jewish Organisation for Jewish Rights - which canvassed support for Jews in Russia, Galacia and Palestine who were suffering indignities or worse - obtained temporary offices at 15 Greek Street, Jacob Weintroub was its secretary.

Weintroub returned to Jerusalem in June 1919 after the British took rule over Palestine. The Institute organised a farewell banquet, gave him a Testimonial Certificate in recognition of his work, and presented with a gold pocket-watch with a Hebrew engraving. Interestingly, when he wrote to Gaster after the Arab riots of 1920 asking if he could help him to return to London, Gaster was discouraging. He said that life had changed for the worse in the West End, and urged Weintroub to be patient until he found work in *Eretz Israel.*

The Beth Sepher opened a temporary synagogue, Shibath Zion, at 82 Berwick Street on 9 August 1916. Weintroub sent Dr Moses Gaster an invitation to the ceremony. 'As our Institute is in no way connected with any of the offical congregations, such as the United Synagogue or the Federation, we hope that you will grant us the pleasure of your presence.' Gaster attended, as did Rabbi Ferber and the Rev H Davids.   The consecration was performed by Messrs Otto and Ernest Schiff.

The Institute moved to 26a Soho Square on 8 December 1918 which appears to be the date on which it adopted the title Beth HaSepher. Several letters were addressed to Gaster asking him to become their Honorary President:

> We are striving to make an ideal intellectual home for the residents of this neighbourhood ... Our Institute has always thought you are the most competent man to preside at a National Institute such as ours

Gaster accepted, and remained a firm supporter able to help in the selection of teachers and in fund-raising. He was their president from 1918 to 1923.

The opening ceremony was conducted by Mr L A Jouques who said that the Institute had experienced a hard struggle but had survived because of the enthusiasm of a few individuals including Mr Weintroub and Dr Gaster. He said the Beth Sepher had created the right Jewish atmosphere, and it was only the forming of such institutions that would teach the children to feel and think as Jews and know what was expected of them by the Jewish nation as they grew up. He claimed that its beneficial influence would have an incalculable effect in raising the standard of Jewish life in the neighbourhood. One of the pupils addressed the meeting in Hebrew in a speech of his own composition.

More than 50 per cent of the membership lived in Soho, but about 20 per cent lived in Fitzrovia, and another 20 per cent in Marylebone. They were overwhelmingly engaged in the tailoring industry.

Like the West End Talmud Torah, the Institute received annual donations towards its Hebrew Classes from the Jewish Religious Education Board which had its offices nearby in Hallam Street. Shortly after the First World War ended the Institute still had more than 100 pupils, but Jack Kahn recalls that by the time he prepared for his barmitzvah there in 1927 they had only about 20 pupils.

Discussions for merger between the Beth HaSepher and the West End Talmud Torah continued over a period of years. After many false starts a full merger of the Institute and the West End Talmud Torah took place in 1948 and the title West End Great Synagogue was adopted.

WEST CENTRAL SYNAGOGUE

The progenitors of Liberal Judaism in this country were Claude Montefiore and Lily Montagu. In 1899, Miss Montagu wrote an article in the *Jewish Quarterly Review* entitled, 'The spiritual possibilities of Judaism today', urging an association to 're-establish a religion which was originally founded on a basis of truth, dignity and beauty'. The Jewish Religious Union, formed in February 1902, was the outcome. Its immediate objective was to hold Sabbath afternoon services for those obliged to work on Saturday mornings but who nevertheless would be able to attend on Saturday afternoons. Men and women could sit together, prayers could be recited in English as well as in Hebrew, some prayers would be added and others deleted, and instrumental music could be used. More than 300 people attended the first public service held at the Wharncliffe Rooms, Marylebone Road, on 18 October 1902. In 1909, the name of the organisation was changed to The Jewish Religious Union for the Advancement of Liberal Judaism, and the first congregation was established in 1910 in a disused chapel in Hill Street, by Dorset Square, just a few yards north of the boundaries of the West End. The first rabbi appointed was the American Israel Mattuck. He, Lily Montagu and Montefiore became known as 'The Three M's.' The congregation moved to St John's Wood in 1925 where its synagogue has recently been rebuilt.

Lily Montagu organised services at the Girls' Club premises on Saturday afternoons. As most of the membership came from ex-Club members there was naturally a shortage of men, and it was not until 1928 that they were strong enough to form a congregation. In the interim period Lily acted as lay minister. On 8 September 1928, the West Central Congregation was formally established at Alfred Place, and Rabbi Solomon Starrels was appointed to serve as minister. Although Lily was the prime mover of both the Club and the Synagogue, she kept the two organisations separate. Services were held in the Club premises because they had no other building. The main hall was transformed into a synagogue by bringing in a movable Ark and Reading Desk. After the building was destroyed by bombing in 1941, the congregation was without a permanent home. Services were held in Whitfield Tabernacle and for many years at the Mary Ward Settlement. In 1954, it moved to 109 Whitfield Street. Over the next two decades, however, the movement away from the West End, combined with an ageing (though loyal) membership, caused the executive to reconsider the situation. In 1970, the building was readapted as headquarters for the Union of Liberal & Progressive Synagogues and other Liberal organisations, while retaining permanent facilities for the congregation.   It was renamed The Montagu Centre. Today it has a membership of 80 families of whom 17 live in the W1 district of London and 8 in WC1.

"My mother was one of Lily's girls, and because of her membership of the Girls' Club, because of her respect and devotion to Miss Lily, she used to go to the services at the Liberal Synagogue started in Alfred Place. I used to go with her. The first services were in the hall of the club. The stage and the balcony were used. My memories are of services mostly in English, a gowned Miss Lily leading the Hebrew prayers in strict unison giving way only to Rabbi Israel Mattuck whose American accent blended strangely with her aristocratic vowels - rather like Edith Evans and Henry Fonda in a duet.

In her wisdom, my mother decided she would hedge her bets. She sent me for an orthodox education at the Talmud Torah, and at the same time I went with her to the Liberal Synagogue which she was devoted to. When Rabbi Ferber took his *shul* to the Scala Theatre in Charlotte Street to accommodate the swollen Talmud Torah congregation on the High Holydays, I would often dash across Tottenham Court Road, and down Goodge Street to join my friends at the more lively Scala service, and then return before the end to join my mother for our walk back to Marshall Street.

Were there ever two more contrasting figures than the Hon Lily Montagu JP CBE and Rabbi Zvi Hirsch Ferber?   Both deeply pious in their own way, and each having a most profound influence on the lives of the Jews of the West End. I like to think that God chuckled a little when he chose to plant these two personalities in Soho and its environs, but then what other place on earth was more appropriate?"

XII - EDUCATION IN THE WEST END

At the beginning of the 19th century there were no government or local authority schools, and Jewish education in London was in a rudimentary state. In the *cheders*, the teachers frequently could not speak English, and certainly did not provide any grounding for a trade. There was the Talmud Torah of the Great Synagogue which, when it was established in 1732, aimed to provide advanced Hebrew tuition to a small number of boys whose parents could not otherwise afford such schooling. In 1788, reading,. writing and arithmetic were added to the curriculum, but it catered for comparatively few pupils, as did the Sephardi schools.

In 1796, a London magistrate Patrick Colquhoun wrote of:

> the deplorable state and condition of the lower order of the Jews in the Metropolis ... Totally without education, and very seldom trained to any trade or occupation by which they can earn their livelihood by manual labour: their youths [are] excluded from becoming apprentices ... and seem to have no alternative but to resort to ... tricks and devices ... to enable [them] ... to live in idleness.   The habits they thus acquire are of the most mischievous and noxious to the Community that can be conceived.

> ... it is earnestly to be hoped that the opulent and respectable [Jews] will lend a helping hand in devising some means of rescuing this part of the nation of the Jews who reside in England, from the reproach, which it is to be feared, has been too justly cast upon them.

Further outside pressure on Anglo-Jewry to take some active steps was provided by The London Missionary Society's Jewish Committee, which opened free schools in the Jewish area of the East End in 1807, 1811 and 1813. Chief Rabbi Solomon Hirschell urged Jewish parents not to send their children to such schools, but between 1809 and 1814 the Society recruited 219 Jewish pupils. Additionally, some Jewish children - in both the East End and the West End - went to charity schools of the National School Society (organised by the Church of England) and of the British and Foreign School Society (organised by the Dissenting Churches).

The unschooled Jewish street children were more than an embarrassment to the community. They were a threat to the established Anglo-Jewish elite, who feared a backlash should the wayward youths not be contained.

Colquhoun's unflattering remarks had made them very uncomfortable, and they decided that the solution was to take their own measures to provide both Jewish and secular education for the children of the Jewish poor.

In 1807, the Jews' Hospital (not to be confused with the London Jewish Hospital) opened in Mile End. It was a combined old age home and trade school, but it catered for only 10 boys and 8 girls. The numbers increased over the next 20 years, but only to 47 boys and 29 girls. It later became known as Norwood.

In 1811, the governors of the Great Synagogue Talmud Torah began to talk seriously about expansion to include a free school, and in 1817 the Jews' Free School opened its doors near Bell Lane, Spitalfields.

The Westminster Jews' Free School was founded in 1820 under the auspices of the Western Synagogue. Its numbers were never more than a fraction of those at Bell Lane but the function it performed was the same. In addition to providing religious and secular education, both aimed to take Jewish children off the streets and put them into a modern Jewish school to learn work skills and English manners.

In 1845, the Reform movement, through the West London Synagogue of British Jews, opened a school for the children of the middle class, the West Metropolitan Jewish School in Little Queen Street. A girls' school followed the next year.

The London School Board came into existence in 1870, but there was no board school in the West End until Pulteney School in Peter Street, Soho, was opened at the end of the century. It immediately became popular with Jewish parents, most probably because it was the only non-church school in the area, and by 1914 it had 440 Jewish pupils. Jewish families north of Oxford Street had to wait until 1914 before a satisfactory council school was available to them. In that year the Upper Marylebone Street (now New Cavendish Street) School opened. As will be seen both schools were blessed with non-Jewish teachers of the highest calibre who gave their Jewish children a first-rate start in life.

Of the Church schools, St Anne's in Dean Street and St James's and St Peter's in Great Windmill Street were the most popular among Jewish residents. Each catered for an average of 150 to 200 Jewish children in the years 1900-12. Comparatively few attended St Patrick's in Soho Square or All Saints' in Margaret Street. St John's in Fitzroy Square had 60 Jewish pupils in 1905, and a few attended All Souls' in Foley Street. After the First World War there was a French Protestant school in Noel Street which had half a dozen Jewish pupils. Strangely, most of its pupils were Roman Catholic Italians.

The Central Schools most attended by Jewish children were Lyulph Stanley in Mornington Crescent, a mixed school, and the Burlington School, which catered for girls. A few attended the Archbishop Tenison School, Marylebone Grammar School and Buckingham.

Overall, the West End furnished its Jewish inhabitants with elementary and central school education that equalled the best.

WESTMINSTER JEWS' FREE SCHOOL
THE BOYS' SCHOOL FOUNDED

In the Brompton Cemetery of the Western Synagogue lies the body of Levi Solomon Graeditz. The inscription on his tombstone reads:

> Levi Graeditz, a pious and selfless man, one of the founders of the school for instructing indigent children in Westminster, who devoted his earnings to charity: died 5th Jan 1827

He was employed by the Western Synagogue, and from about 1811 he taught the children of the poor in subjects other than Hebrew and religion. A small group of synagogue members decided to put his work on a more formal basis.

A school certainly existed from at least the beginning of 1820. In the minutes of 6 December of that year, the founders are quoted as being Messrs L S Graeditz, Israel Solomon and Mark Emmanuel, while the treasurers were Messrs A R Jacobs and Moses Jacobs. The first committee was appointed.

> Nathan Lewis - St James's Street
> Charles Davis - Panton Street
> Moses Davis - Grays Inn Lane
> John Moss - High Holborn
> Hyam Hyams - Dean Street, Westminster
> Moses Levy - Alie Street, Goodman's Fields

Isaac Phillips - Swallow Street
Lewis Jacobs - Nassau Street
Hyman Collins - Cockspur Street
Isaac Josephs - Drury Lane
Jacob Harris - Peter Street, Saffron Hill
John Salmon - Botolph Lane, City
Solomon Sanders - Holywell Street
Abraham Hart - Duke Street, Aldgate

The honorary secretary was Samuel Abrahams.

The aim of the school, as set out in the preamble to the 'Laws, Rules and Regulations of the Westminster Institution for Educating and Clothing Indigent Jewish Children in Hebrew and English instituted A.M.5580 [=1820]', was:

> that *male* children of the Jewish persuasion (whose parents are unable to afford them education) be instructed in Hebrew and English, reading, writing and arithmetic; that the principle of religion be carefully inculcated, and every exertion used to render them good and useful members of society.

There followed some 30 rules and regulations, concluding with a curious resolution, namely 'That Mr Solomon Graeditz *only* be considered the founder of this Institution, and he shall have the privilege of attending at all meetings of the committee and voting upon all occasions.'

The school was funded entirely by voluntary contributions and quite quickly attracted a sufficient number of subscribers to engage teachers at a salary of £50 per annum. Classes were held at the teachers' homes, and the children attended the teacher living nearest to their own home. A prominent early teacher of Hebrew was Hyman Breslau, editor of the *Jewish Chronicle* from 1844 to 1851.

Children were admitted between the ages of 5 and 12, and discharged at 13. Whenever a vacancy occurred, a public notice had to be given 'in the synagogues of the West End of the Metropolis' (at that time only the Western and its secessionist Maiden Lane group). To become a pupil you had to be lucky in a raffle. Candidates were not eligible unless they were recommended by a subscriber, and the method of election, not uncommon in those days, was as follows:

that the election of candidates be by ballot, at which time a name or names of the members recommending each candidate be placed into the wheel, a number of chances to be apportioned according to the amount of subscription, that is to say, the member paying 6s per annum to have one chance; the 12s subscribers to have two chances; the one guinea subscribers to have three; and a life governor to have four chances. And the member whose name may be drawn is to have the choice of the candidate who shall thereupon be admitted to the benefits of the Institution.

A collector was appointed who received ten per cent of the annual subscriptions, but two sponsors had to enter into a Fidelity Guarantee for him as to his *bona fides*. Mr Kasur held the post for 40 years until his retirement on pension, in 1865.

One of the primary duties imposed on the masters, who had classes of about 20 children, was to pay strict attention to the clean appearance of the children; any failings had to be reported to the Committee. The children had to arrive at 9 o'clock in the morning throughout the year, and no parents or friends were allowed to visit them during school hours. Another regulation, passed in 1821, ordained that all the children of the Institution had to attend the Western Synagogue for afternoon prayers each day.

There was a rather macabre duty to which the children were at times subjected. In the case of the death of a member of the Institution, they were obliged to attend the house of the deceased, accompanied by a schoolmaster, and recite Psalms during the progress of the Tahara (the ritual cleansing of the body).

In addition to instruction, the boys received gifts of clothing. In 1825 it was decided that one third of subsequent annual income would be set aside for this purpose and the rest allocated to teaching. Pupils had to return the clothes to the master every Sunday, and he kept them until the following Friday when the pupils were allowed to collect them to wear on the Sabbath. On *barmitzvah*, an entire new outfit of clothes was provided, comprising one suit of cloth ruffle dress, two shirts, two pairs of stockings, one pair of boots, one hat, one neck ribbon and one bag.

School attendance was not compulsory, and in its early days the efficiency of school left much to be desired.   There was a good deal of truancy, leaving without notice, and complaints by both pupils and their parents as to treatment meted out to them.   There were occasional expulsions. After complaints of bad behaviour in public, it was decided that in future a master would attend the afternoon service with the children and march them in crocodile fashion by twos until they reached Trafalgar Square where they dispersed and were allowed to make their own way home.

The Committee became increasingly aware that the   system of using the masters' houses for teaching was inherently defective, and in 1837 they rented premises for a school in Stanhope Street. By 1843 yet larger premises were required, and on 30 April a new school was opened in Greek Street, Soho. The consecration was conducted by the minister of the Western, the Rev A H Henry, and contributions were received exceeding £150, including subscriptions of ten guineas each from Baroness Rothschild and her sons.

THE GIRLS' SCHOOL FOUNDED

The Chief Rabbi, Nathan Adler, was a strong advocate of education for girls. He was also very concerned about the success of the recently formed West London Synagogue of British Jews which had opened in Burton Street in 1842. The *herem* (excommunication) pronounced upon them by his predecessor, Chief Rabbi Herschell, had no effect on their numbers, and indeed they were making substantial progress. On 17 August 1846 they opened a girls' school in Little Queen Street which attracted pupils not only from their own congregation but also from the City orthodox synagogues.

Adler had to act, and he wrote officially to 'The Committee of the Western Institution for Educating Boys', calling attention to the anomaly that they had no girls' school and emphasising the urgent need to remedy this deficiency. A high-powered fund-raising committee was formed under the patronage of the Duke of Cambridge, Baroness de Rothschild and Lady Montefiore. Adler offered to undertake the office of Honorary Superintendent. The first meeting of subscribers raised £200, and their efforts bore fruit when a separate Western Jewish Girls' School was officially opened at Richmond Buildings, Dean Street on 15 October 1846, but shortly afterwards moved to 59 Greek Street. [The original minutes of the meetings of the school governors have recently been discovered, and it is hoped they will throw fresh light on the school's history].

The first officers appointed were: J M Johnson, President; S A Sampson, Vice-president; and H L Keeling, Treasurer. The elected committee consisted of S A Hart, A R Jacobs, A A Goldschmidt Jnr, S Solomon, Leopold Neumegen and Mr Lamert, but Neumegen and Solomon did not take up office and were replaced. The first governess (headmistress) was Miss Caroline Magnessau, who was 'possessed of respectable literary acquirements'.

At the opening ceremony, attended by the Chief Rabbi and the Dayanim, the proceedings continued from 7 pm to midnight, and the occasion was described as 'an unparalleled celebration by West End Jewry'. Mr Johnson said they were starting in a small way but they hoped to progress slowly, but securely, 'for the diffusion of religion and knowledge of moral and social principles among the young and the ignorant'. A Ladies' Visiting Committee was formed which undertook to visit the houses of the poor in order to induce them to send their children to the school. The number of pupils grew from 12 to 63 within just two years, and they transferred to larger premises in Dean Street.

No corporal punishment was permitted. The girls, some as young as five, were described as being of 'clean and healthy appearance'. At the second examination of the children, which in those days was held in public, the examiner on this occasion being the Chief Rabbi, the Duke of Cambridge, their patron, said that great progress had been made since the first examination. The Free Schools in both the East End and the West End had connections with leading Jewish families that enabled them to attract important personages to their examinations and dinners. One visitor said, 'In no other country would you meet with a Prince of the Blood Royal and a child of the humblest parent'.

AMALGAMATION OF THE GIRLS' AND BOYS' SCHOOLS

In 1853, the boys' and girls' schools amalgamated at 60 Greek Street (the freehold was purchased for £1,500) and was called the Westminster Jews' Free School, a title it was to keep for more than ninety years. Throughout the school's existence it had separate boys' and girls' departments. Although it maintained a close association with the Western, the school gradually developed into an independent body.

The headmasters were all long serving, with only four in 80 years. Mr W J Passington was appointed in 1858, and on his death in 1874 he was succeeded by Mr Jacob Woolf who remained in office until 1905. He was followed by Mr Lazarus Weisberg (who later changed his name to Whitehill), who had been a pupil, then pupil-teacher, and finally teacher at the school before his elevation to the headmastership. On his retirement in 1924, he was succeeded by Maurice Silverstone who took over and was still in office when the school was evacuated in 1939. One headmistress, Hannah Herzon, served at the school from 1876 to 1915, and her successor, Gertrude Herzon, from 1915 to 1922.

In 1866, Henry Levy Keeling, a prosperous provision merchant and an office holder at the school for many years, revealed that he had refused admission to many children of respectable tradesmen who were prepared to pay because the School's first duty lay to the children of the poor.

By 1871, the Committee were able to report that several boys who received their first instruction at the school had completed their education at Jews' College (founded in 1855) and held prominent positions as ministers in the community. Others, of both sexes, were engaged as teachers.

The *Jewish Chronicle* was very supportive of all Jewish schools and the cause of Jewish education. Each year, before the Westminster Jews' Free School annual dinner, it would run an article praising the school's progress and urging the wealthy to loosen their purse strings. The editorial of 27 April 1883, written just before the school moved to Hanway Place, was typical:

Last week we briefly called attention to the remarkable testimony borne by Mr Matthew Arnold [the poet, and also a leading government school inspector] to the excellence of the educational work in the Westminster Jews' Free School. The report is all the more notable inasmuch as its author is Mr Matthew Arnold, a critic, as all the world knows, who is both acute and severe.

For a considerable number of years - *many more than most persons are aware* - there has been a large Jewish population resident in the West-Central district. The institution in Soho has admirably provided for the educational wants of the poorer members of this population. But while the wealthier classes have been carried away from the district by the tide of migration which is ever flowing towards the far west, no diminution has taken place in the numbers of the humbler orders. *On the contrary, the poor element is, if anything, more extensive than ever it was;* and hence the necessity of the new building which is being erected for the 'Westminster School'. *No doubt the population served by these schools includes but a small proportion of the very indigent. It does not largely exhibit that extreme poverty which is so prevalent in the City and which is so extensively represented among the children of the great school in Bell Lane.* It is certain however that the poor of the West Central district would be unable to provide from their own slender resources the excellent education which their children are obtaining in the Greek Street institution. The religious part of the instruction they certainly could not provide. In many cases the secular part would be wanting too; for it often happens with Jewish children of the humbler classes that it is the combination of the Hebrew instruction which ensures them sound teaching. Were it not for that, the number of those who are sent to inferior schools would be very much larger than it is. Such special considerations will suffice to establish the many claims of the Westminster Jews' Free School on the sympathy and generous help of the community. We earnestly trust those claims may be satisfied in full measure.

The committee, all middle class or above, shared the prevalent Victorian view that though the wealthy had a duty to assist the poor, they should do so in a way that did not pauperise them: the recipients should pay whatever little they could afford so as not to become so dependent on charity as to be deprived of the will and ability to stand on their own feet. By the 1880s, however, no charge was made for general education.

The President, Louis Davidson, referred to the subject of school meals. Originally, only cocoa and bread had been supplied, but more substantial meals were introduced at a cost to each child of a penny - or less if the family could not afford even that sum:

The committee have been so impressed with the necessity of supplying our children with sufficient food if they have to undergo severe mental strain that they started penny dinners. On an average, 90 dinners are supplied five days a week. Every child pays something towards the dinner provided. The cost of the dinner is 1 5/8th of a penny per head - a not unsatisfactory result. The utensils required have been purchased with money kindly presented by Miss Pinto, *while Mrs Henry Lucas, has, in order to enable the dinners to be paid for, initiated the system of giving out work to the mothers, and the cost of the children's dinners is 'taken out' of the work brought back.* [Hear, Hear]

The Committee was forward looking, and did not limit the curriculum to 'the three R's'. The President gave a review of the school's work at each annual fund-raising dinner, and in 1885 Louis Davidson, who had succeeded Sir David Salomons in the post, referred to drawing lessons which were given on Sunday mornings by J E Jacobs, a Royal Academy exhibitor:

The labour was with him a labour of love, and he had earned the very best thanks of the community for teaching poor children so as to enable them hereafter to earn their living in other directions than in the old overcrowded industries of tailoring, cigar making etc.

Art became a strength of the school. Many recently interviewed pupils confirm that this continued to be so until the Second World War.

By the 1880s, the government was taking a fuller role in education. After some hesitation and against the wishes of some of the committee, the Westminster Jews' Free School placed itself under limited government control. An increasing proportion of its income came from a government grant the size of which depended on the success of the pupils in the annual examination held by government inspectors. Both the girls' and the boys' departments were consistently given good reports, of which the following are typical:

January 1871:

Boys: The work is very well done, and the boys are remarkably well behaved ... **the school takes a very high rank amongst elementary schools.**

Girls: The instruction and behaviour of the children ... is very creditable.

1874:

Boys: The institution is most creditable. Work done in good style and with much accuracy.

Girls: Reading good and intelligent.   Writing and spelling very fair.

THE MOVE TO HANWAY PLACE

Despite praise for the work of both teachers and pupils, there was criticism about the premises. The inspectors were concerned that there was no yard or other playground, and the numbers were too large for the available space, leading to dangerous overcrowding.   It became obvious that the school would not be allowed to remain in the same location and continue to be awarded government grants. Technical advances were being made in school buildings, particularly in the new board schools, and the inspectors put growing pressure upon the governors to bring the Westminster Jews' Free School up to these standards.   Urgent appeals were made to the community for the money necessary   to erect a new school building. Eventually, enough was raised to acquire premises in Hanway Place on an 80 year lease from 25 March 1882 at the annual rent of £200.

The new building was consecrated on Wednesday, 4 July 1883. Sir Julian Goldsmid said the new and larger premises would offer better accommodation for both teachers and pupils, at that time 195 boys and 175 girls, and he had no doubt that the roll would increase and many children would be attracted by the fine building. The total cost would not fall far short of £7,000, and there was still £3,000 to be raised.

Moses Angel, the Headmaster of the Jews' Free School in Bell Lane, and Miss Lipman, its Headmistress, both attended the consecration ceremony. Louis Davidson remarked on the fact that both the Westminster Jews' Free School's current Headmaster, Mr J Woolf, and Headmistress, Miss H Hertzon, had been pupils of Mr Angel. The two schools were completely independent of each other, and not associated in any way, but over the years many teachers came to Hanway Place from its East End counterpart. Indeed, a very high percentage of all the teachers in the Jewish schools throughout the country during the second half of the 19th century had been taught by Moses Angel.

The *Jewish Chronicle* carried a detailed report on the new building. Motives of economy had influenced its conception from first to last and all ornamentation had been studiously eliminated. Above the arcading which formed the playgound ran a band which carried the inscription (still partly visible today) 'The Westminster Jews' Free School founded 1811, rebuilt 1882'. [The date 1811 refers to the early teaching of Levi Graeditz. The school proper dates from 1820]. The boys' entrance was in Hanway Place and the girls' in John Street.

The planning of the building was determined by the peculiar shape of the site and its surroundings. Since Hanway Place and John Street were rather narrow thoroughfares, the school rooms were built to such a height that the buildings on the opposite side would not block the light and air. Moreover, the limited space made it necessary to appropriate as much of the land as possible for playground purposes. The whole of the ground floor was arranged as playground space which was to be fitted with gymnasiums, the gift of Edward Wagg. The ventilation and heating of the rooms were installed upon the most up-to-date principles. Great care had been exercised that each room should be distinct in itself, and to this end the corridor was situated in the rear of all the rooms, heated by warm water to prevent the children catching cold by coming from one atmosphere into another, and also insuring the privacy of each classroom. The staircases were deliberately arranged in very short flights so that in the event of panic or otherwise, it was almost impossible for accidents to arise. The walls were faced, through the kind liberality of the treasurer, Mr Julian Joseph, with dados of glazed bricks to ensure cleanliness. Both staircases and corridors were absolutely fireproof. Great care had been taken with the plumbing and drainage, and all the drinking water passed through filters which had been supplied by the London and General Water Purifying Company.

The building could accommodate 500 children, at a cost, including fittings, of about £13 per head, which contrasted very favourably indeed with the cost of similar school buildings. The building was erected on the designs of Mr H H Collins FRIBA, of 61 Old Broad Street, EC, and they were satisfactorily executed by Messrs Sahey and Sons of 95 Ironmonger Row, St Lukes, E C.

CLOSE THE SCHOOL!

The Education Act of 1870 began the move towards universal compulsory education and to the opening of local authority 'board' schools. Wealthy Jews already paid their rates, so why, many argued, should they dip into their pockets again to support Jewish voluntary schools such as Westminster Jews' Free School? The board schools, it was said, gave a perfectly good education, and the exemption clauses introduced into the various Education Acts ensured that no Jewish child needed to attend Christian services or teaching.   A lively debate arose on the question in Jewish circles.

In 1887, the School hit financial problems. The move to Hanway Place had involved large capital expenditure, but during the previous ten years the community's support had been gradually diminishing. In 1878, it received £207 from annual subscriptions; in 1886 only £140; in 1878, £827 as a result of the annual appeal; in 1887, only £500; and the number of individual donors dropped from 171 to 125.   Expenditure during this period had naturally increased, since the number of children had increased to 457, compared with 311 in 1878. The Chairman reported:

> It should be known that we educate children free of charge, and that the payments we receive amount to only 7 per cent of the annual expenditure. Our record of educational progress during the period from 1878 to 1887 presents very satisfactory and gratifying results. The average number of passes per cent in the Government Examination having risen from 91 per cent in 1878 to over 99 per cent in 1887; further, the report of Her Majesty's Inspector of Schools spoke in the highest terms of the efficiency of the school.

> We venture to think that notwithstanding the arguments of those opposed to denominational schools the closing of the Westminster Jews' Free School, which has carried on its work with such excellent results for 66 years in the West Central District of London, will scarcely commend itself to the community.

This appeal drew a sharp rejoinder in the *Jewish Chronicle* in the following week's issue from 'A True Conservative':

Sir - In your last issue there is an appeal from the managers of the Westminster Jews' Free School. I am not surprised that the support the school has received from the Jewish public has been gradually diminishing for ten years past. I think it shows the good sense of the community that they are ceasing to support Jewish schools ... and I should regard it as an excellent thing if the school now appealed for were closed.

The 457 boys and girls being educated in the Westminster Jews' Free School would be drafted into various Board Schools ... And a capital thing it would be, as then these Jewish children will be educated with the children of the English artisan, the mechanic, the small shopkeeper, the poorly paid labourer, the worse paid clerk. The Board School education may not be, probably is not, quite as good, as that given at the Westminster Jews' Free School - but what is far more important is that these 457 Jewish children, instead of being educated solely together, instead of mixing only with their own race, and as a consequence imbibing daily only one view of everything, and as a further consequence growing up in a narrow-minded, bigoted, sectarian condition, will, if scattered amongst the Board Schools, in all probability grow up without narrow prejudices, on broad lines of thought, able to regard any and every question, not from one point of view only - that of race, but from three or four standpoints, the most important one of which would be - the way in which an Englishman should look at it - in fact these children would become first English working-men, then Jews ...

It is absurd to say that if Jewish children go to a Board School, they can have no religious education. What about the classes arranged to give religious instruction to children attending Board Schools? They are under the management of Mr Henry Lucas and I hear do good work, and personally if, as I hope, the Westminster Jews' Free School be presently closed, I will give five pounds a year for the next five years towards the maintenance of these classes, and more, will guarantee that many other of my personal friends will do the same.

Claude G Montefiore, the Vice-President of the school, replied the following week:

I [agree] that our aim in education should be to produce 'English working men, then Jews' or, as I should prefer to put it, 'English citizens of the Jewish faith.' I, for one, could scarcely with any approach to consistency, support any institution, the necessary effect of which must be to encourage 'narrow prejudices' or to prevent the growth of national and civic patriotism.   But I wholly repudiate the suggestion that denominational teaching must have so lamentable an issue.   I know as a matter of fact that the virtue of Patriotism is earnestly insisted upon in our Westminster School, and that every effort is there made to impress upon boys and girls alike the duties of our common humanity, the love and service of our country, and the moral impartiality of God.

A main aim of Westminster Jews' Free School, and indeed of all the other Jewish voluntary schools in England, was to anglicise their pupils.   The ex-pupils who were interviewed for the purposes of this book confirmed that the claims made by Montefiore more than a century ago were still true at the time that they attended the school.   Patriotism was drilled into them. It was recorded, for example, in the school log book, that on 24 May, 1916, Claude Montefiore addressed the whole school on the significance of Empire Day.   On 24 May 1928, the girls all joined with the boys in listening to the Empire Celebrations on 2LO.   Great attention was also paid to their accents.   Many pupils heard only Yiddish at home.   As early as 1873 Frederick Mocatta, the philanthropist and good friend of the school, said at the annual dinner how pleased he was with the children's accents, particularly as they heard a mixed jargon at home.   In this century Shakespeare Day and Empire Day were honoured to the full.

Despite the views of 'A True Conservative', the school continued to flourish, though not without facing recurrent financial problems. Between 1898 and 1913 the total roll varied between 400 and 600, with 1902 the peak year. A random sample of 500 children taken from the Admission Register of 1915-23, revealed that 65 per cent of the fathers were in tailoring or allied trades.   Next, but a long way behind, were boots and shoes with 5 per cent, tobacco industry 5 per cent, and hairdressers 4 per cent. The small shopkeepers were grocers, bakers and fruiterers, with the occasional publican or restaurateur. In 1914, when the influx of Belgian refugees arrived, the school took in its fair share. Between 1898 and 1913, 80-90 per cent of all the pupils were either born abroad or born in England of foreign parents. Obviously, as time passed, the percentage of English-born pupils increased.

The staff for the 1920/21 educational year were:

Standard Ex VII and VII A.Supperstone (who joined in 1915)

VI	L E Israel
V	R Weinstock
IV	H Orler
III	F Young
II and I	Miss Davidson

"I enjoyed school. There was a structure to it. We had Hebrew four mornings a week Monday to Thursday, and on Friday we had assembly. We also stayed two evenings a week 4.30 to 6 for Hebrew.   On High Holidays the school had its own services - we had our own ark. Various teachers used to come and conduct the services and it was a preference, not a must, that we should go to the school service rather to go and bother our parents wherever they were. It was also a preference, not a must, that we went to *shul* every week. When we went to school on a Monday they asked whether or not we had been to *shul* on the Sabbath".

"We had this prize-giving every year and the school governors came, the Tucks, the Montefiores. There was Claude Montefiore, he was a lovely man, and he used to come to the school. He gave each child a bible when he or she left school. I remember he used to come to our school plays, and I remember his son Leonard also coming to the school. The school itelf was of an extremely high standard and the pupils did very well - extremely high demands were made for courtesy and scholarship. To show how things are changed, when we were sent with a message from one teacher to another we had to knock on the door - go in and say, 'Please Madam, Madam said ...'. Never forgotten that".

"Many boys and girls who should have gone on to higher education did not do so, and I was one of them, because our school had quotas for scholarships. So there were years when people from our school couldn't get into schools of higher learning.   These schools were the North London Collegiate and the big grammar schools.   We were alright for Stanley Central where I could have gone, but I was advised, and I suppose others like me, to wait for the scholarship, but I never made the scholarship. It must have happened to others".

"Mr Whitehouse was the headmaster. The words he used were, 'Come out pest'. 'Pest'. That was his word. He couldn't unbend or wind down. He was too stern and forbidding and too distant. We had little to do with him actually".

"Hebrew was taught at school every day, every morning. The teacher, who also taught me my barmitzvah, was Rev Goldston, and he came to the school every Friday morning just to give lessons to these poor immigrant boys who wanted to learn their *barmitzvah* at the school. He was the minister of South East London Synagogue. One of those typical Anglo-Jewish ministers. His Hebrew pronunciation was very English. A nice person, kind, helpful, and conscientious, who took a great interest in the pupils placed under his charge".

"My first school was Westminster Jews' Free School. The headmaster was a Mr Silverstone, assisted by a number of teachers and in particular Mr Harry Orler whose aspirations to the stage were sublimated by the continuous infliction on the school of plays he directed badly. There were occasional performances by myself which I have yet to live down. I particularly recall a boy of that era, Lionel Harris, who is unique in my experience as someone who knew exactly at the age of nine that what he wanted to do in life was to act and direct. He later became an eminent stage and TV director. I well remember his first part as the Griffin in a school production of Alice in Wonderland. His mother cajoled a reluctant Mr Silverstone to include him in the cast. During the first performance he was heartily sick on stage.

Other teachers at that school were Miss Speilman, Miss Woolfson and Mary Muscat; the last was my first teacher in the Infants'. The Rev Goldstein was the Hebrew teacher and Chaim Lipschitz joined later. My recollection of the school, almost 60 years after, is quite clear and I think I could draw a fairly accurate plan of the building with its cavernous, draughty playground, narrow stairs, and dusty classroooms. Mr Simons, the caretaker, together with his family, lived in a tiny flat on the first floor.

The school was visited from time to time by various beneficent governors, all members of illustrious Anglo-Jewish families. I recall Claude Montefiore, Leonard Montefiore, Miss Jacob and Mr Waley. There were many substantial endowments to the school expressed in the form of cash prizes, books, of some of which I was the recipient.   The Blume Angel Memorial Prize, the Louis Joseph Prize and others indicate the munificence of the patronage of the school".

The school was nowhere near as heavily endowed as the Jews' Free School in Bell Lane, even though it received support from Louis Davidson, Claude Montefiore, the Waley family, and others of similar standing.   There was no one providing such large sums, on such a regular basis, as the Rothschild family did for Bell Lane. Apart from the freehold of the Greek Street premises and a few thousand pounds in stocks, it had no assets.   There were several small funds that supported annual prizes in the names of Sir David Salomon, Louis Joseph, Annie Davis, Louisa Israel, Baroness Rothschild (the Evalina prizes), Mrs Sebag-Montefiore, Philip Waley, Louis Davidson and Messrs Rothschild. Mrs F S D Phillips gave a prize of two guineas in memory of her husband who had been a committee member for 40 years; Mr H Marks gave one guinea in memory of his brother, an old boy of the school who had died in the South African war. Mr A H Wolf, another old boy contributed in memory of his mother. Prizes were given by Mr Arthur Wagg for regular attendance, Mrs Arthur Sassoon for drawing, and Mrs S Sebag-Montefiore for cooking.   There were also prizes in money and books for Hebrew and religion.

"I was not a good pupil by any means, and the only prize I ever won was for proficiency in Hebrew and I was given a book called *Jewish Post-Biblical History*.   That was on 15 July 1931.

Mr Silverstone, the headmaster, was a very nice man, slim with greying hair, but very much an authoritarian.   I remember being caned once in his office. I cannot remember what it was for, but I shall never forget the pain".

"I started at Westminster Jews' Free School in 1926 and left it four years later to join the Lyulph Stanley Central School in Camden Town, but even that short time still provides me with many memories.   Here was my introduction to Jewish education with the learning of Hebrew, the annual festivals and High Holy days, and a cursory knowledge of the bible.   From what I recall the primary education was of a high standard, and compares favourably with that of today.

The building still stands, unscathed by the war, and on a recent visit I stood in the playground which then seemed so large and now so small, where I had my nose broken in an accident and was knocked unconscious, waking up in the headmaster's study.

Many of the pupils later played distinguished roles in the Anglo-Jewish community and not a few shed lustre on it".

"The headmaster was Silverstone. He wore rimless glasses and had a twitch on his face, and he threw chalk if we annoyed him. He was very good with the cane. There was a Miss Muscat, she was wonderful; Miss Speilman; and Buskey who was a very kindly man who took the singing class. There was Mr Orler who ran the religious class. I was there in 1930. There were only four classes: infants, classes 2 and 3, and then the top class which Mr Silverstone took. On *yom tovim* they gave every child sticky buns with a glaze and currants and a bottle of milk".

"The school caps were blue with sections of yellow. We wore little round pins on our lapels with the colour of our house".

"I was captain of the school from the age of 11 to 14. Every Friday afternoon the captain and prefects held court and we were allowed to call out from the class the children who had misbehaved and we sat and gave them various punishments. This was without reference to the masters or headmaster. We would give them lines and they would have to stay behind. This was a special innovation of the school".

"The headmaster was Mr Silverstone and the headmistress Miss Rich. They were both awesome characters. The teacher I remember best was Mr Orler who had a habit of thumping everyone hard on the back for no known reason".

As the distinctions between state and Jewish schools gradually lessened it made little difference to many Jewish parents where they sent their children. Between 1901 and 1911 the numbers at the school declined considerably. It was felt that the successive Education Acts had removed the need for more Jewish voluntary schools, and there was no reason why Jewish children should not benefit from the help given to all citizens by the state. No new Jewish day schools opened until after the Second World War.

School teachers had a high opinion of the immigrant pupils. They were variously described as 'keen and intelligent in all that concerns the welfare of our country', 'bright and superior intellectually', 'excellent workers in school', and 'anxious to learn'. Public educators were impressed by the eagerness with which Jewish children were sent to school in neighbourhoods where generally there was hostility to schooling.

Compared with other schools, there was a lack of extra-curricular activities at Westminster Jews' Free School, with little in the way of organised games such as cricket or football, though there was a Habonim group after school. The school averaged 25-30 pupils per class.

The Admissions Registers show that the last pupil, Alfred Marcel Schneider, joined the school on 27 June 1939.

On the outbreak of war, the school was evacuated to Dauntey, a village in Wiltshire, between Swindon and Chippenham, and although it was not officially closed down until 31 December 1945 it never returned to Hanway Place. The freehold of the Greek Street premises, which had been retained and leased out, was sold in 1949 for £20,750.

"For some years after the war the premises were used for a variety of purposes. For a time they were occupied by a former pupil, Harry Kweller, for his printing and publishing business. The building was later used as rehearsal rooms, but today it is boarded up and padlocked with broken windows and a general air of dinginess and gloom."

In 1950 the assets were transferred to the London Board of Jewish Education.

The Westminster Jews' Free School served the West End community well for 120 years. It provided a haven for the children and reassurance for the mostly foreign parents that here was a school in which their children would be safe from outside hostile elements and given an academic grounding that would stand them in good stead when they entered the adult world.

THE WEST METROPOLITAN JEWISH SCHOOL

The founders of the West London Synagogue of British Jews were anxious to provide education for 'the choristers and other poor children'. Funded by voluntary contributions from its members, a boys' school was opened in 1845 and soon attracted 61 pupils. A girls' school opened in Little Queen Street the following year, triggering Chief Rabbi Adler to urge the Westminster Jews' Free School to open a school for girls. The President of the West Metropolitan said in 1847 that the Western Girls' School in Greek Street owed its origin to the West Metropolitan Jewish Schools, and whatever might have been the cause of the rivalry he was pleased with its *effect*.

The boys' department moved to High Holborn and the girls' to Lamb's Conduit Street, but they merged in 1853 in Red Lion Square. It was not a charity school in the accepted sense. Most parents paid something. It was the first Jewish school in London that accepted Christian children.

Matthew Arnold, the government inspector, was unstinting in his praise. After a visit in 1864 he said, 'I have no girls' school in which grammar is so good. I have none in which the reading is better'. The following year he said, 'The reading from a newspaper by the boys at the top of the school is, I think, the best I have ever heard'. The *Cornhill Magazine* reported favourably on the school in 1860 and said the chief aim of the school was 'to teach the pupils to help themselves and to inculcate an honest self-dependence and independence'.

Despite such glowing reports, the school suffered from its association with the Reform movement and was becoming increasingly unviable. When two children were sent there in 1870 from the Sephardi Villareal School they were withdrawn immediately the Haham learned of it. In 1874, it changed its name to the West Metropolitan Jewish School for Middle Class Pupils and later, in 1878, to the Jewish Middle Class School. The numbers on the roll declined and the boys' school was closed down in 1880. In 1881, the girls' school, now called The Jewish High School for Girls, continued in new premises close to Bedford Square. The cost was defrayed by Miss Isabel Goldsmid, the daughter of the founder of the school,

F D Goldsmid.   In 1897, the school had only 80 pupils in a building designed for 200.   Jews had moved out of the Gower Street area further west.   The need was no longer there, and the school closed.

PULTENEY SCHOOL

Pulteney School in Peter Street (referred to by many West Enders as Peter Street School) was a board school, later taken over by the London County Council, with separate boys' and girls' departments.   It had more Jewish pupils than any school in the West End, with the exception of the Westminster Jews' Free School.   From 1901 to 1912, their numbers varied between 278 and 442, with 1911 the peak year.   The school admissions book for 1912 shows that in that year only 15 per cent were non-Jewish; mainly, judging by their names, Italian and Irish.   From the First World War onwards, Jewish pupils comprised more than 80 per cent of the total, though perhaps its most famous pupil was non-Jewish - Jessie Matthews, the musical star who attended from 1915 to 1921.   It was the equivalent to the schools in the East End, such as Old Castle Street and Settle Street, which were to all intents and purposes 'Jewish' schools, except that it did not have the same proportion of Jewish teachers.

In many ways Pulteney School was situated in a most unpromising area for education.   Just off Berwick Street market, it was surrounded by the growing vice industry, narrow alleys, inadequate housing, noise and dust. Yet, as an educational institution, it shone due to the intelligence and liveliness of its pupils and the outstanding character of its teachers, particularly during the 1920s and 1930s.

Alex Flinder, the architect, who was at the school from 1927 to 1935, and became a world authority on underwater archaeology, could not find words adequate to praise its qualities, and in particular the headmaster of the Boys' Department, J C Whitebrook.   When the Inspectors' Report which follows was shown to him he said it conveyed the position exactly as it was.

"It deserves to be published as a demonstration to modern-day educationalists of the value of good and devoted teachers. In many ways I owe much of what I am (or rather have been) to Whitebrook and the deputy-head Fitch.   Their influence dovetailed in with the Boys' Club and reminds me of what a lucky chap I was. It is strange to compare all this that I had with my grandchildren today, with their private schools and commercial ballet classes and drama classes. All in all the West End was remarkable for some of its personalities - Ferber, Montagu, its teachers, and the people who ran the clubs and societies. Or is this simply an intoxication with nostalgia?"

His comments on the report are interspersed with the text.

Special report to London County Council dated November 29, 1933 after full inspection by council inspectors Miss E.Stevenson, D.A.G.Hughes and Mr A W Pegrum, together with the inspectors of special subjects. Visit was in October 1933

1.   This school lies in a cul-de-sac in the heart of Soho, among garages, film studios, restaurants, and street markets. Though it is the only council school within a wide area its members have of recent years declined rapidly owing to the commercialisation of the district, which is also served by a number of non-provided schools, [mainly the church schools] and it now consists of only three classes, for one of which the headmaster is responsible. The building is old and unattractive, with a small basement playground and one hall shared by the boys and the combined girls' and infants' departments. An unusual but most fortunate addition to the accommodation is the provision in the basement of spray baths, the use of which by the pupils, both in term and during the holidays, has been admirably organised by the headmaster.

[The showers, supervised by the school caretaker, were very popular. One minute was allowed. We were provided with very stiff towels, the gift of the chairman of the school governors, one of the Glucksteins of J Lyons & Co].

2.   The boys are mainly of Jewish parentage and more than 80 per cent are of the Jewish faith. In more than half the homes Yiddish is used preferably, and in some exclusively, as the mother tongue, and there are always in the school some boys who have entered knowing no English at all. The houses in which most of the boys live are old, overcrowded, and often unhygenic, and the streets are naturally the desirable alternative in leisure time, adverse though the influences of a cosmopolitan pleasure haunt are to growing boys.

[I don't think that we were adversely affected by 'the influences of a cosmopolitan pleasure haunt'. We were not very conscious of Soho as a den of iniquity. The streets were safe, the kids were not molested, there were no muggers; though fights by pub drunks were common]

3. Fortunately for his pupils, the headmaster is a man of marked originality of outlook and of keen interest in education, whom the obvious difficulties of his problem have stimulated to find an appropriate though not conventional solution. The characteristic of the school which first arrests attention is the perfectly natural relation that exists between the teachers and the pupils. The boys are free and unrepressed, and as they have a vivacity of temperament characteristic of their stock there is not that degree of formal orderliness which has come to be associated with school life. The freedom given in this school is, however, noted in a spirit of real friendliness and is governed, in most of the pupils, by a refreshing interest in acquiring knowledge, in the best of them by the achievment of educational standards above the average, and in the weakest by co-operation up to their capacity in some of the many activities for which the school gives them scope.

[This passage is beautifully written, and so true. The relationship between the head, L C Fitch, the deputy head, and the boys, was one of respect and reasonable discipline]

4. Recognising the fundamental difficulty for most of the boys is the mastery of English, the headmaster lays great stress on practice in understanding and acquiring spoken English, written work being delayed to the later stages. In the middle class, for which he is himself responsible, oral lessons predominate. These oral lessons, informed as they are by his own wide and often recondite knowledge, are full of interesting matter and on occasion develop trains of thought which are usually considered beyond the comprehension of school children; for example, in teaching arithmetic the headmaster may lead his pupils to explore in thoughtful discussion difficult ideas such as the nature of infinity and the properties of fractions. He is not afraid of taking them out of their depth and they go willingly, finding obvious pleasure in the challenge of their power of thinking and in the sometimes vague mystery of the headmaster's thoughts. In the same way lessons in scripture and history for the two top classes appeal by the wealth and variety of their subject matter and the power of arresting de-

scription to the various sections of the class. Whatever the subject taught by the headmaster, his presentation of it enriches the children's ideas, vocabulary, and scope of language. This broadly stimulating attack is supplemented by careful organisation of the work of individual children who have little or no English, by opportunities for practising connected statement and by natural intercourse between teacher and taught. As a result there is a remarkable advance in knowledge and in command of English within the boys' school life, indicated sometimes in the case of abler boys by the gaining of trade and supplementary scholarships, and in some cases by their entering, through private study, into professional careers. But the attention paid to physical health and development is no less marked and individual. Consciously the headmaster sets out to encourage physical health and physical courage as a corrective, as far as possible, of the social environment of the children, and to set up standards of right and, he would say, 'English' behaviour. On his initiative the shower baths are used daily, and by almost all the boys, not only in term but during holidays. Swimming is carried on during the whole year, and the school runs its own gala; sports are actively pursued, and in both fields the school holds an excellent record. A special remedial gymnastic class is conducted by the headmaster in close co-operation with the school Medical Officer, and hygiene is taught in connection with the swimming and physical exercises.

[Whitebrook excelled in oral lessons. His history lessons were fascinating, anecdotal. He made history come alive. Discussions always followed. A feature was oral classroom quizzes conducted by the head and Fitch in all subjects.]

5. Though the headmaster is, as he should be, the inspiring and directing force of the school's activities, his ideas could not have been made effective without the wholehearted and intelligent co-operation of his first assistant, who, though he has been for 21 years in the school [L C Fitch, also non-Jewish] is full of energy and zest in both school work and social activities. He specialises in science and geography and, in default of anyone with a specialist knowledge, in Art, and is in all subjects a stimulating and sympathetic teacher. In organised games he is indefatigable giving Friday afternoons, after school hours, Saturday mornings and, in summmer, Monday evenings to taking the boys to the somewhat distant parks, which

are their nearest playing fields. His pleasant, cultivated personality rein-
forces the influence of the headmaster in making the school à place of
intellectual stimulus and civilising influence.

*[Mr Fitch was trim in appearance, slight, slim, with a military bearing.
He served in the Machine Gun Corps and we were always asking him for
his First World War stories. He owned one of the early Baby Austins
which he regularly drove to school. His geography lessons matched the
headmaster's history talks. He also took the singing classes, and I can
recall 'Cherry Ripe', 'Where 'ere you Walk', 'Nymphs and Shepherds',
'The Three Grenadiers', 'Land of Hope and Glory', and the overture to
Tannhauser which we 'la-la-la'd'.]*

6. The third mastership has been filled by a succession of teachers. It is
not an easy post for, owing to the small numbers in both departments, the
little boys are promoted between six and seven and the technique needed
in the youngest class is that most frequently possessed by infants' mis-
tresses. The present master has not yet been 18 months in the school. He
is interested in the younger children and handles them sympathetically
and with an appreciation of the importance of his task ...

*[Mr Flower was the junior class master, the only Jewish master I can
recall. He was succeeded by Mr Hillier and then Mr Jones.]*

8. The proper employment of leisure in this neighbourhood is a difficult
one. To meet it the headmaster has established a chess and ping-pong
club, and a school library to which books are supplied by the Westminster
public library.

*[Extra activities were encouraged for all boys. Chess was taken by Mr
Flower. Bookbinding was taught by the head. Part of his 'getting to love
books' approach. Whitebrook and Fitch regularly refereed and umpired
football and cricket matches on Saturday against other schools. Swimming was the head's passion. Many boys obtained the Bronze Medallion
of the Royal Life Saving Society. I still have mine. Table tennis was
played on the laboratory tables. A large stock of plimsoles was kept in a
large box in the corridor for gym sessions on the ground floor.]*

9. On holidays the boys often come back to school to do handiwork jobs or to occupy themselves with reading or games under the headmaster's general supervision, and visits to places of interest in the neighbourhood are paid in and out of school hours. The headmaster's personal influence is also exerted in entering the boys at evening institutes, in finding them suitable jobs, and in keeping in touch with them in after life. **Corporal punishment is rare, and it is significant that the parents enlist the headmaster's help in all kinds of domestic difficulties. He plays indeed in this odd cosmopolitan community the part of a friend and adviser in all that affects pupils' lives.**

[I can recall annual outings to Bushey Park, and visits to the Tower of London, Greenwich Observatory, British Museum, Madame Tussauds, Kew Gardens and the National Gallery.

Whitebrook was a barrister. He had a flat in one of the legal buildings in Lincoln's Inn Fields. His family (I recall two daughters - one called Lucy) lived in the country.

The report says that corporal punishment was rare, but most boys received at least 'one on the hand' at some time.]

10. In general it may be said that the school is giving generously the essentials of a good education, the development of body, mind, and character, by reasonable activities carried out in a stimulating atmosphere created by sympathetic and educated teachers. We should be reluctant to see any changes which would formalise the present vital teaching ...

E M Rich, Education Officer, The County Hall, S E 1.

From before the First World War the school had an annual camp on Limpsfield Common. An inspector visited on 30 June 1925. There were 40 boys (37 of them Jewish), the headmaster (Whitebrook's predecessor), one assistant, and three students from Westminster Training College. Training was given in all details of camp life. The headmaster's wife supervised the open-air cooking and provided a special diet, even under camp conditions.

Every weekend there were visits from parents. The inspector reported that on the Sunday previous to his visit there were about 70. One family of six, who lived in one room in a house opposite the school, made the whole journey by taxi-cab!

UPPER MARYLEBONE STREET SCHOOL

The Upper Marylebone Street (now New Cavendish Street) London County Council school opened in 1914 and was divided into a boys' school, a girls' school, and an infants' school. Its name was changed to Clipstone Junior School in 1937. The three-storey building was described as well-planned, light and pleasing in decoration, and considering that it was in a busy West End quarter, it had a reasonably good playground.

The extant log books and admission and discharge registers (only a few appear to have survived) indicate that from the outset about 40 per cent of the pupils were Jewish, and this remained a fairly consistent proportion until 1939. When the school first opened, almost 90 per cent of the fathers of the Jewish children gave their occupation as tailor or an allied trade. Occupations listed for non-Jewish parents included:

painter, boot repairer, van guard, pastry cook, traveller, police sergeant, milkman, cook, butcher, builder, porter, bus inspector, driver, packer, electrician, dyer, carman, cabinet maker, greengrocer, brass worker, labourer, postman, hairdresser, compositor, timber merchant, fruiterer, accountant, chauffeur, warehouseman, waiter, undertaker, gas company worker, brassfounder, plasterer, and telephonist.

The school managed to attract teachers and head teachers of the highest calibre and provided its pupils with an elementary education of the best possible quality. Most remarkably, it succeeded in transforming children born abroad, or in England of foreign parents most of whom spoke Yiddish at home, into young men and women whose English, pronunciation and grammar, was superior to that of the local-born children of English parentage. It inculcated a love of books and of reading in its pupils. It was also noted that the children of foreign origin were healthier and better fed than their native compatriots. London County Council District Inspectors were not averse to making the strongest criticism, though not harshly, should the circumstances justify it. For this reason, the praise heaped on Upper Marylebone Street (and also on Pulteney Street School) was quite remarkable:

Report on Girls' School dated December 15, 1923:

1. Miss E M Horsley has been in charge of this Grade II Dept since the school was opened in May 1914. During this period of nine years she has built up a fine school from very mixed material, for some ten nationalities are represented amongst the girls and many of them come from very poor homes.

2. There is one feature, the elocutionary and dramatic work, which is of such outstanding merit that even if the other features were mediocre (which this report will show they are not) it would alone serve to give distinction to the school

a) Poetry Society's Examination in the Art of Speaking Verse 8 girls were awarded silver medals, 23 bronze, and 42 certificates

b) North London Musical Festival - held on November 23, 1923 at Northern Polytechnic. 38 girls entered elocution competitions open to children of elementary school age. They won every silver and bronze medal that was awarded, and in two classes extra awards were given on account of the excellence. In all they were awarded 3 silver medals, 9 bronze medals and 25 certificates

c) Scholarships
        Incorporated London Academy of Music [2]
        Trinity College of Music [2]
        Marylebone Scholarships, tenable at the Metropolitan
        Academy of Music [3]

One ex-pupil, Celia Shinowitz, who is now attending the Burlington Secondary School, has just gained the Bronze Medal [elocution] of the Incorporated London Academy of Music, a high distinction for a girl of 15, after a brilliant record in the competitions of the Poetry Society, and the British Empire Shakespeare Society.

Beautiful and gracious speech is not confined to a few girls or a few classes, but is an attribute common to the girls throughout the school. There is little doubt that many of the children have a natural gift of dramatic expression (a majority are of foreign extraction) but that gift could not have been cultivated to its present degree of excellence without the most skilful training, and without some unique source of inspiration. It is quite clear that this source of inspiration is the head mistress.

3. English - very praiseworthy ... The children are encouraged to read widely, and to keep a record and brief critical description of the books they have read. The high merit of the composition exercises is due no less to this careful reading than to the vigilance with which the teachers detect and eliminate errors. *Better, perhaps, than the actual achievement in the field of written and spoken English is the manifest enjoyment with which the children study English literature and enter into its spirit.*

4. History and Geography - very satisfactory, (but not as good as the English)

5. Arithmetic - very well taught - well above average for similar schools

6. Science - satisfactory

7. Art - Commendable success - none of the classes weak, and in some classes extraordinarily good

8. During the interval between arranging and carrying out the inspection Miss Horsley was appointed to a Grade IV school, but we carried out inspection none the less.

9. The all-round efficiency of the Girls' Dept may also be indicated by the variety of scholarships gained. They include Christ's Hospital; LCC Junior Art; Trade Scholarships; LCC Junior County; LCC Domestic Economy; Foundation and Free Place scholarships at St Martin's High School and Burlington Secondary School; scholarships (17) tenable at St Martin's School of Art, as well as those mentioned in para 2. Nor are the girls' activities confined to scholastic attainments. Considerable sums of money have been raised for various charitable objects and for the purchase of savings certificates; they do exceedingly well in swimming and games, whilst there is a strong Old Girls' Club.

11. Miss Horsley's promotion is well deserved, but is a serious loss to the school. It is to be hoped that Upper Marylebone Street will be given a leader who will be able, not only to conduct the school efficiently, but to maintain and develop those features which the late headmistress, by her skill and enthusiasm, backed by the whole-hearted support of a loyal and efficient staff, brought to a remarkably high standard of excellence. *There can be no doubt that the girls who have passed through this school have had as broad and liberal a training as is possible within the limits of an elementary school education.*

Signed: L Brooks; P B Ballard; John Brown.

Report on Boys' School dated January 25, 1926

1.   ... A large number of the boys are of foreign extraction, and many nationalities are represented. There is very little poverty in the homes of the boys, but overcrowding is common, with the result that many suffer from insufficient rest and sleep.

2.   Under the able and vigorous direction of the headmaster, the department has made considerable progress in all directions. Among its special features may be mentioned the excellent work in English, Art and Music; an efficient Prefect system; a carefully planned scheme of educational visits covering the last four years of school life; two violin classes; and a prosperous National Savings Club. It is very creditable that during the past five year 68 boys have been transferred to places of higher education.

The instruction in English, Art, and Music are the strongest features of the teaching. *To some extent this is due to the marked foreign element among the boys,* but it is also due to the head master. The presence of a large number of boys of foreign extraction makes the instruction in English specially difficult, but this difficulty is partly counterbalanced by the fact that the boys had a great natural aptitude for clear speech and for dramatic utterance. The head master has taken full advantage of this fact, and has made the reciting of poetry a specal feature of the school.   Not only do the boys take a great interest in recitation and dramatisation, but they reach in this subject an extraordinarily high level of merit.   Almost equally praiseworthy is the way in which the difficulties of writing English have been overcome.   The composition at the top of the school, in spite of frequent errors in spelling, indicates a careful training in the subject through-out the school. Reading is wisely encouraged, and the older boys borrow books extensively from the Marylebone Public Library as well as from the school library ...

Some of the boys show remarkable ability in drawing and painting ... we are of the opinion that this is a school where a highly qualified specialist in Art would find ample scope for his abilities.

The organisation of the teaching of Music is on novel lines. A School Choir of about 80 carefully selected boys from the four top classes com-prise one group. The remainder of the boys from these classes are taught in separate groups. The work of the Choir reaches a very high standard in all branches of the syllabus, and its members are receiving an excellent elementary training in Music. Signed: L Brooks; P B Ballard; E P Bennett

Report on Infants' School dated March 20, 1928

1. ... A large number of the children are of foreign parentage, drawn from many nations, and about 40 per cent are Jewish. In many of the homes English is not spoken. Housing conditions are bad throughout the dis-trict, and in many cases both parents go out to work. *The English children are poorer in physique and social class than those of foreign origin, who are generally well fed and well cared for.*

2. The head mistress was appointed in 1922 ... she rightly stresses the importance of training in good habits, and such matters as luncheon and playtimes, personal cleanliness and good behaviour receive special atten-tion and are well organised.

5. ... Though the children have some special difficulties they are in gen-eral bright and responsive, and we think there has perhaps been a ten-dency to exaggerate the difficulties presented by the foreign extraction of the children and to expect less of them than they are capable of doing.

Signed: G H Gater

Report on Girls' School dated December 20, 1929

1. This school is situated between Tottenham Court Road and Great Portland Street *in a quarter in which the most prosperous residents are of foreign extraction, and the poorest and least successful of English stock.* These two elements are found within the school. Of the 245 girls on the roll in December 1929, 121 were of Jewish race, many of them of Polish or Russian origin, and 117 were non-Jewish. Of the non-Jewish children, 77 were English, the remaining 40 being chiefly Italians, with representatives of the Southern and Central European peoples and one or two children of Indian and Chinese strain.

2. The school is therefore confronted by the problem of making English citizens of children, a large number of whom are foreigners in respect of their home language and their social and cultural traditions. All departments are dealing effectively with this difficulty; the girls department is selected for special report because the head mistress, who is now in her sixth year of office, has built up, on sound foundations already laid, a school of marked individuality and interest in its aim and its achievement.

3. Her aim has been two-fold: to make good English a natural form of expression for these foreign children and so to give them a share in English culture, and at the same time to give scope for the development of their own charactersistic gifts.

4. ... training in speaking English is the core of the teaching and this is based on systematic speech training and on the study of good prose and poetry in which memorising, recitation and acting play a very important part. The temperament of the foreign children responds eagerly to these opportunities for expression and the less articulate English girls expand under the influence of their gay and animated companions, *though it is found that the children whose language is foreign often attain finally a higher standard of English speech than the child handicapped from birth by hearing vulgar and slovenly English.* The school takes part annually in the examination in the Art of Spoken verse conducted by the Poetry Society, and is very successful not only in gaining high individual awards but in the large number of certificates won at all stages.

5. Music, Dancing and Art are also very well taught ... and within the last year a course in bookbinding has been well begun. The danger of resting content with merely showy work in the progressive arts has been well recognised by the head mistress, and thoroughness in them and in the fundamental subjects is stressed and ensured by careful guidance and supervision. External evidence of this is given by the steady increase in successes, which include Junior, Trade and Supplementary Scholarships, free places and Art and Music Scholarships ...

7. ... The head mistress has a strong team of able and enthusiastic assistants to whose several abilities she has given full scope, and who respond as a whole with eagerness to the example she sets of hard work, enthusiasm and a progressive outlook on education ... *Stress has been laid on the scholastic side: it should be said that in this school studies pass over into manners and conduct, and that there is every indication that the influence of the school leaves a permanent impress on its pupils.*

Signed: G H Gater

ST ANNE'S SCHOOL, DEAN STREET

St Anne's was a Church of England school. The boys' school was founded in Frith Street in 1699 for 'the poor boys of the parish'. A girls' school was founded in 1797 and an infants' one in 1847. The combined departments moved to Dean Street in 1872.

There were Jewish children in all departments, and in 1899 it was reported by the School Committee that about 60 Jewish pupils were in attendance, chiefly in the Infants' School, and it 'was a somewhat strange thing that ... very few of them are withdrawn from religious instruction'.   Between 1900 and 1912 the number of Jewish children, according to reports sent by the school to the publishers of the *Jewish Year Book,* fluctuated between 115 and 190, with 1911 the peak year. A teacher from the Western Synagogue provided regular tuition in Hebrew.

Compared to the glowing inspectors' reports on the Pulteney and Upper Marylebone Street schools, St Anne's fared badly, but it nonetheless gave its Jewish pupils a reasonable start in life.

The Rabbi gives regular religious instruction to the Jewish children at the same time that the Christian children receive theirs. The Christian and the Jewish children are on the best terms, and last year a Jewish boy gained the popularity prize. The Jews receive the clergy very courteously, and are anxious to join any institutions of the parish which are open to them ... [and] while we wish that they were Christians we do not make any direct effort for their conversion. We think it best to commend the cause of Christ by the work and life of the Church rather than by an aggressive propaganda.

[From *Twenty years in Soho. A review of the work of the Church in the Parish of St Anne's, Soho from 1891 to 1911* by Rev J H Cardwell, rector of St Anne's. 1911].

W J Reece, the headmaster, wrote a separate chapter in the book:

... But let us leave this side of the subject and catch a glimpse of the interest to be found in the odd ways and queer names of the little foreigners amongst us.

Not many years ago there was a representative in the schools of every important European nation, but now the foreign element is smaller, and consists principally of Jews. To admit a foreign boy is often quite a business. A mother arrives with her boy, but neither can speak English: then four boys, dubbed interpreters because they know French, German, Italian or Yiddish well, are called, and one or other soon gets the required information.

It may be of interest to see a few names taken at hazard from one page of the admission register:

Marino Emiliani, from Modena; Pierino Vercesi, from Pavia; Pietro Desimoni, from Turin; Achille Cremonsi, from Paris; Isidore Rottenberg, from Warsaw; Fritze Halbritter, from Switzerland; and Timon Shargriski, from Russia.

This foreign element comes and goes rapidly. They are birds of passage. Today a lad from Durban is admitted, and tomorrow farewells are being given to a boy whose family is seeking better fortune in Winnipeg. It is no little knowledge of the various countries they have visited that they bring to the geography lesson, but the trouble is that they sometimes have to be taught English before they can relate their experiences.

... Despite these peculiarities some of the cleverest children in the schools are of foreign extraction, and we should not care to be without them.

"I went to school with my brothers and sister at St Anne's School in Dean Street.   Most of my contemporaries went to Pulteney, but Dean Street School was only 30 yards from where we lived, and that is why we went there. We had prayers in the morning, but the Jewish children waited outside.   We had all the Jewish holidays that you could think of off".

LYULPH STANLEY CENTRAL SCHOOL

"At the age of 11 I went in for the scholarship and passed.   Soon I was measured for the special green school blouses. I shall never forget my first morning there; I was sitting in the front row of the class. The first words the teacher said was, 'Are there any Jews here?' I raised my hand and looked around - I was the only one.   At 10.30 in the morning in the playground I was quickly surrounded by other girls all shouting at me, 'Jewey, Jewey'. This was my first experience on my own in a non-Jewish environment. I did not enjoy my schooldays there at all. I was so shocked when older Jewish girls from another class joined in the hymn-singing at Assembly. I expect they wanted to belong, but that was not for me. I was pleased when scripture time came and the Jewish girls were allowed to go into a separate room to read the Old Testament. The long day over, I was back on the underground - Mornington Crescent Station to Goodge Street Station - round Catesby's on the corner (the furniture shop with the huge animal in the doorway), into Whitfield Street, turning right into Windmill Street and *I was on home ground again"*.

"It was a marvellous school. Very strict.   If you misbehaved you got the cane. You were sent to the headmaster, no messing about. Two schools, one for the boys and one for the girls. Entirely separate. Next door to each other in Mornington Crescent, in Crowndale Road. There were about 30 children in each class.   There were not a lot of Jewish boys. About four or five in our class and we were taunted a bit, but we got over that.   We took the Jewish holidays off; no problem.

I used to jump on a 24 or 29 bus at Tottenham Court Road, or go by tube. It was 9-12 with two hours for lunch.   Then we started again 2-4".

"I enjoyed my time there.   The school provided a very good education. The examinations were very stiff.   One of my friends there, Jack Kruchevsky, became a consultant surgeon.   He lived in Berwick Street. Another, Lou Cohen, became right-hand man to Joe Coral for the football pools, and Alec Vichinsky became an art director for films".

ARCHBISHOP TENISON SCHOOL

"I got a scholarship to Archbishop Tenison School which was then in Leicester Square. It was the choir school for St Martin's-in-the-Fields. When I joined the school the choirmaster was a famous organist. He played a tune on a piano and said, 'sing it'. So I sang one octave and he said, 'You have no ear for music' and he chucked me out.   I had no problems being Jewish at that school.   There were only three or four other Jewish boys. No real trouble about being a scholarship boy either, but I did not play football because they played on the Sabbath".

BURLINGTON SCHOOL

Burlington School in Boyle Street, off Regent Street, was a fee-paying girls' school originally intended for the middle class. Indeed, for many years it was called the Burlington Middle Class Girls' School. It attracted many Jewish pupils, both fee-paying and on scholarship, and was regarded as a very superior school.

"I went to Burlington from a council school. My parents didn't wait for scholarships but decided I must leave then and there [apparently because of anti-semitism at her then school]. I liked it. I liked learning. We had very good English teachers and the books they gave us to read certainly gave me much pleasure.   Jewish children had their prayers in a separate room although they were only a small percentage of the whole".

"My first school was St Anne's.   One of the teachers there was Dr Ripker who was instrumental in getting my parents to send me to the Burlington, which I attended from the age of 12 to 14, 1927-1929. It was just off Regent Street, next to Savile Row police station.   Subsequently it moved to Wormwood Scrubs; from the sublime to the ridiculous, I would say".

"I was just bewitched by Ada, a daughter of Rabbi Ferber. [He married her.] She went to one of the poshest schools in England, the Burlington in Mayfair, direct from a council school. She used to meet Lady So-and-so and the Hon So-and-so and she was close to them and the teachers. They were keen on getting her to go to university, but her father would have none of that. 'A Jewish daughter should stay with her mother at home'. That was their tradition".

"I stayed at Pulteney until about 11, and then went to Burlington. I used to go through Marlborough Street, Foubert's Place, cross over to Regent Street and turn into the Burlington - it was only a short walk. There were a few Jewish girls. I went in on a scholarship. There were quite a lot of paying pupils, including Jewish girls, the daughters of business people. I think it was about five guineas a term, not that much really. If you had a shop, you could afford a fiver, and you would sent your daughters there. There was a very nice atmosphere at the school, and it was very well equipped, with a big gymnasium, and we were taught French and other subjects which were not available at Pulteney".

REGENT STREET POLYTECHNIC

"Unfortunately my father bought a shop in Berwick Street in 1919, and he pulled me out of school to work on the stall outside the shop. I didn't think much of it so secretly I joined the Polytechnic evening classes to continue my education. I worked on the stall during the day. I used to go every evening to the Poly from 7.30 to 9.30. My parents didn't believe in education; they thought it would harm my brain or something! So I didn't make a big deal about it. I learned French there, and business methods and all sorts of subjects, including book-keeping. I was about 14½ and I went there for two years. My mother said, 'Don't break your head.'"

XIII - WEST CENTRAL JEWISH GIRLS' CLUB AND MISS LILY MONTAGU

"It was not only the friendships which were generated, it was an eye-opener to the different ways of living which was most remarkable about the club".

"Everyone who came under Lily Montagu became 'a somebody'".

"In the Club we have to make amends on behalf of society for defects in home circumstances".

The West Central Jewish Girls' Club, founded in 1893, was one of the best-loved institutions in the West End. Its principal leaders, The Honourable Lily Montagu C B E [1873-1963] and her elder sister Marian [1868-1965], were looked upon by the members with a mixture of awe and extreme affection. The Club gave young girls, mostly foreign-born, or born of foreign parents, an opportunity to broaden their horizons and initiate life-long friendships. It excited comments from its members such as 'My mother regarded it as her second home' or 'I don't know what I would have done without the Girl's Club'. Miss Lily, as she was fondly called by her members, devoted almost her entire working life to the Club and was its prime influence for a period covering three generations and extending over seventy years. Her other great achievement was the establishment, together with Claude Montefiore, of the Liberal Jewish Union (out of which grew the West London Hebrew Congregation) in 1902. Her success in both fields gave her the greatest satisfaction of her life.

By the last quarter of the 19th century, reformers were becoming increasingly aware of the needs of young working girls. However caring and loving the parents might be, large families and overcrowded houses or tenements, many of which doubled as workshops, meant a complete lack of quiet and privacy for the homecoming worker. Many girls yearned for a place where they could find companionship and friendship, escape from the dreariness of their work, enlarge their outlook and experience, find an outlet for their untapped ability, and generally do something better with their lives. The concern of the Jewish community was that such girls, if not provided with an adequate opportunity to fulfil their needs, might be lost to the community. The Jewish establishment were ever anxious to ensure that the children of the poor should grow into Englishmen and Englishwomen of the Jewish persuasion - that they should be anglicised but still retain their Jewish identity - and took great care of their needs while they were at school. The East End and the West End each had its Jews' Free School. Some local authority schools were 'Jewish' in all but name, and even in the board schools and Church schools where Jewish children were a minority, steps were taken to give them separate religious and Hebrew teaching. But what was was going to happen when the schooling stopped, usually at 12, 13 or 14? How could the community ensure that their Jewishness remained intact? How could they reduce the much-feared risk of intermarriage? The situation was considered to be particularly acute in the cosmopolitan West End where additional temptations, such as music-halls and 'low dancing saloons of dubious morality' could lead them astray.

The youth club was seen as the answer, the means by which the gap between adolescence and adulthood could be bridged in a safe Jewish environment. The first clubs were single sex, but mixed social events where Jewish boys would meet Jewish girls were arranged and carefully supervised. The theory was that once safely married to a Jewish husband the Jewish wife - and through her the Jewish family - would continue intact.

Lily and Marian were two of ten children of the Liberal MP, Samuel Montagu, the first Lord Swaythling. He was a self-made man whose fortune flowed from the banking firm of Samuel Montagu & Co, which he had started in 1853 with his brother-in-law, Ellis Franklin. Their mother, Ellen, was a daughter of Louis Cohen and a grand-niece of Sir Moses Montefiore. The Montagus, Montefiores, Cohens, and Franklins were part and parcel of the Jewish 'cousinhood', well represented in all Jewish institutions and numerous enough to be formidable supporters of any new organisation in which one of their number became interested. However, initially Lily did not enjoy their totally unqualified support for her club work.

The ten Montagu children were given the best of education and provided with all the comforts of an upper-middle class family living in 'Millionaires' Row', as Kensington Palace Gardens was, and still is, known. After finishing their schooling, Lily and Marian spent one day a week helping at the Jews' Free School in the East End. In so doing they were engaging in the type of charitable work common amongst those of their class. The middle-class, upper-middle class and the aristocracy, all had ladies who, as Chaim Bermant has described them, 'descended on some poor quarter for an afternoon once a month - sometimes even once a week - patted a child here, gave a guinea there, scattered smiles and sympathy everywhere - and were then off back to Kensington as quickly as their carriages could take them'. It is true that many were dilettantes employing their superior station in life in condescending social charity, doing their bit 'for their less fortunate sisters' and at the same time quenching their social consciences. But there were others - and Miss Lily was one of their number - who wholeheartedly and genuinely devoted their time and efforts to bettering the lot of those who did not start with the advantages they enjoyed. Miss Lily went even further. She sacrificed a comfortable social life and, most probably, her prospects of marriage. Even the Rothschild ladies, whose devotion and attendance at the Jews' Free School in the East End exceeded normal bounds, could not match Miss Lily's sympathetic identification with her girls. Without the activities of such ladies, however much or little time they devoted and whatever the motive which drove them, the growth of the girls' club movement would have been delayed, and in some instances perhaps not have occurred at all.

Fathers, husbands and friends provided the financial backing for causes 'the ladies' espoused. In addition to Marian, Lily recruited her niece Sheila Conrad and Sheila's husband Eric who gave lectures on current affairs ('Auntie Lily was awfully keen on involving anybody she could'); her sister Netta (Franklin), who loaned her Bayswater and Irish homes for Club use; her sister-in-law Firenza, who was active in the drama classes; and her nephew Bryan (Firenza's son) who played a leading role in the later years of the Club's life ('the best she could do, as I was completely unmusical, was to put me in charge of the operatic class').

Lily was not the first on the scene. The redoubtable Lady Magnus formed the Jewish Girls' Club in the East End in the mid-1880s. More commonly known as Lady Magnus' Club, it operated out of Gravel Lane Board School, and sought to cultivate the three Rs: *Religion, Refinement, and Recreation*. The Club enrolled girls from 14 to 18 years, and the aim, as Lady Magnus described it, was:

to awaken a sense of pleasure in what is restful and beautiful ... to direct lagging feet to really profitable paths ... to civilize and to spiritualize rather than to stimulate these keen-witted boys and girls, as, fresh from school discipline, they enter on their university of the streets.

Lily adopted many of her principles but was also very keen to stimulate interest in further education.

When Lily was just 19 her cousin Beatrice Franklin introduced her to Miss Emily Harris, a social worker in both the East End and the West End. Emily had for many years been holding Sabbath classes for young working girls in a small room in Devonshire Street, and sought out 'ladies' to provide 'occasions' for her girls on Sundays. Lily obliged with well-received and appreciated Shakespearean readings. About 20 local working-class girls attended, and after a while the girls said that if a move could be made to larger premises they were sure that there would be many others who would welcome the formation of a club. In 1893, in response to this, two large rooms were rented at 71 Dean Street, and this was the foundation of the West Central Jewish Girls' Club. Its stated object was 'to bring brightness and refinement into the lives of Jewish working girls'. Its motto, based on Hillel, was later embroidered and displayed in the entrance hall of the club: 'If I strive not after my own salvation who shall strive for me? If not now, when?'

A committee, consisting largely of family friends, assisted in running the Club. Emily was appointed the first President and Lily was given the title of Honorary Secretary, but it was Lily who was in effective charge from the start despite her youth. Her right hand was Marian, 'my better half ... wise and beloved ... who has accompanied me step by step in my travels in Clubland. Our lives are entirely entwined ... By thousands of members our Miss Marian is respected for her wisdom and unselfishness - and loved for all the tender beauty of her character'. Bryan Montagu described Lily as the leader and Marian as the anchor.

A third member of their team was Constance Lewis who played an essential role in their personal and Club life. She lived with them, and was their *aide-de-campe,* secretary, companion and friend. 'She has looked after our home and relieved us of great responsibility while interesting herself in all our work ... she supplied the happy, peaceful background which has meant so much to us'.

At the Club Miss Lily was known as 'mother', Miss Marian as 'auntie' and Miss Lewis as 'father'. Miss Lewis was responsible for starting the employment bureau which placed hundreds of girls in suitable positions that did not require Sabbath work.

Members were encouraged to bring guests, and soon the space was ovewhelmed by the numbers wishing to attend. The Club moved to 8 Frith Street, next to a brothel, and stayed there for a short period until, in 1896, a house was rented at 8A Dean Street where the Club remained for 17 years until its move to Alfred Place.

Lily and Marian's parents were beginning to have considerable reservations about the project. They were worried about the neighbourhood in which their girls were proposing to spend so much of their time, about the effect it would have on their social lives if they became too involved, and about what their own friends might say. A sensible marriage, preferably to someone within the cousinhood, was what they had in mind for their daughters. Lily and Marian were becoming too seriously immersed in the club work for Samuel and Ellen's liking. At first they had given their daughters every help and encouragement, but that lasted only until they discovered to their dismay that Lily 'was not merely intent upon a good deed, but had entered into a vocation'. When it became obvious to them that the Club was beginning to absorb Lily and Marian's lives they became agitated. As Lily wrote in 1941 in her book *My Club and I*:

The accepted life's programme for every girl in my set was that she would go out as much as possible, know plenty of people, and settle down in an early age in marriage. My complete failure to conform with this widely supported plan brought much disappointment and anxiety ... mother's visiting circle, though generally kind and sympathetic, did not approve of my mode of life and outlook. Because I worked very hard, dressed badly, went out very little, was always shy and backward at social functions, I was held up as a warning to my mother's acquaintances.

Her mother was warned 'by kind relatives':

... that Soho was a part of London which was fraught with dangers for young girls of good family. I knew at this time nothing concerning social evils. My girls taught me a great deal later on. But I could not see why, because I was better bred and better educated than the Club members, I should be less qualified than they to resist the temptations which were vaguely talked about in hushed whispers in my presence. Finally, it was agreed that my sister and I could visit the Club on certain evenings in the week, but not more than once in the same week. The rule that we could never go in the streets alone was adhered to with particular strictness when we wanted to visit the danger zone of Soho.

The pattern the Club was to follow was set at the very beginning. [See Appendix IV]. Practical experience taught Lily the principles by which to run it. She endeavoured to influence every phase of the members' lives, the keynote to which she called 'sympathetic sharing', and she had regard for the girls not only as individuals but in the context of their family:

It is important that each member should count ... She came to us because she knew we were interested in her. She could talk to us. My approach to the girls was so very simple, just the kind of friendliness given by one girl to another like herself, and they gave me affection in generous measure'.

From very early days, girls entered their names as they came into the Club, and careful lists were kept of absentees. 'We wrote them postcards before many days had elapsed, and we did our best to show them that they were always missed if they stayed away.'

She and Marian were allowed to invite girls to their own home:

In the days of strong class separation, we were told that by inviting the girls to our home we roused discontent among those who were ill-housed and lacked so many things necessary for material and physical well-being, to which, indeed, they were entitled as part of their human heritage. We in our large houses had all we needed and much to spare. Although, here and there, it may be possible that feelings of discontent were roused, I think, on the whole, we did much more good than harm in establishing the right relationship between us. We were simple people, and the spirit of our hospitality was sincere. Our guests were brought near to us through our showing them the beauty of our home. They were not estranged.

A genuine relationship between privileged women such as Miss Lily and the working girls who lived in the area might seem unlikely. It might be thought that the difference in upbringing and wealth, particularly in Victorian and Edwardian times and after, would make such an alliance impossible, with condescension on one side and deference on the other. Lily recognised the possibility of disaffection. The girls were within a stone's throw of some of the most luxurious houses and places of entertainment in London. 'It is small wonder', she wrote, 'that we had to cope with a certain amount of restlessness and a sense of injustice in girls who came from drab and wretched homes'. However, the almost unanimous testimony of the girls and their families that Miss Lily and Miss Marian were good and true friends cannot be disregarded. Very few considered they were being patronised.

HOME VISITING

The Montagu sisters started the practice of home visiting as early as 1895. For the next 60 years it became a common sight to see these two formidable ladies, still dressed in Victorian fashion long after the Old Queen died, stalking the streets of the poorer sections of the West End, acknowledged with respect even by those who had never spoken to them, quietly and resolutely going about their splendid business of spreading education, goodwill, and community spirit among all sections of the population.

They soon came to appreciate that the main problems facing their members were poor housing and poor working conditions. Lily described the housing conditions in which 'her' girls lived at the turn of the century as among the worst in London.

Our people lived mostly in badly constructed, ill-ventilated houses in small streets in Soho, St Marylebone, and St Pancras. There was no possibility of privacy or of entertaining at home. The tenements were overcrowded, and in many of the courts the houses seemed to bend over and shut out both light and air ... Our members had to depend on outside agencies for their social life. Soon after Miss Lewis started her flower guild in 1901 through which seeds and plants were distributed for home use, a little girl was seen standing in the street clutching her plant. 'I thought it better to take it outside because it wanted air and light'.

She said that poverty was general and vermin impossible to eradicate, but the mothers, who often acted as runners to the shops for which the fathers worked, kept their homes as clean as conditions would allow. Clothes were hung on the door, covered by a sheet, because there was neither the space for wardrobes nor the money to buy furniture.

When the club started, girls leaving school began their working life at an average wage of 2/6d a week; for women the average was 12/-. Wages were so low that it was not surprising that girls and women regarded their working life as a temporary evil rather than a career in which it was desirable to be as efficient as possible. Most of the girls were tailoresses whose average working hours were 8 a.m. to 8 p.m. with an hour for dinner and half an hour for tea. Girls employed as milliners worked equally long hours. Many of these girls were the mothers and grandmothers of the West Enders who were interviewed for the book. To Miss Lily it seemed remarkable that they could survive the strain of such protracted sedentary occupations, and she appreciated the vital need for an outlet after long days of repression.

CLASSES

The Club arranged an outstanding variety of classes, both educational and recreational, eventually totalling more than fifty. It was made clear that members were expected to join at least one class, and not to use the Club solely for social activities. Lily classified the classes and their advantages as she viewed them, into **physical training** for a healthy body; **domestic science** 'which prepared for satisfactory home keeping'; **technical** 'to give the girls the opportunity to learn subjects which would provide them with an alternative trade'; **art** 'which afforded an outlet for creative feeling'; **music and drama** 'which afforded an emotional outlet, intellectual training and recreation'; **literature** 'which supplied intellectual food'; **knowledge of public affairs** 'which helped train the members as citizens'; **languages,** including French, German, Spanish, Russian and English for foreigners 'which helped the girls in their work'; and **university tutorial classes** conducted under the auspices of the Workers' Educational Association.

Teachers were provided by the London County Council (and later by the Inner London Education Authority). Club members assisted, and several eventually became class teachers and Club managers. 'We learned that the aim of the Club should indeed be self-development through service'. Girls who worked in certain trades all day found real enjoyment in teaching an evening class in subjects in which they had expertise.

The Club classes came under the Education Department in 1895, and the first government grants were received the following year. In thanking the teachers, Miss Lily said that she appreciated that it was not easy to teach a girl who had just finished a ten and a half hour day. The classes were held in a serious, but friendly and relaxed, atmosphere:

> The capacity of club members for talking is something astonishing and it is immeasurable. Club noise is cheerful and it is clean. It expresses good fellowship and a complete oblivion to the nerves of those who are not actually taking part. The flow of talk is quite inexhaustible. There are no lulls. The high-pitched voices go on and on - bless them! Well, noisy classes are very popular, and the successful teacher does not try to still conversation so long as it is compatible with progress in education.

She was particularly delighted that the teachers of literature were able to convert girls into book lovers and that the study of sculpture, always a feature for small groups, was undertaken with feeling and a genuine appreciation of aesthetics.

PHYSICAL TRAINING

Over the years there were considerable changes in physical training and the girls' costumes.

> There was a time when drill tunics were worn well below the knee. I was often severely criticised for allowing shorter garments. I remember at one club exhibition a lady coming to me and applauding all our work, the wonderful behaviour of the girls, their demeanour and happiness, that was until an eurhythmic display followed. She was so affronted that we had

to return her subscription of ten shillings. She said she could no longer be connected with a club which showed such depravity. But the girls rejoiced in the greater freedom of movement.

DRAMA

There was a strong dramatic section at the Club embracing plays, reviews and operetta. 'Jewish girls and boys seem especially gifted for this form of art' said Lily, who felt that creative work was particularly important for those who were part of a great machine in which all industrial processes were minutely sub-divided:

> At the beginning we were anxious lest we should give a handle to our critics, who warned us that we were harming our girls by making them eager for the stage; we were therefore careful to restrict the number of dramatic classes and the amount of time devoted to rehearsals. Girls took the part of boys, and we were very particular about the choice of plays but ... as time went on we became more ambitious. No good plays could be produced unless boys and men took the male parts. We began mixed classes with much fear and trepidation. We even had men teachers! ... Today [1941] we have several students who actually come up to stage standard.

The senior dramatic classes of the 1930s alone produced:

> John Slater - Stage, TV and radio personality. 'Z Cars' stalwart
>
> Jeffrey Segal - TV and radio appearances, script writer, currently appearing at the National Theatre
>
> Harold Lang - in films, he had his own travelling Shakespeare company
>
> Miriam Brickman - film casting director
>
> Lionel Harris - TV and theatre producer
>
> Maxwell Shaw - TV, films, Joan Littlewood's Theatre Productions and Course Director at the famous Rose Bruford School
>
> Michael Segal - several West End productions, TV and films

Annual displays were given to which subscribers, parents and members were invited. Originally these took place at the Club, but later the Misses Montagu were offered the Royalty Theatre in Dean Street that stood almost opposite where the West End Great now is in Dean Street. Excitement prevailed for weeks before the event. Acting on a real stage, in a real theatre, was too wonderful for words, and the whole district was involved, though some parents were against it, fearing, horror of horrors, that their daughters might want to become actresses.

A concert party was formed in 1930 which gave several successful entertainments to charitable organisations as well as to members. Also in the 1930s there were three drama classes. The Juniors' was run by Marion Ross, a tutor at the Italia Conti Stage School and the Intermediate and Senior Classes were under the direction of Stanley Chappell. During the Second World War Rose Segal took over from Marion Ross.

The Operatic Class's productions included *H M S Pinafore*, ('John Slater gave an outstanding performance and should go far in Drama or Opera'), *Merrie England, Les Cloches de Corneville* and extracts from popular operas such as *Carmen*. The Dramatic Class presented several Shakespearean productions, including *Julius Caesar, Richard III* and *Romeo and Juliet*. The producers selected established classics by Barrie, Galsworthy, Kaufman, and Priestley, in particular plays with large casts so that as many people as possible could participate. In 1938 Rita Ross produced *The Sights of London* 'as good as anything Noel Coward could produce'. Even during the Second World War the classes continued and there were presentations of *The Scarlet Pimpernel* and *Berkeley Square*.

The Club's Golden Anniversary was marked at the Scala Theatre in June 1943 by a pageant written and produced by Firenza Montagu, the Misses Montagu's sister-in-law, depicting scenes from *My Club and I*. The cast consisted of past and present members and in the final scene Miss Lily, Miss Marian and Miss Nellie Levy appeared on stage as themselves.

Ten years later another pageant, *If I Strive Not,* written by Jeffrey Segal and produced by his wife Rose, whom he had met through the Drama Class, was presented at the Scala Theatre to mark the Diamond Jubilee. Nellie Levy wrote:

The play ... was unique in all its aspects, written by a past Club member - a Club grandchild - produced by another Club member, stage managed by another Club member grandchild, the principal characters, representing our Founders and the Club Leader, were all Club grandchildren, the costumes were all produced, altered, adapted, renovated, under the supervision and direction of a Club member worker with assistance by Club members; the Box Office was under the management of Club member workers. The Diamond Jubilee Committee were 99 per cent Club members, and member workers. Members took part in the celebrations from 'Darby and Joan', and original members, to great-grandchildren. The appeal was made by John Slater, a grandchild, and past Club member.

A third pageant to mark the 75th Anniversary, again written by Jeffrey Segal, was presented at St Pancras Town Hall. Sheila Levy and Joan Phillips took the parts of the Misses Montagu as they had done in the 60th Anniversary celebration.

The practice of two or three major productions a year continued after the Second World War but were put on in small outside theatres. The Drama Class was one of the very last officially-recognised classes to go when the Club ceased functioning.

JUDAISM IN THE CLUB

Lily Montagu had firm views about the place of religion and Jewish identity in the Club. The recitation of a prayer or the singing of a psalm every evening at the close of the Club's activities was of great importance to her. She had fond memories of her own Friday evening dinners, when the whole Montagu family unfailingly gathered, and for many years she struggled to preserve the observance of the Sabbath eve among Club members. She even established a Guild of members pledged to remain at home on Friday evenings. Miss Lily knew she could hope to win only the few, and this she and Miss Marian were determined to do by holding Liberal services on Holy days and Saturday afternoons (rather than mornings - which was traditional - because the members were usually at work on Saturdays until 1 o'clock). In those days the sisters would not ride on the Sabbath, so they walked from their home in Kensington Palace Gardens to the Club and it became the tradition for some members to meet them at Marble Arch and accompany them to Dean Street.

Miss Lily realised that her efforts made little headway among club members, but she was fond of saying, 'If the penny drops once in a thousand times then it is all worth while'. She drew comfort from the fact that:

The religious feeling in the club has been shown in significant ways. Our members pay Judaism homage when they profess allegiance to our club ... If challenged, they jealously guard the Jewish character of our club.

Lily was at loggerheads with her father over religion. He was strictly orthodox, the founder of the Federation of Synagogues and for many years chairman of the Building Committee of the United Synagogue. Rigid in his views and unable to comprehend, let alone approve of, his daughters' liberal approach, he did not cut them off financially, but made it clear that under no circumstances should anything they received from him be used to promote the Liberal religious movement. To an extent, he supported the Club's work, and Lily and Marian were careful not to antagonise him further by using the Club to forward the Liberal religious cause. Indeed, Lily took extreme care not to influence anyone at the club who held orthodox views. On the contrary, she encouraged their attendance at their own synagogues.

MIXED BOYS' AND GIRLS' CLUBS

Lily was in favour of single-sex clubs, though from the earliest days she encouraged members to introduce boys and men for social purposes and certain educational work. Within just a year or two of the opening of West Central Jewish Lads' Club in 1898, invitations were extended and accepted for joint lectures and dances, but she believed that more was achieved if the boys and girls were given the opportunity to realise themselves as separate groups. She thought the mixed clubs dealt less thoroughly with character training:

We have to decide whether our primary object is to give our young people through the club the best possible time, or to train them for the highest citizenship. The adolescent period, at which most of our young people join our clubs, is greatly affected by sex emotion. Our members should have the chance to know themselves and to allow their characters to attain a certain stability before they share all their activities with boys. In this way, each sex finds the other more developed and self-controlled when they do seek closer social contact. We get the best out of our boys and girls when they have this contact as a privilege rather than as a right.

The first invitation for members over the age of 17 to bring a man friend to one of the concerts evoked consternation among some workers and parents, including Lily's, but it was put into effect, though not without some trepidation on Lily's part.   'We asked our near relations to come and help to keep good order at the first dances.   Gradually we learned that good order as well as pleasure and sociability could only be secured if the members themselves managed their own dances, and a mixed committee acted as hosts and hostesses'.

Sex instruction was not a forbidden subject, and Lily's views were enlightened. In 1924, a series of ten lectures was given, the first in any club.

I have always approved of sex instruction in clubs and unrestricted questions after each lecture.   I do not deny that such instruction, however well given, is only second best, though we try to get the finest lecturers who approach the subject from the religious as well as the medical angle, and give to the consideration of childbirth all the reverence it deserves.   The best is that given by the mother to her little child long before adolescence. The child is thus saved from associating the beginning of life with anything sordid or unclean, but there again, the Club must compensate the girl for the inability of her home to supply her with adequate education for the development of her life'.

The Second World War marked the beginning of the end of separate clubs. The objectives of the club, as set out in the *Jewish Year Book* of 1935 were, ' ... to provide evening classes, recreational and social facilities for *girls* principally living in the West Central District ... to develop the Jewish religious spirit among girls'. The 1940 *Year Book* referred to *'facilities for girls and men ...* to develop the Jewish religious spirit among members'. The Club was now referred to as the *West Central Jewish Club*, not the *West Central Jewish Girls' Club*. In 1940, the number of associated young men members doubled, and in 1945 full membership superceded associate membership for youths and men.   There was a further surge in male members after the West Central Jewish Lads' Club effectively ceased to exist in 1953.

CLUB HOLIDAYS

Miss Lily considered Club holidays an important factor in cementing the members' bond with each other and with their leaders.

Their sister Netta and her husband Ernest Franklin, owned a house in a quiet corner of Donegal, with large grounds and a lake where there was fishing, and tennis. Occasionally four to six girls were taken for a short holiday, and expeditions arranged for them in glorious countryside. Some found the experience at once bewildering and overwhelming. 'My eldest sister went and everything was very posh. When she came home it was 'did you know that?' or 'did you know this?'. It was all she could talk about'.

Lily sought a permanent site for the annual holidays. In about 1900, with her friends Sister Mary Neal and Sister Emmeline Pethick (later Mrs Pethick Lawrence) and other social workers, she persuaded her father and Mr Pethick Lawrence to provide the funds to purchase the *Green Lady Hostel* in Littlehampton which she thought would be ideal. At first the owner, a retired army man, refused to sell if Jews were to make use of it, so she went to her friend Canon Wilberforce, and asked him to use his influence. He advised, 'Don't touch the place, it is stained with prejudice'. But she wanted it, persevered, and the property was purchased. Club members spent one or two weeks' holiday there. They saved up the 12/- charge through the Penny Savings Bank. Clubs of all denominations rented the hostel and enjoyed the advantage of being looked after by an efficient hostess, while club leaders concentrated on organising the holiday as they thought best.

The *Green Lady Hostel* had a large and pretty garden backing on to a field, with the countryside stretching beyond it. Pleasant strolls were within reach, and the members enjoyed excursions, particularly on the river. Because the girls lived such sedentary lives they were not good walkers. Lily and her sister would change partners as they walked along so as to get to know well as many people as possible. Every day some time was spent at the beach, just ten minutes walk away. Lily and Marian, both good swimmers, gave lessons. Miss Lewis taught the girls a large variety of fancy handiwork as they sat in the garden or on the beach. 'Every girl who has been on a club holiday will remember the joy of making lavender sachets by intertwining ribbon round the stems which were folded to enclose the flowers'. These were the only presents they could afford to take home with them. In the evenings there were discussions on the Jewish religion.

Everyone had to be in by 9 p.m., and latecomers were severely repri-manded.   Many girls went to listen to the band that played on the front every evening, but they were given strict instructions not to 'pick up' any males standing by.

The walls of the hostel, if they could speak, would tell of scenes of the greatest happiness.   It did not matter that in some years the catering was curious and unsatisfying, that the comforts of the house were few, that the windows were somewhat inadequate, and that the mattresses could never have been described as soft; that the piano could never have been new, and the cups and saucers must always have been chipped.   No house in the world could ever have entertained happier groups of girls and women.

We were so intensely happy that we actually wept when the holiday came to an end.

After Miss Nellie Levy became club leader in 1925 she arranged holidays in many parts of England and Wales. Schools were rented, some palatial, for which she did all the catering. Holidays for mothers were also organ-ised and much appreciated.   The first foreign holiday was taken in St Cast, Brittany, and this was followed by trips to Switzerland and Italy. Later, West Central was the first club to go on a trip by air. On all holidays Friday evening and Saturday services were a constant feature, and they found that hotel proprietors always took endless trouble to arrange a spe-cial room for the purpose. The majority of members never ventured be-yond the West End, so day outings were arranged to such 'far distant places as Bushey and Harrow'.   Parents assembled at the Club to wave goodbye to their children amid great excitement as they were driven off in horse-drawn brakes.

"I was born in 1906 and was one of Miss Lily's children. She and Miss Marian came to my daughter's wedding. There is nobody in this world who was her equal. She influenced everyone who was in contact with her. That is why I do a lot of good. I make aprons and bake and knitting and the money I raise I give to cancer research".

"I am 91. They never spoke down to us in any way although they came from a different strata of society. They were like twins, always together, and apart from being sisters they were great friends. I am ever grateful that my life was enriched by them".

"My grandmother came from Russia around 1908, and as a youngster went to 'Lady Montagu's Club' to learn English.   Years later I went myself. What a wonderful place this was, and how we learned so much in this club where we had every facility.   Putting on plays, tap dancing, learning, all the time.   We were surrounded by the affection of Lady Lily Montagu, and her sister Lady Marian.   Lady Lily at the time called us her grandchildren, we were her children's children and we all had a great love and affection for her".

"The Miss Montagus were tall majestic ladies, in long black gowns, but Miss Levy was on our level and still actively around when I in turn took my two daughters to the club in the 1950s and 1960s".

"My sister told me she didn't like the West Central Girls' Club. She liked to stand on her own feet and didn't like to be made to feel dependent on their charity.   She seems to have resented the kind of people who were too obviously charitable".

"Most of our life was spent at the West Central Girls' Club, and when I say most of our lives, I mean it.   My father used to say, *'Thank God we've got Friday night - they come home'*.

"The boys were only allowed in on Sundays, and they had to pass through and be vetted.   You could go to the Sunday evening socials only if you had attended classes in the week".

"She used to come round with her sister and Miss Lewis. They used to go to all the houses where the children were. See what jobs they were doing, and take them to Mayfair and the dressmakers and the milliners, and apprentice them all there, but on condition, that they didn't work on Friday afternoon and Saturday.   She was always walking around.   If anyone was ill they would find a convalescent home to send them to.   They would do things to help".

"*I don't know what we would have done without the Girls' Club*. My friend was only five when she lost her mother and Lady Montagu took such an interest and involved herself with her.   If my mother was ill, there was Lady Montagu with a bunch of flowers. I don't know how she even knew my mother was ill".

"I remember if you were not very well they would visit you. Miss Lily came and she would want to know how you were, and they took such a personal interest in every individual. After my sister got married she went to live in Cricklewood. One morning she was sitting in her dressing gown reading the newspaper and Miss Lily turned up. She was making the rounds of all the girls that had gone to live further away".

"You had to sign in. If a member had been away for some time, well they gave you only a little while, they would write you a note. And quite often if they did not hear from you the two Miss Montagus would turn up and want to know why you had not been. I think that was rather nice".

"We had dances on a Saturday night, in Alfred Place. It was a huge hall, and a lot of *shidduchs* were made there. If one of the members got married they would take a personal interest. They came to the *chuppa* and gave a little present. My niece had a lovely painting and I have it now".

"My mother was a born - , well how shall I put it? ... she went round to everybody to see how they were getting on, to see whether she could help in any way. I think she tried to copy the Montagus".

"The whole of our life was pivotal to the West Central, mine included. Now this is very interesting, the effect of the Girls' Club on mother. Everything was always nicely set at table. She had learned that. When visitors came she had very nice sandwiches, very nicely arranged. And her nephews and nieces, whose mother, her older sister, was really very careless, appreciated it, and they insisted that their mother should do the same thing, but she didn't. *But they did.* They learnt from my mother, and she was taught this at the club".

"I knew Miss Levy as the club leader, and of course we knew the Misses Montagu. There were other helpers, like Dora Isaacs, Hannah Feldman, and I think there were the Tasch sisters. Miss Levy was there basically every night. Outings were arranged. I remember going to the *Daily Express* building and to the BBC for radio recordings. There was always something on in the Club".

"They had Silent Friends. The class representatives collected from everyone in the class, whatever you wanted to give. That money was handed in at the end of the evening and it was amazing, no one was ever told how much was collected. But it went to a member of the Club who needed the money. Miss Levy explained it to me. There were a lot of people who needed money and they were too proud, for want of a better word, to ask or tell you. But they had a way of finding out. Everyone was taught that you had to help other people".

"There were about eight bathrooms in the Club. Most houses never had baths, and you used to have to go to the public baths. But Club members could have a bath there and that was a marvellous facility, and I don't think you had to pay anything.   There was also a dentist, a doctor, and a chiropodist. We paid a small amount, but not as much as outside. There was a group of the Hospital Savings Association. It was very good because if you went into hospital you had to pay. The HSA covered you.   *What I am trying to say is that they thought of everything"*.

"Miss Lewis was in charge of employment.   One evening I mentioned to Miss Levy that I wasn't very happy in my job and she said 'why don't you see Miss Lewis'. I did, and that's how I got a job where I stayed for many years. After the war when I needed staff I got them through Miss Abrahams who was Miss Levy's closest friend.   That's how the circle went".

"At the end of the evening we had what we called Assembly in the Hall. Miss Montagu or Miss Levy or Hannah Feldman would give out general notices.   Then they would have a nice little prayer and then everybody joined in the *Shema;* that's how the evening ended, and it was a wonderful feeling - a feeling of togetherness".

"I only got involved because during the war my Aunt Lily started writing to me when I was in the services. She said that after the war it was no longer going to be the West Central Girls' Club, it was going to be mixed, and would I look after it? One always thought of the club as liberal Jewish, but of course it wasn't Reform, Liberal or Orthodox. It was simply Jewish".

"Lily had an absolutely incredible following. She really had a real love for the girls - her children and grandchildren. Of course, not being married, there was a fulfilment".

"Looking back it seems it was the big thing in my life, and I know it does to so many more, especially the 'Old Girls'. We were so united, just a big family, and anything that happened to anyone of us was keenly felt by all". [Letter written from Melbourne in 1929 by a former member.]

"We still attended the West Central, housed at Hands Court, Holborn after the original club was bombed during the war. Our girls had fun, but it was the ghost of the richness it offered us in the past ... by then the paucity of Jewish life in the West End could never, ever, give them the rich tapestry of life that I knew".

"My last memory of it was a remarkable show and concert put on by the club, I think in 1940, with its own orchestra. I recall the *Cigarette Chorus* from *Carmen* and a scene from *Trial by Jury*. There was also a small ballet. Finally a chorus line of some of the club's girls singing *'It's a lovely day tomorrow'*. Alas tomorrow was brought to an end by the building suffering a direct hit by a German bomb a short while after, resulting in the loss of 28 lives".

Miss Nellie Levy who took over as Club Leader in 1924, wrote an outline of the Club's history to 1967. Most of the following are random extracts:

1903

Employment agency started under direction of Miss C P Lewis.

1905

At the Annual display Miss Lily thanked L & H Nathan for supplying the costumes. About 80 in the English for foreigners class.

Club subscription raised from 1d to 1½d. Medical Club had been formed and visited by a lady doctor. Old Members' Guild established. Ramblers Club started. About 70 families were visited every week. Matron of the Emily Harris Home was a club member.

Mr Felix A Davis praised the club which 'afforded innocent and whole-some recreation in a district where, as they knew, were many dangerous attractions and grave temptations. Those who knew Soho before the Club was formed would recognise its value to the district.'

1910

March - Opening of Emily Harris Home for Jewish Working Girls at 60 Frith Street, Soho, to perpetuate the memory of the late Miss Emily Harris. Mrs Eichholz said had been searching for premises for many months to be near enough to enjoy the benefits of the Girls' Club [then at Dean Street]. But rents were high and they also wished to be as far as possible away from the amusements in the neighbourhood. The rooms were light and airy and girls paid 8/- per week. A two course dinner was available for 5d. In the basement was a cheerful sitting room. Bedrooms had 'neat bedstands with scarlet nightdress bags making a cheerful colour on the dark blue and white quilts'.

Dora Isaacs joined club and was a student in Miss Levy's shorthand class, then became her assistant, and later became the teacher. Miss Helen Franklin [Mrs Norman Bentwich] took an active part, firstly by teaching English to foreigners, helping Miss Lily with clerical work, and then with home visiting and holidays at the Green Lady Hostel.

1914

Lease in Dean Street terminating. Families were migrating from Soho to Holborn, St Pancras and Marylebone and when piece of land found in Alfred Place, off Tottenham Court Road, it was considered a most suitable site on which to build a club. Ernest Joseph was appointed honorary architect. A Gentlemen's Appeal Committee was formed with Sir Philip Sassoon as chairman.

The new premises, next door to the Emily Harris Home with which it worked in close co-operation, were opened on Tuesday 4 February by HRH The Princess of Teck. Accompanied by Lady Swaythling, the President of the Club, HRH went to the platform as the National Anthem was sung. Sir Philip Sassoon. The Chief Rabbi and Lord Reading were present.

Mrs H Irving said that just some of classes available on one particular evening were: drama, cooking (in a model kitchen), basket work, blouse making, pattern drawing, needlework, lace making, knitting, double entry book-keeping, artificial flower making, current affairs discussion, library and rest-room. 'Multiply that by five to obtain an idea of what is available'. At the time the Appeal Committee disbanded there was still £4000 owing to the bank. After their mother died in 1919 the Misses Montagu paid the overdraft off out of their legacies. Club work continued throughout the War without a break, though membership and attendance were affected.

1918

Miss Marian formed a cricket club, members playing at Wormwood Scrubs on Sunday afternoons.

1919

After the death of Lady Swaythling, Mrs L B Schlesinger became President.

Misses Montagu moved from Kensington Palace Gardens to The Red Lodge, Palace Court, Bayswater, where Miss Lewis joined them. Their home became a centre for many club activities.

Employment bureau reported having obtained posts for 428 members, including:

177 tailoresses and buttonhole hands
207 clerks
35 home helps
9 corset makers

The Settlement offered families living in the district the facilities of the Sick Room Help Association, a dentist, a doctor and a chiropodist. Clothes were collected and distributed to the needy.

1920

The Children's Club, later called the Play Centre, grew. Mrs Gerald Montagu organised it.

1923

Great change. After 30 years Misses Montagu and Lewis delegated control of evening work to representative members, but maintained their service to the district and the Settlement. The presentation made to them on the occasion included the words:

During your work among us you have become the greatest influence in our lives, and this influence has extended into our homes, where your names are lovingly respected.

1924

Miss Levy appointed Club Leader.   She had been member, worker, teacher and evening superintendent. She immediately initiated an Associate scheme for men members. A number of mixed activities were arranged, including dramatic and operatic classes, whist and conversaziones.

Membership reached 697 - of whom 600 attended classes weekly.   The average evening attendance was 250.

Meeting held at the Misses Montagu's home, Red Lodge in Bayswater, of prominent workers to review the year's work.   Similar meetings then held annually until Lily's death.

1926

Visits to museums and art galleries.   Ernest Franklin [Netta's husband] met the parties and explained exhibits.

Exhibitions of club work were held annually at Red Lodge. Buyers were subscribers and their friends. Entrance 3d for members, 6d non-members.

The Club Magazine 'Club Link' started.   Many copies sold to married members in London and abroad.

A club brooch, badge and tie decided upon after weeks of earnest consideration.

1928

Unexpected visit by LCC inspectors.

... We were delighted and full of praise for the many activities offered, and the friendly atmosphere which prevailed, in fact we have no faults to find.

Canteen managed by Fanny Abraham, made a profit despite having to work under extreme difficulties from a space at the bottom landing outside the kitchen and main hall.

Attendances were increasing. Miss Levy enlisted assistance of Misses Feldman, Isaacs and Tasch for special evening duties. [They were still working for the Club in 1967.]

10 Club members placed on LCC panel as teachers of Club classes.

590 members belonged to Health Insurance Branch and 303 to the penny savings bank.

Entrance fee for Club membership 1/- and subscriptions 5d per week. Mixed dances held every other Sunday evening.

1929

Membership 754. Library contained over 3,000 books. 51 classes available.

Mothers' party organised at Seaford.

1930

Misses Montagu and Miss Lewis went to the Convention of the Union of American Hebrew Congregations in Philadelphia representing the World Union for Progressive Judaism. During two weeks spent in New York they met former club members and inaugurated the Montagu Club of New York. [It was still in existence in 1967.] Members kept in touch with the London Club and gave hospitality to visitors and sent money for Club funds.

Membership was becoming very varied. 'It included heads of business houses, teachers, musicians, bank clerks, as well as the little errand girl, the motherless undersized wage-earner, and the foreigner seeking refuge in our hospitable shores'.

The changing nature of the area in the late 1930s affected the club:

With the changes which have been effected in recent years in our district, the houses have in many cases been transformed into business premises, and the living accommodation has been still more restricted. The domestic workshops are now fast disappearing. Our local members come from St Marylebone, St Pancras and Holborn, as well as from Soho. *During recent years the club, although still catering for the needs of local groups, has become more a Central Club than a West Central Club.* We are easy of access, and the girls of today are accustomed to keep quite late hours. So we have members from all parts of London. Some come from comfortable homes, and their families and friends supply them with social outlets; they are not so dependent on club entertainment. *There is something, however, which the club gives which cannot be supplied elsewhere and which counts for a good deal in the girls' lives. This something is made up of personal sympathy and understanding, and an opportunity for corporate service which stimulates the individual girl's self respect.* Through belonging to the club she becomes of greater importance to herself, and feels that she may be needed in the great world outside. There are people, even outside her home, who care very much that she should be good and happy. In the club, and especially through our visiting, we have established relations with our girls, and from this intimacy it has been quite easy to create a delightful community of feeling. We have succeeded in securing a really happy tone, which is quickly noticed by everybody entering our building.

1931

Room furnished 'The Montagu Room' for members 25 and over as 'a rest and quiet room'.

Judith Norman, a club member, acted as accompanist to singing class, later renamed the Operatic class. [She was still helping in 1967.]

Mrs Schlesinger died [she had always given generous financial assistance] Miss Lily's niece Hon Joyce Montagu succeeded her as President.

Advice given in *Club Link*. 'Old tooth brushes are very useful for putting polish on fire grates as they get into the crevices so easily'.

1932

First summer fete held in grounds of Sir Robert Waley Cohen's house in Caen Wood Towers, Highgate. £160 raised. He was a cousin of the sisters.

1934

Badminton in Club Hall for over 19s. Unqualified success.
Miss Levy, assisted by Fanny Abrahams, visited every member's home when an application was made to join the club, and devoted practically the whole of each Sunday for the purpose.

Advice given in *Club Link*. 'It is often difficult to clean the holes in a gas cooker. Asbestos pipe cleaners are very useful for this job and prevent soiling the hands.

1935

Annual *Chanukah* party for children aged 4-12 organised by Miss Hannah Feldman.

New sporting activity, a rowing club. Meetings at Regent's Park Canal.

1937

Tennis courts and a pavilion purchased at Boston Manor. Mr Meyer Taylor was a leading force. Miss Lily awarded OBE for her club work. Junior Advisory Committee of 15 juniors [aged 15-19] formed. It was hoped it would prove a training ground for future club workers.

Michael Franklin offered the Club the use of a hut which could accommodate four, in Box Hill in Surrey, for weekend relaxation. A Club member acted as secretary and arranged bookings which were eagerly sought.

Canteen opened midday for light lunches, or for those who brought own sandwiches and simply wished for rest and cup of tea.

Garden Fete raised £166.

1938

Gerald Stitcher organised Thursday Evening Socials. Afternoon classes for married members and parents of members were introduced in dressmaking, upholstery, keep fit and novelties.

Miss Madeleine Simonis appointed children's section organiser and had 115 names on register. Girl Guides, Brownies, needlework, handicrafts, dancing, gardening, painting, acting and gym.

Miss Feldman introduced a 'Make and Mend' class, later carried on by Lucy Press, Dinah Lippy and Mrs Ferris.

1939

Miss Montagu's home became an 'open house' for any refugees who wanted to consult her. Regular correspondence was kept up with those unable to attend the club. District visiting increased. Because of air raids open only two nights a week. The basement was opened as a shelter, as they were advised that it was as safe as could possibly be obtained. 25-30 there every evening. Canteen remained open.

For children still in London, Children's Club re-opened two afternoons weekly.

Later in year decided to open the club from 6-8 pm. The Club became something of a clearing house for refugees.

West Central Fellowship of Jews and Christians formed.
Club recognised as training centre by National Council of Girls' Clubs.

1940

Club Link, January. The Club is open from 9 a.m. to 9 p.m. Miss Levy is always in attendance. 'Come out of the dark into the Club's friendly and happy atmosphere, where friends congregate together assured of friendship and understanding sympathy.'

1941

Everywhere we heard 'thank goodness for the Club; what would we do without it?' Sadly, as Lily Montagu was to record in her book:

Towards the end of March 1941 we decided to take advantage of the longer evenings and to open the Club for educational work from 6 to 8 o'clock. The L.C.C. gave us every encouragement. Our young people were delighted to return. By April 16 much of our work had been resumed, and we were all very happy. Miss Levy looked radiant in spite of the marks of anxiety the war had already made in her face. We were all glad that Wednesday night as we said good night to our shelterers and residents, and to dear Miss Paynter and Miss Hetty Lewin who had come to do their firewatching. That night of April 16 brought one of the worst raids of the war. Soon after 2 o'clock our building was struck by a landmine and completely demolished. With it went the lives of the 27 friends who were there. The terrible tidings were brought to me at 6 o'clock in the morning.

There is a small plaque, now in the London Museum of Jewish Life, commemorating the Club members who died in the raid on the night of April 16/17, 1941:

We remember those Club members who lost their lives when the Club building was destroyed in 1941. Their memory remains with us:

Milly Cohen   Celia Goodstein

Julia Hertz   Lena Jacobson

Ray Jacobson	Sadie Kram
Betty Levy	Hetty Lewin
Lena Patursky	Donia Rudikoff
Annie Silver	Bertha Stricker
Ray Weiswall	Winifred Ida Paynter
	(settlement secretary)
Yetta Jacobson	
Samuel Jacobson	housekeepers

AFTER THE BOMBING

Members and residents collected £1200. Dr Israel Feldman raised £800. Personal friends sent £200. 'All for a new building which we decided MUST be opened.'

"After our catastrophe we were housed by one who has ever been the friend of the Club - since her sister founded it in 1893 - The Hon Mrs Ernest Franklin, who put 50 Porchester Terrace, W2 at our service twice weekly for classes and at week-ends for social purposes. We were then offered the use of Whitfield Day Nursery in Whitfield Street where we crowded in as many activities as possible and remained there for eighteen months, until the Nursery required the premises for its own use".

1942

Mrs Norman Bentwich President. In April Club moved to Clergy House in Fitzroy Square. 'Its rooms are small, its passage narrow, and there is not too much room, but the spirit of the Club has not changed'. It was close to West Central Boys' Club and a joint committee arranged mixed activities.

1943

The Club's Golden Jubilee.

1944

Red Lodge partially bombed

Miss Hilda Schlesinger became Hon Treasurer with Mrs Sylvia Tuckman as her assistant. The Club moved to 80/82 Charlotte Street where they took two houses on a long lease.

1945

Resolution at AGM. Full membership superceded associate membership for youths and men.

Club Link, which had been suspended during latter years of war, resumed. Miss Lily resigned as Hon Sec and became President.

Frank Austin became the treasurer. 17 of the 20-member Executive were former club members, and 18 out of 25 on the Advisory Council.

1949

First mixed weekend party organised.

Miss C P Lewis died.

1950

Building in Charlotte Street declared a dangerous structure and Club forced to move at short notice. Used two rooms at Boys' Club during the day and Netley Street Infant School in evening.

1953

HRH The Duchess of Gloucester performed the opening ceremony at new premises at Hands Court in November.

West Central Jewish Lads' Club ceased to exist - many joined the Girls' Club.

1955

Miss Lily awarded CBE

1954/55   First Annual Report of the West Central Jewish Club & Settlement (Incorporated); Thirtieth Annual Report of the West Central Jewish Day Settlement; Sixty-first Annual Report of the West Central Jewish Club.

Settlement activities: Darby and Joan Friendship Club; Old Folks' Annual Holiday; English for foreigners; Hospital Savings Association; Home Visiting; Maude Nathan Home for Children (founded 27 years ago by the Misses Montagu); Married Members' Guild; Married Members' Dance Committee; Montagu Club of America.

1956

'Over 30's' group, later 'Over 27s', started.

1958

Lily Montagu retired after 65 years' service.   Became Life President and Marian Vice-president.   Bryan Montagu became President.

1962

Miss Olga Lazarus died.   She had devoted 50 years service to the Club.

Miss Lily died in January 1963 and Miss Marian in July 1965.

Lily Montagu left a letter to be read after her death:

My dear friends,

I am writing this to you, dear club members, as my message to you when I pass away ...

I have been most happy working with you and for you. I began work when I was a girl of 18 and have found that work brings a great deal of happiness through friendship which is the best of all blessings.   Although I had no previous training in social work, I think I began on the right lines. The main object was to make the Club members develop their capabilities and to learn to serve each other.

... I am glad that through the Club some of you have learned to appreciate and discover the true meaning of Judaism ... Do try and cling to your Faith and live by it, and express it in your lives.

Then I have tried to bring before you a high ideal of friendship and of continued education. The Club classes have given you a wider outlook and opportunities for relaxation.   I have endeavoured during my Club life to show you the things that are eternal, don't accept anything that is cheap or vulgar ...

... make your membership worthy of the Club, give of your best to it and to one another ... Let our Club be a Jewish Club because only the best will be found there, that Judaism and its teachings will be appreciated and lived by, otherwise why a Jewish Club?

Finally I would ask you to make our Club a happy place, a place of peace and hope, wherein happiness can be sanctified and sorrow softened through friendship.

And now, dear children, goodbye and God bless you and help you in all you try to do. I know you won't forget your Club Mother very quickly, she loves you all and will continue to do so from her new home. She leaves you her work unfinished and very imperfect so that you can complete and improve it.

Your affectionate friend and Club Mother,

Lily H. Montagu

The Club more or less dwindled away in the late 1960's and early 1970's - there was no further local call for its services.

Miss Lily and her sister Marian had an immeasurable impact on the lives of thousands of young girls and young women who lived in the West End. Their influence spread from their Club members to members' families, and then to their members' children and even grandchildren. Possibly no other persons had such an influence on the future lives of West Enders as these two indomitable sisters.

XIV - WEST CENTRAL JEWISH LADS' CLUB

"It was a wonderful institution. In many ways it served as a university. Speak to any of the old boys and you will find that they think of it with great devotion. The people who ran the Club had a profound effect on me, profound".

Following an inaugural meeting of about 100 persons the West Central Jewish Lads' Club started its life in January 1898 in the basement and ground floor of 38 Fitzroy Square. Its initial membership was 80. The *Jewish World* told its readers that the previous use of the premises had been as a night club of the very worst class. 'A cursed habitation, a veritable hell upon earth, one of those dens where men gamble away their health and manhood, and girls their womenhood.' It had been raided several times by the police, but had reopened under another guise. 'The house formerly the centre of sin and ruin has become the hub of regenerating and strengthening work.'

Many of the principles that governed the West Central Girls' Club applied to the Boys' Club. The basic differences between the two, apart from the sex of their members, was that, although the Boys' Club over the years attracted first-rate managers, it never acquired anyone quite like Miss Lily and her sister, nor did it enjoy the benefit conferred by having a leader who remained with the Club for over sixty years. Nor was the Boys' Club so concerned with further education as was the Girls' Club.

The objects of the Club, as set out in its Rules, were to provide recreation and instruction for 'Jewish Working Lads resident or working in or near the West Central district'. Its First Annual Report was presented at an Annual General Meeting held on 5 February 1899. Claude Goldsmid Montefiore was President; P S Waley, Vice-President; W L Seligman, Honorary Treasurer; and H B Cohen, Honorary Secretary - all members of well-known Anglo-Jewish families. The Honorary Secretary of the management committee was F Morley, and the committee consisted of G G A Cohen, R Q Henriques, S Lesser, W Levy, B B Mocatta, D A Moss, L Pyke, E H Samuel, H M Schloss, O J Simon, A Steibel, L Weisberg, and J Woolf. Woolf and Weisberg were respectively the headmaster and future headmaster of Westminster Jews' Free School.

The well-supported activities included gymnastics and drill, boxing, draughts and chess. The cricket team, which played at Acton, won five and lost seven of their games, and swimming sessions held on Monday evenings during the summer proved popular. At the beginning of the winter they had no funds to cover the expenses of running a football team, but an anonymous donor gave generously, and a team was able to play from January 1. Debates and Sunday evening concerts were well attended. However, classes in French, shorthand, drawing and English literature had to be abandoned because of lack of interest. The reason proferred was that the long hours the boys spent at work rendered them unfit to give the concentration needed for such subjects. This was in distinct contrast to the progress made at the Girls' Club. It is not clear whether this was because the girls' working day was not quite as hard as the boys', or whether, as is more likely, the girls showed greater resilience and determination.

Club Rules

7. Club to be open every evening except Friday 8-10.30 and Sunday 7.30.-10.30.

20. Members who have been six consecutive months members of the Club shall be eligible as 'senior members'.

22. Any lad wishing to join the Club must be proposed by one member and seconded by another.

25. The Club subscription shall be 2d per week or 7d per month, due on Mondays and payable in advance.

29. Visitors are permitted on special nights, but no visitor can be intro duced more than once a month.

30. No lad shall remain a member of the Club after 19, unless specially re-elected by the General Committee, such re-election to be for the period of two years only.

31. No gambling, betting, or card playing shall be allowed in the Club, and any member found breaking this rule shall be expelled forth with from the club.

In that first year, the rent was £110, salaries and wages £88, and the total expenditure £231. Among the subscribers and donors were to be found most of the well-known names: Beddington, Behrens, Cohen, D'Avigdor Goldsmid, Franklin, Henriques, Jessel, Lousada, Lucas, Mocatta, Montagu,

Montefiore, Raphael, Rothschild, Samuel, Schloss, Seligman, Steibel, Van de Bergh, Waley.   Like so many Jewish institutions, the West Central Jewish Lads' Club would not have started, let alone have succeeded, without the assistance of the, sometimes maligned, wealthy Jewish establishment.

Towards the end of 1900, the Club joined the London Federation of Working Boys' Clubs and was to do well in Federation competitions, both sporting and cultural.   Later, in the 1903 Report, the comment was made that 'although there are only four Jewish Boys' Clubs in the Federation against over thirty others, a large number of challenge cups and medals have lately been won by members of the Jewish clubs, and in competitions where they have not actually come first, they have done very well.'

At the Second Annual General Meeting in 1900 membership was 80, and about half attended every evening.   An extra hour had been added to the Sunday opening hours, and the general behaviour of the boys was said to be extremely good.   The public school attitudes of the managers, which they tried to instil in the boys, was reflected in the report by Claude Montefiore. The boys, he was delighted to say, 'played football and cricket in a fair and gentlemanly way, and took defeat in the right light'. He gave a silver cup for the gymnastic champion, to be held for a year, or permanently if won in three successive years.   Harriers were formed, and inter-club matches were played not only at football and cricket but also gymnastics, billiards, draughts and chess. The Girls' Club had invited them to join them at Dean Street for a lecture on Dreyfus and for a dance, and reciprocal invitations had been accepted and enjoyed. A dramatic society was started, and it gave performances at the Club, at the Girls' Club, and for three charities. The library was growing, and the frequent debates diminished the reluctance to speak, and led to a distinct improvement in the quality of the speeches delivered. A delightful day was spent at Gunnersbury at the invitation of Mr Leopold de Rothschild. The only discordant note was that boys were going off to the Army to the war in South Africa.

The Club's lease was due to expire in September 1900, and was not renewable unless they took over the whole building which they could not afford to do. It was Claude's mother, Mrs Nathaniel Montefiore, who came to the rescue. She bought the property for £4,500 and said she would not want any rent from the Club 'for the first five years at any rate'.   The management remained the same, and the four boy representatives were J J Smith, M Symonds, E Spiegal, and S Blumenthal. Chief Rabbi, Dr Adler, attended the opening ceremony on 6 October 1900, and expressed the hope that the new club would not neglect what he considered a very important subject - physical training.   But he earnestly hoped also that at least some portion of the time would be devoted to reading and study. The premises were described as old-fashioned and substantial.   Besides an excellent concert room with a well-fitted platform, which was also to be used as a gymnasium, there was a comfortable library, a recreation room, a smoking room, and various commodious other rooms. There was also a set of rooms set apart for senior members, the managers of the club and the committee.   Electric light had been installed.   The *Jewish World* reporter said that no one could look at the boys, 'those bright, clean, lithe young Jews', without a feeling of pride, and 'one did not need to be a very deep thinker to reflect what excellent work was being done in providing them with a place where they had the opportunity to cultivate the upright frame of the athlete and its almost universal corollary, upright bearing in their daily dealings with their fellows.'

In his speech, Montefiore called upon the members 'not to disgrace by any actions their race or their religion ... a Jew committing an offence of any kind reflects the wrong on the whole community.'   He also appealed to the boys to uphold the tone of the Club.   He said he wanted to see prevailing the spirit which obtained in the great public schools, so that a boy might say with pride that he belonged to the West Central Jewish Working Lads' Club.

A brass plate was affixed in the gymnasium expressing the boys' appreciation to Mrs Montefiore.   Membership had by the beginning of 1901 increased to 200, with an average attendance of 80.   It was now open from 6.30 on Saturdays as well as on Sundays.   Successful French classes were held weekly by Mr Gerald Montagu, and lectures by Miss Morley on English literature were well attended. A second football pitch was acquired at Acton to accommodate the increased numbers who wanted to play, and the Club joined the newly formed Jewish Sunday league.   There was another visit to Gunnersbury during the year.

The 4th Annual Report in January 1902 reported that Mr A Stiebel had taken over as chairman.   An increasing share in the management was given to the members, who also assisted in maintaining order. Cecil Sebag-Montefiore presented the club with a miniature rifle range.

The Jewish establishment was anxious, if at all possible, that the boys should enter trades other than the traditional Jewish trades of tailoring, shoemaking and cabinet making. Many boys were apprenticed to a wide variety of trades under the auspices of the Jewish Board of Guardians. The Club played its part in encouraging the parents to allow their sons to follow this course rather than allowing them to become tailors or errand boys. Several of the managers of the Club were also Visiting Guardians of the Board, so close contact was kept with the boys once they had become apprenticed. In accordance with their usual practice, the Board required repayment of the premiums they paid on behalf of the apprentices, and arrangements were made for this to be done at the Club instead of the boys or their parents having to make the journey to the East End offices of the Board.

The *Green Lady* Hostel at Littlehampton, used for holiday trips by the Girls' Club, was booked for a week in July, and it was hoped that up to 30 boys would avail themselves of a seaside holiday. The football team came second in the Jewish league.

The 5th Annual Report, 1903, noted, with regret, a tendency to gambling. Fortunately it was limited to a small section and had proved to be the chief evil the managers had to contend with. They were pleased to record that they had received considerable assistance from some of the boys in putting down the offence.

Since there was no men's club in the district for the over nineteens, 29 members were allowed to remain at the club for another year because the Committee felt that boys reaching manhood constituted serious problems. This was remedied in February 1905 when the West Central Jewish Working Men's Club was opened at 113 Tottenham Court Road. The impetus for such a Club came from Rev Michael Adler shortly after his appointment as minister of the Central. The *Jewish Chronicle* of 10 February 1905 reported that it would fill a long felt need for those leaving the girls' and the boys' clubs. Mr Felix Davis was the first President and Leopold de Rothschild and Claude Montefiore its Vice Presidents and the initial membership was 80.

The Boys' Club committee encouraged other organisations to make use of the premises. Westminster Jews' Free School held 'Happy Evenings', and on Sunday mornings the Beaver Company of the Jewish Lads' Brigade met there. Every spring, a tea party was given by members for their younger brothers and sisters, with members providing the funds and making the arrangements. A Club magazine was started, edited by S Blumenthal, and a Savings Bank established. The Club came second in the Jewish Athletic Association Sports competition held at Walthamstow, Brady taking first place, and the trip to the *Green Lady* Hostel at Littlehampton proved a great success.

As the years passed, so the Club prospered. In 1905 Claude Montefiore said that he was prepared to allow the club to continue at No. 38 rent free, so long as he was satisfied with the way in which it was run. He was not in favour of mixed religion clubs, and defended the position of separate Jewish youth clubs in order to maintain a high moral and religious tone. However, as with the Girls' Club, no religious viewpoint was thrust upon the members.

In 1908, the Club celebrated its 10th birthday. They now had nearly 250 members and had had to close the waiting list. Montefiore said people who came to the Club were impressed 'but they did not and could not fully realise the necessity of a club like that, and he would ask them to think of the conditions of life and the temptations to which their young men and women were exposed in that neighbourhood'. The view had been expressed some years before that Jewish lads who lived and worked west of Temple Bar were better off than those whose lot was cast in the East End, but, he said, they were nonetheless dependent on suitable recreations provided by a well- managed club.

They may even need them more because the West End of London with its thousand and one amusements is more alive with temptations against which growing lads have to be guarded, than the far east where the conditions of life are harder and more serious. It is an excellent thing to encourage the

Jewish working classes to settle in a neighbourhood like the West End district, where they will be less congested than in Whitechapel and can demand a higher wage.

During 1908 the Club stayed for two weeks at St Helen's College, Southsea. Two parties, each of 46, spent a week there. Given that many of the boys (aged 13-19) had never seen the sea before, or even been away from home, their behaviour was considered to have been excellent. Only very limited restrictions were placed on them, but prayers were held every morning and evening. Each boy contributed 10/- towards expenses.

When the Girls' Club moved to Alfred Place in 1913 it meant that both Clubs were now situated north of Oxford Street, which was an incentive for the youngsters living in Soho to cross the divide and mix with 'the foreigners' to the north.

The Club was successful throughout the inter-war years. In 1939 Rev Michael Adler of the Central Synagogue was chairman, R M Norton and H Silbert the trustees, and H R Samson the Hon Sec. During the war its activities continued but the Club's premises were damaged by enemy action and the Club moved next door to no. 39. The end of the War spelled out the beginning of the end for the Club. It could not be immune from the outward movement of the Jewish population from the West End. It remained successful for a few years just after the War, but the Annual Report for 1954/5 indicated that it had ceased to function as a Club in April 1955 because of the ever-dwindling Jewish membership. Its history during this period, and of the lingering Old Boys' Section, is set out by 'A West Central Old Boy' who remains anonymous.

GONE WEST

Last rites are always a sad affair, and Sunday, 23 February 1986 was one of those occasions. It marked the formal closure of active life of one of the oldest and most famous Jewish institutions in British life, the West Central Jewish Lads' Club.

Not long after the destruction of no. 38, in 1940 the club restarted next door at no.39 on the premises of the defunct St Christopher's Club, and here it remained throughout the war, finally being ejected shortly afterwards because the lease had expired. Then it moved to temporary quarters in the basement of Woburn House before settling in at the old Westminster Jews' Free School in Hanway Place. But during the early post-war years it soon became apparent that the Jewish residential population of the West End was drifting out to the suburbs at a rate so fast that the days of a Jewish Youth Club in the district were numbered. Finally, the club was wound up in the mid-1950s, leaving behind a large number of ex-members to maintain their links. The Old Boys' section, established in 1934 with premises in the basement of the Central Synagogue equipped by Sir Isaac Wolfson, became the last tangible evidence that the Club had ever existed. By early 1947 it was meeting regularly and putting football and cricket teams into the field with great success.

An Old Boys' section with no new membership from an active youth club cannot survive indefinitely, and February 1986 will be known to social historians of British Jewry as the date of its last re-union dealing with current affairs. For some time during the 1950s the Old Boys survived in the old Dean Street [West End Great] Synagogue. While the synagogue was being rebuilt, between 1962 and 1964, the Old Boys became guests of the West Central Girls' Club in Hand Court, Holborn - a club with parallel history in the West End. Then they returned to the basement of the new Dean Street Synagogue. The Club's flourishing existence here came to a summary end in 1966, since which time the Old Boys have functioned only as a cricket team.   Advancing years and the gradual dropping-out of members moving away have now caused even the cricket club to wind up its affairs, nearly ninety years after the Montefiore family first made the idea of a club a practical proposition.

When state education does much of the work once undertaken by youth clubs, one may assume that the usefulness of organisations like WCJLC ceases. Old members may disagree, knowing from personal experience that in a well-formed club the blend of responsibility, freedom, broad education and, above all, an atmosphere in which life-long friendships can be forged, are part of the uniqueness of club life that no other educational or welfare organisation has ever approached. Anglo-Jewry's genius for club life has been one of the most benign curiosities in its history, and the gradual decline of one of the oldest youth clubs in the country - from a club, to an Old Boys' section, to a cricket team, to a scattered membership with no focal point - is a sad and sorry business.   Inevitable perhaps, but very sad and very sorry for all that ....

The Club constituted one of the most important aspects of the children's lives, as testified by the following comments of former members.

"As youngsters of about 10,11,12 we went to the Boys' Club.   It cost a penny if you were a junior and twopence if you were a senior, I think when you became 14. *It was one of the greatest things in my life.* Most of us went there. There were maybe only one or two of my friends who did not.   The activities that went on for the Jewish boys were absolutely wonderful.   We used to go running from Fitzroy Square round Regent's Park in a circle, the outer circle.   If you did the inner circle it was no good, but if you went round the outer circle you were good.   Every year we had the Club camp in the Isle of Wight; a junior paid 27/6 and a senior 37/6.   You paid a penny a week towards the camp and as you got nearer you built it up to twopence or fourpence".

"I will not talk too much about my home life. That turned out to be rather difficult and sad. It was a very unhappy home.   However I overcame that by going to the West Central Jewish Boys' Club".

"I was a member 1927-30. I remember going to camp for 8 or 10 days to the Isle of Wight and to Bognor which I enjoyed very much. As Club librarian I covered hundreds of books with canvas. When we went there we were just living, we did not appreciate until later just how wonderful the Club was".

"I was a member of the West Central Jewish Lads' Club from about 1933 up to the outbreak of the war.   It is only in one's later years that those of us who were lucky enough to be there at that time have come to appreciate fully the lasting benefit that we derived from 'the Club'.   Each 'old boy' will have his own memories and recollections. Here are some of mine.

Jimmy Warner, the Club's PT instructor, he happened also to be the caretaker. Ex-Army, straight backed, he could walk on his hands as well as he walked on his feet. ''Allo, my young lad, welcome to the club; I shall expect to see you regular in the gym, plimsoles and shorts, healthy mind in a healthy body, remember regular now!'   All the new kids attended 'regular' until we got wise to the fact that gym was not compulsory. But by that time our biceps had expanded substantially, and we had been introduced to 'the noble art of boxing'.

Billiard tables in the basement, and two table tennis rooms on the first floor. In those years, table tennis was dominated world-wide by Jewish players - Barna, Bergman, Ruth Arons, UK's Ernie Bubbly and West Central's contribution, Ben Marcus and Hymie Rosenbaum, British doubles champions.

The four 'houses' - Montefiore, Moccatta, Waley and Morley, named after Anglo-Jewish worthies of the day and club benefactors, gave every kid the chance to participate in sports at all levels, including cricket, football, swimming, gymnastics, athletics, boxing, all the indoor games and even small-bore shooting. From these activities sprang natural leaders, such as Alf Mendlesohn, the epitome of the best type of cricket captain, and Arnie Tucker, authoritative soccer centre-half skipper, and brilliant individuals such as Morry Dennis, British Amateur Middle-weight champion, and Monty Shefsky, London Federation Champion.

And there were the cultural activities, debates led invariably by Henry Morris, David Pela, and Wolf Feldman, and the drama section directed by Briggs MacKean whose Shakespearian productions won festival after festival over a period of many years.   MacKean inspired his classes of working-class kids to act the Bard's words with such enthusiasm that James Agate, the most distinguished drama critic of the day, on seeing West Central's excerpt from *Henry VI, Part II,* remarked 'never was the wretched Lord Say dispatched with such realistic vengeance by the bloodthirsty mob'.   Two members of that mob went on in later life to distinguish themselves as film producers: Michael Klinger and Lewis Gilbert, who also directed the highly praised *Shirley Valentine* and many of the better *James Bond* films.

The competitive spirit engendered by the house system was not unique. It was repeated throughout London by Jewish Youth clubs such as Oxford and St George's, Stepney, Cambridge and Bethnal Green, Brady, Stamford Hill, Hackney, and North West. All competed against each other under the aegis of the AJY and the London Federation of Boys' Clubs, with such clubs as Eton Manor, Mary Ward, Repton, Crown, Athan Thirty-One, Dockland Settlement, names which bring back to me many nostalgic memories of the thirties.

The annual summer camp in the Isle of Wight - two weeks under canvas - was the year's big event.   Inter-tent competitions, camp fire singsongs, concerts, rambles and 'chatting-up' the local girls, a very harmless pursuit when compared with today's norms. The 'grub' prepared by ex-army cooks was pretty good, and regularly received the lads' own Grace after meals":

We thank the Lord for what we had

If we'd had more, we would have been glad,

But as the times are very bad

We must put up with what we've had.

Amen.

"You see, the Boys' Club in Fitzroy Square was the main feature of my life. The Club was housed in what had once been a grand house, and it gave you a sense of perspective, I think. It broadened my outlook a bit, to see that not everybody lived three in two rooms. There was other life going on. The people who ran the Club had a profound effect on me, profound. I was a clever boy, and I won a scholarship from my elementary school which was in Upper Marylebone Street, and I went to a grammar school ... but I never got on with them - *my education took place at the Boys' Club.* I played the saxophone before an audience for the first time in my life there. I learned to speak in public there. Once a week there was a discussion and an LCC guy would come round on a Thursday night and say, 'Tonight we'll talk about so and so', and we would all be hopeless, but it taught us a little about standing up.

And I don't want to sound priggish, but I learned a bit of civic responsibility. I took the minutes of the meetings at the Club, and I became the editor of the Club Magazine, and as the captain of football and cricket teams I had to get the team lists out on a certain night and tell people where they had to be. I was 15, and I wasn't the only one who benefitted. They taught you a sense of responsibility. That did wonders for everybody, it really did. If other people rely on you, you have got to do it. Looking back it was marvellous, marvellous. I was so happy there.

I was in the Club from 1942 to 1946. The club leader was a man called Harold Sampson, and he had gone into the army when the war started and Bertram Cohen took it over. He was a marginal figurehead, the people who ran the Club, they called them managers, were Old Boys of the Club. Some were young Old Boys, about 20, just become too old to be members of the

Club, but others were middle-aged, and they ran the place, and they delegated a huge amount of responsibility to the boys and that was where we learned a great deal.

It was a social life that I reckon was more or less perfect. You had a lot of sporting activities which I was absolutely fanatical about, and there were dances and socials where you met people from other clubs, and there were visits.

To be honest it took me several years to get over the fact that I didn't belong to the Club any more. But the infra-structure of Jewish life there went, vanished, because the Jewish community had packed up and gone. It happened to all the clubs. The club doesn't play the function in people's lives that it did, which I think is a great pity because I think that society took the wrong turning when it turned its back on the youth clubs. It was better than schools that are compulsory. It was more civilised than the forces which are compulsory; it was voluntary and it was wonderful. I was very, very happy there and made friendships that have lasted ever since.

Boys of all classes were thrown in together. But the point was you found once you were in a club you were just a boy, and there was no question of whether or not you had any money.

The Club was started by the Jewish aristocracy. It was their patronage, they wanted to provide somewhere for working boys in the slums to go. By the time I joined that did not really apply. We were all taking our examinations, a lot of us were going to school till we were 18. But the function of the club remained, and it was a very powerful function. It was really a training for citizenship. It sounds like a little thing, but if you lost a football match, you learned to say 'Well played' to your opponents and go on your way. No bitterness, no fighting, and no arguments, and that is hard for a pugnacious boy to do. However we were told that was the way it had to be. If you lose, you lose. Someone is going to beat you. Those lessons were priceless".

"I used to go to the Boys' Club as a child, at eight or nine. We used to have a session between 4 and 6.30. in the afternoon where we would wrestle and do P T and play games in the gym with Mr Warner who was the caretaker cum physical training instructor. We grew into the culture of the Boys' Club from the earliest possible age. When we were older we went four nights a week and later, when it opened on Sunday, five nights a week. *It was the happiest period that I can remember.*

All my brothers were members of the Boys' Club and all my sisters of the Girls' Club. It was inevitable that the girls from the Girls' Club would marry the boys from the Boys' Club, and that is exactly what happened. It was a wonderful start to life".

"I cannot remember any formal link between the Boys' and Girls' Clubs, but this was made up for by the regular weekend dance. Who will ever forget the Ladies' and Gentlemen's 'excuse-me' waltzes, and the observant sitters-out chatter 'look who's getting busy with you know who'.

Imagine what the club meant to the Jewish kids of the West End, many of whom were first-generation sons of immigrant parents. It helped them to develop their self-esteem, their individual talents and potential, and their responsibility to society. It filled that vulnerable vacuum between childhood and adulthood with many good and lasting things.

But none of this would have been possible without the dedication of the Club's sponsors, and in particular the 'managers', nowadays called 'leaders', who voluntarily gave up their time to run the club. In my day they were headed by Harold Sampson, and then there was Kaufman, Bertram and Phillip Cohen, Harry Errington who was awarded the George Cross in the war, and Hillier Field, killed in action in the Western Desert. To these and so many others whose names I cannot now recall, but whose faces still remain clear, thank you all".

SCOUTS

"At the age of 8, I joined the cub pack of the 46th Westminster troop which met in a dark, dingy basement of the Beth Ha-Sepher Synagogue situated in the south-east corner of Soho Square. My cub master was Sam Lubin, and the year must have been 1929. Later I became a scout and the names I recall are 'Borneo' Wildman -the group scout master who always wore a World War I officer's jacket and carried a woven-wood walking stick resembling a caduceus, and a rather clever, older boy than myself named Greenberg. He kept his first name secret and preferred to be called 'G'. He later qualified as a doctor. There was 'Fatty' Wax. I attended a summer scout camp in

Shoeburyness in 1933. The troop merged with the 24th Marylebone, to which I gave my enthusiastic support and we continued to meet in the basement of the Great Portland Street Synagogue."

13   "Miss Lily" and club members enjoying a holiday at *The Green Lady* hostel, Littlehampton.

Debbie Seedburgh

14   West Central Jewish Lads' Club, 1931. Boxing played an important part in the club's sporting activities.

Harry Errington

15   Berwick Street market, a focus for the community.

Museum of London

16   The Kerner family outside their shop at 81 Berwick Street in 1903.
      In the 1930's more than 70 per cent of the shops in the street were
      Jewish-owned.

Geoffrey Janes

17   S Marks, grocery and provision dealers on the corner of Foley
      Street and Candover Street, opened in 1908. It became famous
      for its pickled cucumbers.

Isabel Marks

18   A typical local fruit and vegetable shop c 1920.

June Lewis

19   Stalls in Berwick Street.

Phil Franks

20   Samuel King's tailors' trimmings shop at 60 Berwick Street. He
stands proudly at the entrance.

Sally Fiber

21   Kahn's Kosher Restaurant at 5/6 Sherwood Street, c 1938. Just
one of the several Jewish restaurants and salt-beef bars in the
district.

Jack Kahn

22   The West End was alive with street characters. Everyone knew "Prince" Monolulu who wore an Indian headdress and sold racing tips. "I Gotta Horse! I Gotta Horse!"

23   1932. The annual outing to the country for 500 local children,
organised by Judah "Pop" Kleinfeld of *The Fitzroy Tavern* in
Windmill Street, was one of the most eagerly awaited events.

Sally Fiber

24   Oxford Street by Oxford Circus, 1910. Jewish immigrants coped
well with the transition from Polish or Russian village to the
"hub of the Empire".

The Marylebone Gallery

25 Bourne & Hollingsworth moved to Oxford Street in 1902. Hyman & Co was one of the earliest Jewish owned shops in the street.

The Marylebone Gallery

26 There were two distinct self-contained communities north and south of Oxford Street. It was "The Great Divide" that many did not venture across. 1930's.

The Marylebone Gallery

XV - COMMUNAL INSTITUTIONS

One hundred and fifty years ago almost all Anglo-Jewry's communal institutions were in the East End of London. The main synagogues - the Great, the New, the Hambro, and Bevis Marks - each had its headquarters in the East End Jewish quarter. The largest Jewish school - Jews' Free School - was in Bell Lane; the Jews' Infant School, in Gravel Lane; the Beth Hamedresh and the Jews' & General Literary Society in Leadenhall Street. The three Sephardi schools - Villareal, Gates of Hope, and National and Infant - were grouped in Heneage Lane. The principal charity for the relief of the poor from 1859, the Jewish Board of Guardians, operated from Middlesex Street. Also in the area were Jews' Hospital at Mile End, Jewish Orphan Asylum in Goodman's Fields, Beth Holim Hospital in Mile End, Hand-in-Hand Asylum in Wellclose Square, and three groups of Almshouses.

As the 19th century progressed, the wealthier sections of the community moved westwards. So, inevitably, did the institutions.

The centre of Jewish learning and culture in London left the City. University College, founded in Gower Street in 1826, attracted much of the intellectual life of the metropolis, and was of particular importance to Jews because it was the first college in England in which no religious tests were enforced. Jewish students were free to attend and take degrees without restriction. Its establishment owed a great deal to Jewish benefactors, prominent among them Sir Isaac Lyon Goldsmid.

Jews' College, founded in 1855 in Finsbury Square, did not have sufficient funds to provide a secular education high enough to place its graduates on a par with ministers of religion of other denominations. Co-operation with another institution was essential, and no institution fitted the bill better than University College, itself just a few hundred yards from the British Museum with its Oriental Room and vast collection of Judaica. It made sense for Jews' College to move to the West End to be closer to both. In 1881, Jews' College moved to Tavistock House in Tavistock Square, and in 1900 to Queen's Square. It made two further moves within the West End, to Woburn House and Montagu Place, before coming to rest in its present premises in Albert Road, Hendon. A high proportion of Jews' College students graduated at University College.

The Jewish Historical Society of England was founded in 1893 and it, too, found a home at University College. In 1905, it presented the College with the library of Frederick David Mocatta which had been entrusted to it, and in 1932 the College constructed the Mocatta Library to house it. At the same time the Gustave Tuck Lecture Theatre was dedicated. Today the Library is housed in Jewish Studies at the College, and scholars world-wide use it for research into Jewish history and culture. In 1953, the Institute of Jewish Studies was founded at University College by the late Professor Alexander Altmann. Its wide range of lectures and conferences bring together scholars, students and academic institutions from inside and outside the United Kingdom.

By the end of the 19th century the general offices of the United Synagogue were in Charlotte Street, as was the Jewish Religious Education Board. The Jewish Association for the Protection of Girls and Women was in York Place and later in Baker Street. By the 1930s Woburn House, still today an institutional centre, accommodated the offices of the United Synagogue, the Central British Fund, the World Refugee Organisation, the Jewish Memorial Council, the Anglo-Jewish Association, the Board of Deputies of British Jews, the Union of Jewish Women, the Union of Hebrew & Religious Classes, the Educational Aid Society, the Jewish Health Organisation, the German-Jewish Aid Committee and the Jewish Museum. The Federation of Jewish Relief Organisations was at 33 Soho Square. O R T was at 133 High Holborn.

English Zionist organisations always had their strongholds in the West End, and the 4th Zionist Conference, the first to be held outside Basle, took place at the Queen's Hall in Langham Place in 1900. For many years the British Zionist Organisation and associated organisations were based at 77 Great Russell Street. The London Bureau of the Zionist Organisation was set up at 175 Piccadilly in 1917 and Dr Chaim Weitzmann and other Zionist leaders lived and worked there. The Balfour Declaration was delivered to Lord Rothschild at his Piccadilly address. The World Jewish Congress had offices in Hertford Street in the 1920s, and the Jewish National Fund in Southampton Row. The Anglo-Palestinian Club was established at 43 Great Windmill Street in 1919 as a social club and cultural centre for Zionists and played host to many Palestinian Jews visiting London, providing a centre where they could relax and chat. Habonim was represented in the West End. A group met at the Beth HaSepher and two *gedudim*, one for boys and one for girls, met at the Rehearsal Rooms in Poland Street.

Many important institutions, listed below, are still in the West End, but now the general move is from the West End to the suburbs. Jewish Care, the Ravenswood Foundation, the Initiation Society and British Ort are in Golders Green, the Federation of Synagogue's offices and Jews' College in Hendon, the London Museum of Jewish Life, the Zionist Federation of Great Britain and the Reform Synagogues of Great Britain are in Finchley, and the Association for Jewish Youth in Wembley. The Jewish Museum and its rich collection of objects and antiquities of artistic merit illustrating Jewish life, history and religion is shortly to move from Woburn House to Camden Town. The Rabbinical Council of the United Synagogue is even further out at Borehamwood, and doubtless that will be the pattern for the future.

Currently the West End houses five synagogues, the Central, Western Marble Arch, West End Great, West London Synagogue of British Jews and West Central Liberal Synagogue. Other West End institutions include:

> Board of Deputies of British Jews in Woburn House, Tavistock Square. It would seem more probable than possible that the Board, and the other institutions sharing Woburn House, will move out before many years have passed.

> Anglo-Jewish Association, Woburn House

> Association of Jewish Friendship Clubs, Woburn House

> Association of Jewish Women's Organisations in the United Kingdom, Woburn House

> League of Jewish Women, Woburn House

> The Chief Rabbinate, Office of the Chief Rabbi, Adler House, Tavistock Square

> Beth Din, Adler House

> United Synagogue, Woburn House

Jewish Committee for H.M.Forces, Woburn House

Jewish Memorial Council, Woburn House

Rabbinical Commission for the Licensing of *Shochetim*, Adler House

Union of Liberal and Progressive Synagogues, Whitfield Street

Central British Fund for World Jewish Relief, Gordon Square

Jewish Educational Development Trust, Adler House

Jewish Historical Society of England, Seymour Place

Ben Uri Art Society and Gallery at Dean Street, sharing premises with the West End Great Synagogue

Association of Jewish Sixth Formers, Endsleigh Street

B'nai B'rith Hillel Foundation, Endsleigh Street

Union of Jewish Students, Endsleigh Street

Institute of Contemporary History and Wiener Library, Devonshire Street

Department of Hebrew and Jewish Studies, University College

British Wizo, Gloucester Place

British Library

XVI - THE TWO WORLD WARS

THE FIRST WORLD WAR

Between 1914 and 1918 air raids and bombing were comparatively minor, and most Jewish residents remained in the West End, sheltering in underground, police and fire stations when necessary.

"My eldest brother was about 13, my other brother just a baby. We used to go to Oxford Circus tube every night when the warnings were given. A policeman paraded the streets with a board, 'Enemy planes sighted on the coast', which meant we had half an hour to get to the tube. If we couldn't get there in time we we went into the fire station or the police station in Great Marlborough Street. We slept in half of our clothes. We rode on the tube to all our relations till the trains stopped at midnight. We saw our aunts on the platforms at Notting Hill Gate and our friends on another station, and had the times of our lives. But raids were infrequent and irregular, not every night like the Second World War. The zeppelins didn't come in great numbers".

Only 57 of the 218 children on the roll attended school. Due to air raid during early morning many children kept by their parents in shelters till 4 p.m. (*Log book of Westminster Jews' Free School, 1 November, 1917).*

"After the raids we found shrapnel in the streets, still warm, which we used to collect in boxes and sell amongst ourselves".

The West End Jewish population actually increased during the First World War because of an influx of refugees from Belgium. In 1914, a large number of Jewish refugees fled Belgium and came to this country. Unable to house all of them in the Jews' Temporary Shelter in Mansell Street, the relief organisation appealed to the Home Office for assistance. The former Westminster Union workhouse building at 49 Poland Street (now the Poland Street Garage) was made available as a temporary measure and many families were housed there. The name of the street was very appropriate as most of the families actually originated in Poland. They made a significant contribution to the orthodox community of Soho. One of the children of this group of settlers, Rabbi Dr Isadore Epstein, was appointed principal of Jews' College in 1945.

"At 49 Poland Street, in the Soho district of London, stood a disused workhouse, a practically derelict building known as The Old Poland Street Institution. Early in September 1914, the Metropolitan Asylum Board handed over this workhouse to a voluntary committee to accommodate some of the refugees, Mr Ernst H Schiff being placed in charge.

By December 1914, the refuge accommodated 842 souls. Through Mr Schiff's unsparing efforts, and with the assistance of his little band of helpers whom he had recruited, the refuge now formed into one homogeneous colony, having two dining rooms, a sewing room, a boot repairing workshop, a carpenter's shop, a dispensary, a hospital, a nursery, a library and a school.

In the school the curriculum was in English. Some of the children spoke French, some Flemish, and some were trilingual.

Some marriages were solemnized there under the auspices of the Central Synagogue, and appear in the synagogue's register. In 1920 there were 180 children attending classes of the Jewish Religious Education Board Poland Street Refuge".

From *We Must All Fight* by Beth Mayer-Ber [1973].

"There was a big workhouse in Poland Street that was empty. So one weekend they came in buses, open buses, crowds of Jewish people, from Antwerp, and they put them in there. We all brought tea and sandwiches for them. But gradually they became very discontented with living that way. They hated it, and they all moved out bit by bit. They were educated, they had trades. It took them a while but they found their own homes and they prospered. They were lovely citizens who had lost their identity".

Communal organisations continued to function during the war. The main worry, shared with the general population, was the fate of the fathers, husbands, sons and sweethearts who were serving in the armed forces. No fewer than 297 former pupils of Westminster Jews' Free School, 7 officers and 290 men served in the forces in the First World War, and 16 died on active service.

"Many of our boys had joined up and anxious mothers would bring their letters to my father's shop in the hope of finding a reader among his Yiddish-speaking customers. These private letters became public property by the time they were read and re-read, and a family's grief turned into communal sorrow within minutes of a telegram's arrival. I recall too the grave elderly Jewish faces all in a huddle at street-corners, raking over the news from the battle-fronts as it reached them, stale and second-hand from their Yiddish newspapers".

THE SECOND WORLD WAR

The Second World War disrupted Jewish life in the West End much more decisively than did the First World War. In particular it led to a depopulation of the Jewish West End. Children and whole families were evacuated, others joined the Forces, and a high proportion did not return. Workrooms and small factories turned to war work. Bombing, though not on the scale experienced by the East End, was nonetheless extremely heavy. The buildings of several institutions, including the Girls' Club, the Boys' Club, the Western Synagogue and the Central Synagogue were destroyed by bombing. Buildings were replaced, but the West End community never revived.

"The war came and our lives were changed. Families moved away. For those who stayed evenings were split between sheltering from air raids or braving it at home. The small factories around us turned over to war work. I made leg braces in Tottenham Street, examined parachutes at Heal's, and later rivetted wing-flaps for Beaufort fighters in Great Portland Street where once kettles were made. We managed to have some social life throughout, including dancing at the Paramount or the Cricklewood Palais. Our friends were soldiers and airmen away from home, English and overseas troops, and delighted to come into a Jewish home. My mother was the centre of their hearts, and they would often give her more attention and gifts than we received".

"I had friends who lived in Paramount Court, and when the war was on the Paramount dance hall was an official shelter, they had an entrance from the flats. Sometimes we would go down the tube, at Goodge Street. We would go down at 5 or 6 o'clock, sometimes you could see people queueing at 2 p.m. to get a good place for the night".

West Enders were rightly proud of Harry Errington, the only Jew during the Second World War to be awarded the George Cross, the highest civilian award for acts of courage in circumstances of extreme danger.

SUPPLEMENT

TO

THE LONDON GAZETTE

of TUESDAY, the 5th of AUGUST, 1941

Published by Authority

CENTRAL CHANCERY OF THE ORDERS OF KNIGHTHOOD

St James's Palace, SW1.

The KING has been graciously pleased to award the GEORGE CROSS to:-

Harry Errington, Auxiliary Fireman, London Auxiliary Fire Service.

High explosive and incendiary bombs demolished a building. Errington and two other Auxiliary Firemen were the only occupants of the basement of the building at the time of the explosion. The blast blew Errington across the basement, but although dazed and injured he made his way to the other two Auxiliaries, whom he found to be pinned down, flat on their backs, by debris. A fierce fire broke out and the trapped men were in imminent danger of being burnt to death. The heat of the fire was so intense that Errington had to protect himself with a blanket. After working with his bare hands for some minutes he managed to release the injured men and dragged them from under the wreckage and away from the fire.

While he was so engaged, burning debris was falling into the basement and there was considerable danger of a further collapse of the building. He carried one of the men up a narrow stone staircase partially choked with debris, into the courtyard, made his way through an adjoining building and thence into the street.

Despite the appalling conditions and although burned and injured, Errington returned and brought out the second man.

Both Errington's comrades were severely burned but survived. He showed great bravery and endurance in effecting the rescues, at the risk of his own life.

Experiences of the Second World War are naturally still deeply etched in the minds of West Enders, particularly when recalling those killed during the bombing or those who died while serving in thc Armed Forces. The following is a partial list:

Rfmn Sidney Beskin, King's Royal Rifles

Sgt Mick Cashman, Royal Air Force

Rfmn David Cohen, King's Royal Rifles

Pte Emanuel Cohen, Queen's Own Royal West Kent

Sgt Lionel Cornbloom, Royal Air Force

Sgt Hillier Field, King's Royal Rifles

Rfmn Jack Grossman, King's Royal Rifles

Pte David Jacobson, Middlesex Regiment

Sgt Harry Kleiner, Royal Air Force

S Messer, Merchant Navy

Pte Henry Phillips (Pitzkoon), Border Regiment

L/Cpl Manny Rosen, Royal Fusiliers

Fus Hyman Ruttman, Royal Fusiliers

Lt Laurence Savitt, Royal Artillery

Pte Ralph Schneiderman, East Surrey Regiment

Pte Barnett Shooster, Sussex Regiment

Pte Benjamin Silver, King's Royal Rifles

Gnr Alfred Sorsky, Royal Artillery

Gnr Samuel Walters, Royal Artillery

Pte Simon Yospur, Royal Army Service Corps

APPENDIX I

WEST END JEWRY IN LIFE AND DEATH
Sidney Budd

INTRODUCTION

To turn around a well known phrase, "In the midst of death there is life". To walk round the Streatham cemetery is to relive old days - here are my grandparents, over there my favourite uncle, to my left the landlord who kept the shop under our flat and was forever complaining about the noise made by my brother and me.   And nowhere, also, is this inverted phrase more true than in trying to study the demography of a Jewish community. For however much or little a Jew lives as a Jew, a Jew is likely to die as a Jew. For this reason burial records provide the most accurate estimate of the size and structure of a Jewish community.

WHAT CONSTITUTES THE WEST END?

Amongst the Jewish residents of the West End it was generally perceived that there were two distinct *shtetlach*, one in the Soho area and the other in Fitzrovia. However, Jews were also resident in significant number in adjacent areas such as Bloomsbury, Regent's Park, Marylebone, Mayfair and Covent Garden.

References in the literature give sketchy and inconsistent values for the Jewish population of the West End. Lipman* refers to a calculation of the number of Jews in London using an assumed death rate (e.g. 20 per thousand). This was the method used earlier in this century, but it has since been subject to refinement.

Lipman also quotes from evidence given to the Royal Commission on Aliens which indicated that in 1901 there were over 11,000 Russians and Poles living in Westminster, although clearly not all were Jews.

*Lipman, V D (1954) *'Social History of the Jews in England 1850-1950'*

The basic problem in reconciling such figures devolves on the definition of the "West End". In this study it is defined as the area bounded by Edgware Road/Park Lane on the west, Kingsway/Southampton Row on the east, Euston Road/Marylebone Road on the north, and Strand/Piccadilly on the south. For the purpose of carrying out a demographic analysis the West End can be regarded as consisting of six zones.

Zone 1: Soho, bounded by Charing Cross Road, Oxford Street, Regent Street and Coventry Street.

Zone 2: Fitzrovia, bounded by Tottenham Court Road, Oxford Street, Regent Street/Portland Place, and Euston Road.

Zone 3: Bloomsbury, bounded by Tottenham Court Road, Euston Road, Woburn Place/Southampton Row, and New Oxford Street.

Zone 4: Covent Garden, bounded by New Oxford Street, Kingsway, Strand and Charing Cross Road.

Zone 5: Marylebone, bounded by Marylebone Road, Portland Place/Regent Street, Oxford Street, and Edgware Road.

Zone 6: Mayfair, bounded by Oxford Street, Regent Street/Haymarket, St James Street/Piccadilly, and Park Lane.

REVERSE MORTALITY STATISTICS

The use of this technique is well established. It has been described by Haberman *et al* in their attempt to estimate the size of the total Jewish community in Britain*. The research technique was deceptively simple. Burial records at all the relevant burial societies were inspected for the years in question. For those deaths recorded with a West End address note was taken of the sex and age of the deceased.

It was helpful at the same time to keep a note of the particular area in which the deceased lived, and also whether or not the deceased was a member of a synagogue affiliated to the burial society. The results then had to be put into a form where they could be compared with the mortality statistics for the general population of the West End in the relevant years, which were obtained from the reports of the Registrar General.

* Haberman, S, Kosmin, B A, and Levy, C, (1983), "Mortality Patterns of British Jews 1975-79: Insights and Applications for the Size and Structure of British Jewry", *J R Statist. Soc, 146,* 294-310

THE REALITY

Now if all that sounds easy, let me detail the difficulties. Not every burial society has records in a form which allow accurate interpretation of data. Home addresses were not always given, and in those cases a guess had to be made on whether or not it was a West End address from the office at which the death was registered. Ages at death were not always given - presumably they were not always known. The early records of the *Chesed v'Emeth* Burial Society (Streatham cemetery) are in Yiddish. Fortunately there is a summary in English in alphabetical order (not date order) which gives the required information, albeit somewhat difficult to extract. The most serious difficulty was the virtual absence of records of the Western Synagogue Burial Society for the period of our investigation. Whether the records were destroyed during an air raid in the Second World War, or whether they became "lost" during the merger of Western and Marble Arch Synagogues is not clear. It was therefore most fortunate that the Secretary at Western Marble Arch was able to find a small volume summarising the burials carried out in 1900 which has enabled a 'guestimate' for the total Jewish population of the West End in that year to be obtained.

In the event, several thousand records were examined, and details of the relevant ones were stored on a database. Summaries by sex and age bracket were produced, and these were then plotted as mortality patterns, which give the probability of survival to various ages of those that died, and this can be used to provide an estimate of the living population.

MORTALITY PATTERNS

Figure 1 shows the mortality patterns for United Synagogue burials of West End residents in 1900. The patterns are typical for those of the general population of London, and from this we can deduce that the living Jewish population from which these burials occurred was about 5,000-6,000. We shall shortly consider the burials from other societies, but for the moment look closely at Figure 1. We see that one out of every three deaths was of a child of five years or under. Notice also that the lines for men and women do not coincide - that for women lying to the left. This corresponds to women, in general, having a higher age at death. But notice also a discontinuity in the line for women at age 20-40, where the line

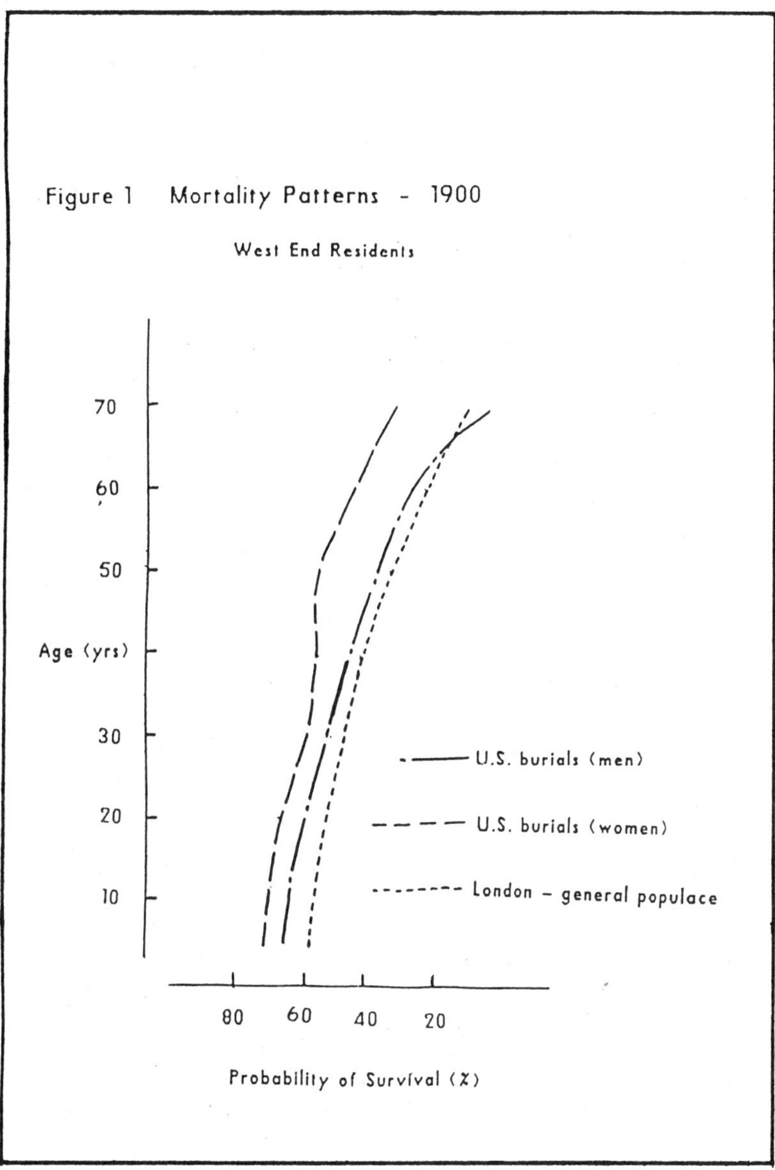
Figure 1   Mortality Patterns - 1900
West End Residents
70
60
50
Age (yrs)
30
20
10
U.S. burials (men)
U.S. burials (women)
London - general populace
80   60   40   20
Probability of Survival (%)

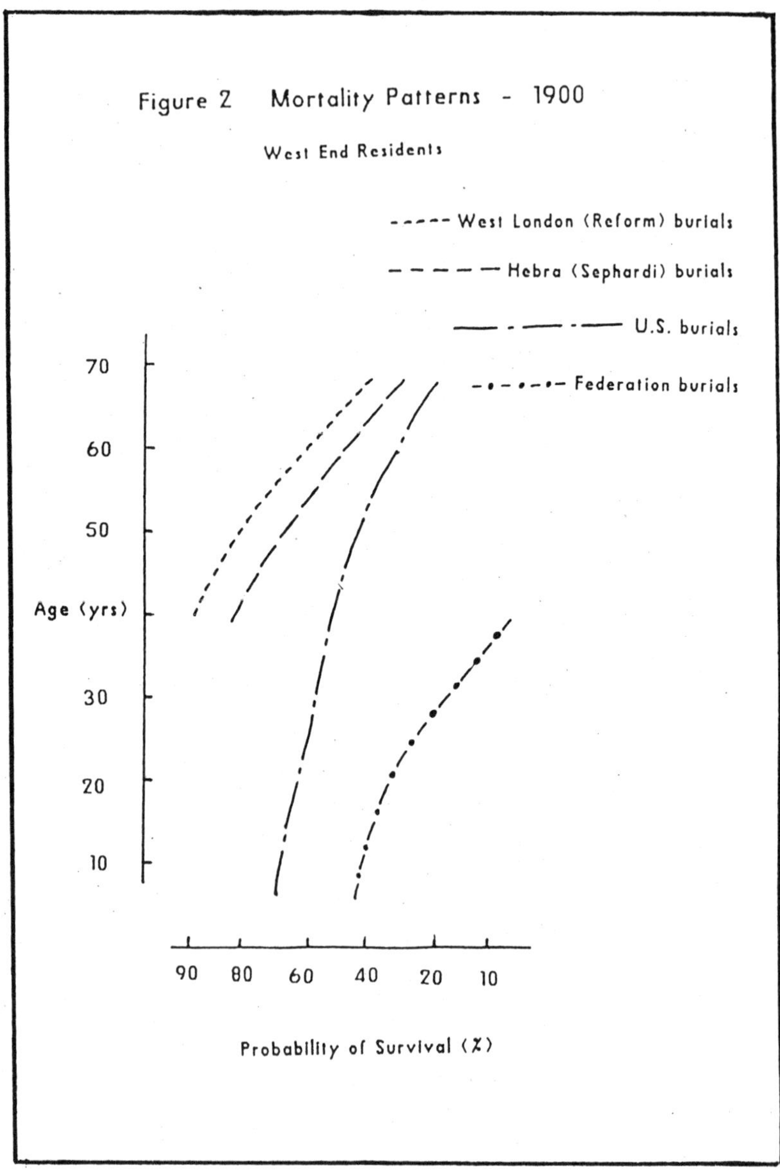

Figure 2   Mortality Patterns - 1900
West End Residents
West London (Reform) burials
Hebra (Sephardi) burials
U.S. burials
Federation burials
70
60
50
Age (yrs)
30
20
10
90 80 60 40 20 10
Probability of Survival (%)

temporarily veers to the right. This feature is common in all women's mortality patterns, more particularly further back in time, and is due to the greater likelihood of women of that age dying because of childbirth.

What I have just described in cold statistical terms comes over rather differently when actually going through the burial records. When entry after entry describes the death of a child from pneumonia or diphtheria it is possible to appreciate how far we have come medically, even in 60 years, and the fortitude our forbears possessed in facing the loss of so many precious children.

Figure 2 shows the mortality patterns for West End residents in 1900 from the records of all the burial societies. For ease of presentation I have not given separate lines for men and women. Remembering that moving to the left corresponds to a higher age at death, we can see a wide variation. Burials by the Federation of Synagogue's society come from a population having the lowest age at death - over 50% being at five years or less, and 80% at the age of 30 or less. These burials were primarily of people living in Soho, for example Berwick Street, Livonia Street, Broadwick (Broad as it was then) Street, etc., and also in the Covent Garden area.

At the other extreme, on the far left, is the line for the burials conducted by the West London Synagogue (Reform) society. Here there were no child deaths and 50% of deaths were at 60 years of age or greater. The addresses of the deceased were all in 'better class' areas - Mayfair, Regent's Park, and in north-west Marylebone.

The Sephardim (*Hebra* records), which showed high age at death, also tended to have addresses in north-west Marylebone, while the United Synagogue deceased tended to have addresses in central Marylebone (i.e. near the Great Portland Street Synagogue), and also in areas of 'better class', such as north-west Marylebone and Bloomsbury, as well as in Soho, Covent Garden and St Pancras.

HOW MANY JEWS?

The average number of burials of Jewish West End residents carried out each year in the period 1899-1901 under the auspices of the United Synagogue, Federation of Synagogues, West London, and Hebra Burial Societies was 138. This was much too low a number to use in the detailed method of Haberman *et al*, but the overall mortality pattern was very close to that of deaths recorded in 1900 for inner London, and the London mortality rate of 18.7 per thousand was assumed to apply to the Jewish population of the West End, which corresponded to a living population of 7.000-7,500.

However, this is, literally, only half the story. The Western Synagogue Burial Society recorded 144 burials of West End residents in 1900. On the reasonable basis that the age/sex make up of Western Synagogue burials was similar to the overall average of that of all the other burials recorded for that year, then we arrive at a total Jewish population of the West End, in 1900, of about 15,000.

We can obtain some sort of check on the veracity of this figure by estimating the total Jewish population in the whole area covered by the Burial Societies. In 1900 this was primarily the East End, but it also included other areas of inner London in which Jews were resident. Again using a mortality rate of 1.87% this comes out at about 120,000. This figure is more or less in line with other estimates made* and lends confidence that the estimate arrived at for West End Jewry is a reasonable one.

THIRTY YEARS LATER

The mortality patterns for 1930 show broad similarities to those of 1900, but also some important differences (Figure 3). By this time *Chesed v'Emeth* had become an important Burial Society; the patterns for its burials and those of the United Synagogue and the Federation of Synagogues' Societies had become close together. Only 10% of deaths occurred at five years of age or less, and some 60% of deaths occurred at age 50 or greater. The "maternity kink" was still evident, more so for those burials by *Chesed v'Emeth* and Federation societies; these were likely to have been of the poorer class. As in 1900, the lines for the West London Synagogue society and *Hebra* (Sephardi) were quite separate. In both cases there were no recorded deaths under 40 years of age.

*See, for example, Lipman, V D, (1990), *A History of the Jews in Britain since 1858,* Leicester University Press, p. 49

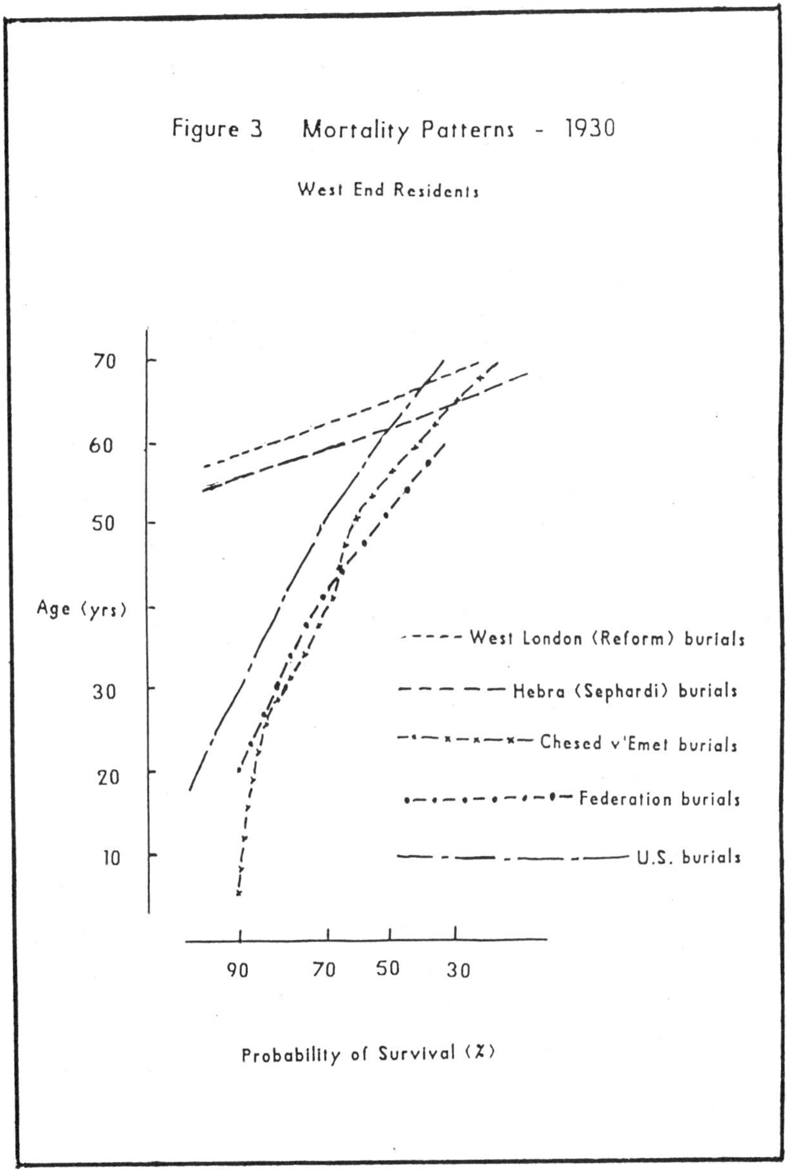

Figure 3   Mortality Patterns - 1930
West End Residents
70
60
50
Age (yrs)
30
20
10
90   70   50   30
Probability of Survival (%)
West London (Reform) burials
Hebra (Sephardi) burials
Chesed v'Emet burials
Federation burials
U.S. burials

An estimate of that part of the Jewish population of the West End derived from the records of all the Burial Societies except that of the Western Synagogue led to a figure of about 14,000. This was based on an average of 176 deaths per annum over the period 1929 - 1931, and a mortality rate of 1.23%, which was the rate recorded in the combined Boroughs of St Pancras, St Marylebone and Holborn in 1930, the mortality pattern of which was very close to that found from the burial society records.

This is about 90% higher than the corresponding figure for 1900, and in the absence of records from the Western Synagogue we have to ask whether this percentage increase is a true reflection of the increase in West End Jewry, since, if so, it would put the total estimate at about 28,000. In deriving this figure it is implicitly assumed that the proportion of burials carried out by the Western Synagogue society was the same as that in 1900. Unfortunately we cannot check this directly, but we can look at other data which may help to verify the accuracy of our estimate.

We can obtain a clue by estimating, as before, the total Jewish population covered by the burial societies (and by this time significant numbers were living in outer London). This comes out at about 160,000, which is somewhat lower than the figure obtained in other estimates*. The increase over that of the year 1900 was some 35-40%, and it is reasonable to accept that the Jewish population of the West End increased over 30 years by at least this amount. This would put the minimum figure of West End Jewry at 21,000.

But was there a growth in the Jewish population of the West End over and above the general rate of increase in the Jewish population? An answer to this question may be derived from the way in which the burial society affiliation changed during the period from 1900 up to 1938. Table I.1 shows the estimated West End Jewish populations obtained by reference to United Synagogue burials on one hand, and to the total of Federation plus *Chesed v'Emeth* burials on the other. The increase in United Synagogue burials over the period ties in reasonably with the general rate of increase given above, but the rate of increase in Federation / *Chesed v'Emeth* burials was many times greater. Since the latter societies were strongly

* Trachtenberg, H L, (1933), "Estimate of the Jewish Population of London 1929", *J R Statist Soc., 96*

associated with East End Jewry this suggests that, in addition to the general growth in the Jewish population of the West End, there was significant migration from the East End.

Table I.1 Estimated Jewish West End Populations attributed to United Synagogue and to Federation / Chesed v'Emeth burials

Year	Synagogue	Chesed v'Emeth
1900	5300	800
1920	6000	3000
1925	8200	4100
1930	6600	6000
1934	7200	5300
1938	8100	3900

Lacking data from the Western Synagogue Burial Society, which almost certainly dealt with a significant number of burials of West End Jewry, it is impossible to arrive at a reasonably accurate estimate of the inter-war Jewish population. On the basis of what we do have, we know that there was a substantial growth over that at the beginning of the century (when the population estimate was 15,000), and the figure for the inter-war years was probably around 25,000. As far as trends during the inter-war period itself are concerned, on the assumption that the population attributed to Western Synagogue burials did not markedly change, the Jewish population from 1925 to 1938 would appear to have remained fairly steady.

DEMOGRAPHY OF WEST END JEWRY

Reference was made earlier to the problem of defining the "West End", and for this purpose it was considered as consisting of six zones. Table I.2 shows the percentage residency of Jews taken from burial records for 1900 and 1930. It should be borne in mind that these data refer to the residency of those who died, and do not necessarily correspond to the percentage residency of the living population at the time, because the deaths in general came from the higher age group.

Nevertheless, we can learn something about the change in residency over the thirty year period 1900 - 1930. Two sets of figures are shown in Table I.2 for 1900, including and excluding the Western Synagogue records. For 1930 the figures available do not include Western Synagogue records..

Table 1. 2 -   Percent Residency in West End Zones

Zone	1900*	1900**	1930**
1 (Soho)	42	35	12
2 (Fitzrovia)	11	23	27
3 (Bloomsbury)	17	18	27
4 (Covent Garden)	9	0	1
5 (Marylebone)	11	14	23
6 (Mayfair)	109	10	10

* including burials by Western Synagogue

** excluding burials by Western Synagogue

The main demographic change over the thirty year period was a reduction in the proportion of burials from Soho and an increase in the proportions from Bloomsbury and Marylebone.

CONCLUSIONS

1. The use of burial records to obtain mortality patterns of West End Jewry has demonstrated differences between class strata, in particular the incidence of child mortality.

2. Population estimates suggest a Jewish population of the West End of about 15,000 in 1900. By 1925 it had risen to about 25,000 and remained at around that level until 1939.

3. Between 1900 and 1930 a demographic shift occurred, with a lower proportion of West End Jewry in Soho and a higher proportion in Bloomsbury and Marylebone.

Appendix II

SURVEY OF MARRIAGE REGISTERS OF
SEVEN WEST END SYNAGOGUES
1827-1945
Rachele Kalman.

The synagogue registers examined were within the boundaries of Marylebone/Euston Road to the north; Grays Inn Road to the east; High Holborn/Shaftesbury Avenue/Piccadilly to the south; Park Lane/Edgware Road to the west.

This area was divided into the districts of **Soho, Bloomsbury, Fitzrovia, Marylebone**, and **Mayfair** approximately corresponding to the present postal districts of W1 and WC1. Where the synagogue concerned, for example the Western, originally in the Haymarket, had a significant association with the district known as WC2 this is included.

The synagogues are listed in order of seniority of their marriage records:

The Western Synagogue from 1837

The West London Synagogue from 1842

The Central Synagogue from 1871

The Maiden Lane Synagogue from 1896 (although founded in 1821 the marriage registers available at the Board of Deputies date from 1896)

The West End Talmud Torah and Bikkur Holim Synagogue from 1917

The Beth HaSepher Synagogue, Soho Square from 1925

The West London Hebrew Congregation (however, there were no records with West End residency)

The information given in this survey is extracted from the details shown in the marriage registers. The aim is to show the centre of Jewish habitation in the West End 1837-1945, the approximate number of marriages in which one or both of the couples resided in these areas and in which district (Table II.1), ages (where shown in the registers) of the brides and bridegrooms (Table II.2), and occupations of brides (where shown) and bridegrooms (Table II.3).

Other synagogues in the area, the Bloomsbury Synagogue at 40 Lamb's Conduit Street, the West Central Liberal Jewish Congregation, and the Bevis Marks vestry in Wigmore Street and later Bryanston Street, are not included because they were not authorised to perform marriages.

Table II.1 Marriages and Residency District

Western Synagogue

	Total	Soho	Holborn B'bury	Cov.Gdn WC2	Mayfair	M'bone	Fitzrov
1837-50	73	16	12	19	5	10	11
1851-70	70	15	25	10	4	7	9
1871-90	67	16	24	8	4	11	4
1891-1910	114	78	10	6	2	4	14
1911-22	107	49	23	3	0	4	28
1923-30	108	46	16	7	0	4	35
1931-35	63	17	15	0	0	1	30
1936-41	69	21	19	2	0	3	24
1941-45	10	0	5	0	0	3	2

West London Synagogue

	Total	Soho	Holborn B'bury	Cov.Gdn WC2	Mayfair	M'bone	Fitzrov
1842-70	56	1	40	3	1	9	2
1871-1900	69	5	26	0	7	29	2
1901-20	69	5	21	0	17	26	0
1921-35	36	2	5	0	8	19	2
1936-45	28	2	6	0	0	16	4

(For period 1842-1945 - total marriages 1649, of which 258 West End resident)

Central Synagogue

	Total	Soho	Holborn B'bury	Cov.Gdn WC2	Mayfair	M'bone	Fitzrov
1871-1900	287	37	155	15	10	45	25
1901-20	175	49	60	5	3	23	35
1921-35	188	52	31	5	3	31	66
1936-45	96	6	20	1	2	33	34

West End Talmud Torah & Bikkur Holim

	Total	Soho	Holborn B'bury	Cov.Gdn WC2	Mayfair	M'bone	Fitzrov
1917-41	204	88	20	0	1	9	86
1942-44	34	12	7	0	0	1	14

Beth HaSepher

	Total	Soho	Holborn B'bury	Cov.Gdn WC2	Mayfair	M'bone	Fitzrov
1925-42	28	5	1	0	0	5	6
1943-45	4	2	0	0	0	1	1

Maiden Lane Synagogue

Only 9 marriages in total - 4 resident in Fitzrovia/Soho, 4 i n Bloomsbury and 1 in Marylebone

Western Synagogue

	Under 21		21-25		36-50		51-65		Over 65	
	M	W	M	W	M	W	M	W	M	W
1837-50		16	73	57						
1851-70		18	51	49	17	2	2	1		
1871-90		16	60	50	5	1	2			
1891-1910		16	112	97	2	1				
1911-22		17	98	89	8	1				
1923-31	2	11	119	113	4	1				
1932-45	1	13	113	110	11	2	1			

West London Synagogue

	Under 21		21-25		36-50		51-65		Over 65	
	M	W	M	W	M	W	M	W	M	W
1842-70		8	52	48	4					
1870-1900		13	56	55	13	1				
1901-20		19	52	54	17	2				
1921-35	1	6	27	27	7	2	1			1
1936-45		2	22	23	6	3				

Central Synagogue

	Under 21		21-25		36-50		51-65		Over 65	
	M	W	M	W	M	W	M	W	M	W
1871-1900	2	65	171	138	38	10	4	2		
1901-20		27	161	144	12	3	2			2
1921-35	3	24	166	160	13	3	5	1	1	
1936-45	1	14	88	78	4					

West End Talmud Torah & Bikkur Holim

	Under 21		21-25		36-50		51-65		Over 65	
	M	W	M	W	M	W	M	W	M	W
1917-41	4	31	176	156	18	15	4		2	2
1942-44	4	6	17	20	9	7	3		1	1

Beth HaSepher

1925-45	4	10	25	16	2	6	1	

Maiden Lane Synagogue

	2	1	6	8	1

Table II.3 - Occupations

Western Synagogue - Tailors and Allied Trades

	Soho/ Fitzrov		M'bone		B'bury		Mayfair		WC2	
	M	W	M	W	M	W	M	W	M	W
1837-76	7	1	1	0	1	1	0	0	7	0
1877-1900	27	6	1	0	1	1	3	2	3	0
1901-17	56	8	2	0	5	2	0	0	1	0
1918-35	25	21	1	0	3	2	0	1	1	0
1936-45	31	8	0	0	4	1	0	0	0	0
Total	146	44	5	0	14	7	3	3	11	0

Western Synagogue - Other Trades 1837 - 1900

	Soho Fitzrov		M'bone		B'bury		Mayfair		WC2	
	M	W	M	W	M	W	M	W	M	W
Tradesmen	3	0	3	0	4	0	1	0	3	0
Merchants	3	0	3	0	11	0	0	0	0	0
Craftsmen	5	0	0	0	7	0	1	0	4	0
Salesmen	3	0	0	0	2	0	0	0	4	0
Gen Dealers	8	0	1	0	2	0	1	0	2	0
Tobacco	2	0	2	0	0	0	0	0	2	0
Jewellers	5	0	2	0	2	0	1	0	0	0
Clothier	4	2	0	0	0	0	0	0	0	0
Hairdresser	2	0	0	0	0	0	0	0	0	0
Commercial	1	0	1	0	0	0	0	0	0	0
Teacher	1	0	2	0	2	0	0	0	1	0
Art/Antique	2	0	2	0	0	0	1	0	1	0
Medical	2	0	0	0	2	0	3	0	0	0
Furrier	2	0	0	0	1	0	0	0	0	0
Pawnbroker	0	0	2	0	0	0	0	0	0	0
Manufacturer	10	2	0	0	0	0	0	1	0	0
Stockbroker	0	0	0	0	1	0	0	0	0	0
Entertainment	0	0	0	0	0	0	0	1	0	0
Bullion	1	0	0	0	0	0	0	0	0	0

Western Synagogue - Other Trades 1901 - 1917

	Soho/ Fitzrov		M'bone		B'bury		Mayfair		WC2	
	M	W	M	W	M	W	M	W	M	W
Tradesmen	3	0	1	0	0	0	0	0	0	0
Merchants	2	0	0	0	1	0	0	0	0	0
Craftsmen	4	0	0	0	0	0	0	0	0	0
Salesmen	5	0	0	0	0	0	0	0	0	0
Gen Dealers	0	0	0	0	0	0	0	0	0	0
Tobacco	3	0	0	0	1	0	0	0	0	0
Jewellers	0	0	0	0	1	0	0	0	1	0
Clothier	1	0	0	0	1	0	0	0	1	0
Hairdresser	8	0	0	0	2	0	0	0	2	0
Secretarial	2	0	0	0	1	0	0	0	0	0
Commercial	2	0	0	0	0	0	0	0	0	0
Teacher	0	0	0	0	0	0	0	0	0	0
Art/Antique	1	0	1	0	0	0	0	0	0	0
Medical	1	0	0	0	1	0	0	0	0	0
Furrier	1	0	0	0	0	0	0	0	0	0
Pawnbroker	1	0	0	0	0	0	0	0	0	0
Manufacturer	0	0	0	0	0	0	0	0	0	0
Stockbroker	0	0	0	0	0	0	0	0	0	0
Entertainment	1	0	1	0	0	0	0	0	0	0
Hawker	1	0	0	0	0	0	0	0	0	0
Catering	2	0	0	0	0	0	0	0	0	0
Civil Service	1	0	0	0	0	0	0	0	0	0
War work	1	0	0	0	0	0	0	0	0	0
Armed Forces	10	0	0	0	0	0	0	0	0	0
Artist	0	0	0	0	1	0	0	0	0	0
Solicitor	0	0	0	0	1	0	0	0	0	0
Electrician	0	0	0	0	1	0	0	0	0	0

Western Synagogue - Other Trades 1918 - 1945

	Soho Fitzrov		M'bone		B'bury		Mayfair		WC2	
	M	W	M	W	M	W	M	W	M	W
Tradesmen	8	1	1	0	1	1	0	0	0	0
Merchants	2	0	0	0	0	0	0	0	0	0
Craftsmen	1	2	1	0	0	0	0	0	0	0
Salesmen	10	5	0	0	5	3	0	0	1	1
Gen Dealers	2	0	0	0	3	0	0	0	0	0
Tobacco	4	0	1	0	1	1	0	0	0	0
Jewellers	1	0	1	0	1	0	0	0	0	0
Clothier	0	0	0	0	1	0	0	0	0	0
Hairdresser	7	0	3	0	5	0	0	0	1	0
Secretarial	2	10	0	0	1	5	0	0	0	0
Commercial	3	1	0	0	3	2	0	0	0	0
Teacher	0	0	0	0	0	0	0	0	0	0
Art/Antique	0	0	0	0	0	0	0	0	0	0
Medical	1	0	0	0	2	0	0	0	0	0
Furrier	4	1	0	0	0	0	0	0	0	0
Pawnbroker	0	0	0	0	0	0	0	0	0	0
Manufacturer	3	0	0	0	0	0	0	0	0	0
Stockbroker	0	0	0	0	0	0	0	0	0	0
Entertainment	6	1	0	0	3	0	0	0	0	0
Hawker	0	0	0	0	0	0	0	0	0	0
Catering	2	0	0	0	0	0	0	0	0	0
Civil Service	0	0	0	0	1	1	0	0	0	0
War work	0	0	0	0	1	0	0	0	0	0
Armed Forces	5	0	0	0	0	0	0	0	1	0
Artist	0	0	0	0	0	0	0	0	0	0
Solicitor	0	0	0	0	3	0	0	0	0	0
Electrician	4	0	0	0	0	0	0	0	0	0
Writer	1	0	0	0	0	0	0	0	0	0
Publican	1	0	0	0	0	0	0	0	0	0
Milliner	2	9	0	0	0	2	0	0	0	0
Theatre admin	0	0	0	0	3	1	0	0	0	0

West London Synagogue - All Trades 1842 - 1857

	Soho		B'bury		Mayfair		M'bone		Fitzrov	
	M	W	M	W	M	W	M	W	M	W
Merchant	0	0	1	0	0	0	0	0	0	0
Gentleman	0	0	1	0	0	0	0	0	0	0

West London Synagogue - All Trades 1858 - 1900

	Soho		B'bury		Mayfair		M'bone		Fitzrov	
	M	W	M	W	M	W	M	W	M	W
Tradesmen	1	0	1	0	0	0	0	0	0	0
Merchants	0	0	21	0	2	0	4	0	0	0
Craftsmen	0	0	2	0	0	0	1	0	0	0
Salesmen	0	0	2	0	0	0	0	0	0	0
Gen Brokers	0	0	1	0	0	0	1	0	0	0
Tobacco	0	0	1	0	0	0	1	0	0	0
Jewellers	0	0	2	0	0	0	1	0	0	0
Tailoring	0	0	1	0	2	0	1	0	0	0
Hairdresser	0	0	0	0	0	0	1	0	0	0
Commercial	0	0	0	0	0	0	2	0	0	0
Art/Antique	0	0	3	0	0	0	0	0	0	0
Medical	0	0	1	0	0	0	0	0	0	0
Manufacturer	0	0	1	0	0	0	1	0	0	0
Stockbroker	0	0	3	0	1	0	3	0	0	0
Artist	0	0	1	0	0	0	0	0	0	0
Solicitor	0	0	1	0	0	0	1	0	0	0
Barrister	0	0	2	0	0	0	2	0	0	0
Banker	0	0	0	0	0	0	2	0	0	0
Bookseller	0	0	1	0	0	0	1	0	0	0
Optician	0	0	2	0	0	0	0	0	0	0
Gentleman	0	0	5	0	0	0	3	0	0	0

West London Synagogue - All Trades 1901 - 1920

	Soho		B'bury		Mayfair		M'bone		Fitzrov	
	M	**W**	**M**	**W**	**M**	**W**	**M**	**W**	**M**	**W**
Tradesmen	0	0	0	0	0	0	0	0	0	0
Merchants	1	0	3	0	4	0	1	0	0	0
Craftsmen	0	0	0	0	0	0	0	0	0	0
Salesmen	0	0	1	0	0	0	0	0	0	0
Gen Brokers	0	0	1	0	0	0	0	0	0	0
Tobacco	0	0	0	0	0	0	0	0	0	0
Jewellers	0	0	0	0	0	0	3	0	0	0
Tailoring	0	0	4	0	0	0	0	0	0	0
Commercial	0	0	2	0	1	0	0	0	0	0
Art/Antique	0	0	0	0	1	0	1	0	0	0
Medical	1	0	3	0	0	0	1	0	0	0
Stockbroker	0	0	0	0	4	0	1	0	0	0
Artist	0	0	0	0	0	0	0	0	0	0
Solicitor	1	0	0	0	0	0	1	0	0	0
Barrister	0	0	0	0	2	0	2	0	0	0
Banker	0	0	0	0	1	0	2	0	0	0
Bookseller	0	0	0	0	0	0	0	0	0	0
Optician	0	0	0	0	0	0	0	0	0	0
Gentleman	0	0	0	0	1	0	2	0	0	0
Surveyor	0	0	2	0	0	0	0	0	0	0
Gen Agent	0	0	1	0	0	0	1	0	0	0
Theat. Costum	0	0	1	0	0	0	0	0	0	0
Publisher	0	0	0	0	0	1	0	0	0	0
Milliner	0	1	0	0	0	0	0	0	0	0
Furrier	0	0	1	0	0	0	0	0	0	0
Shipowner	0	0	0	0	0	0	1	0	0	0
Army Officer	0	0	0	0	1	0	0	0	0	0
Lord Mayor of Norwich							1			

West London Synagogue - All Trades 1921 - 1945

	Soho		B'bury		Mayfair		M'bone		Fitzrov	
	M	W	M	W	M	W	M	W	M	W
Tradesmen	0	0	0	0	0	0	0	0	0	0
Merchants	0	0	0	0	1	0	7	0	0	0
Salesmen	0	0	2	0	0	0	2	0	1	1
Gen Brokers	0	0	1	0	0	0	0	0	1	0
Jewellers	0	0	0	0	0	0	1	0	0	0
Tailoring	0	1	0	0	1	0	2	1	0	0
Commercial	0	0	1	0	0	0	3	0	0	0
Art/Antique	0	0	0	0	0	0	0	0	0	0
Medical	0	0	1	0	0	0	1	0	0	0
Stockbroker	0	0	0	0	0	0	1	0	0	0
Solicitor	0	0	0	0	0	0	2	0	0	0
Barrister	0	0	0	0	0	0	2	0	0	0
Banker	0	0	0	0	0	0	0	0	0	0
Gentleman	0	0	0	0	1	0	1	0	0	0
Secretarial	0	1	0	1	0	0	0	1	0	0
Publisher	0	0	0	0	0	0	0	1	0	0
Bill Broker	0	0	0	0	1	0	0	0	0	0
Architect	0	0	0	0	0	0	1	0	0	0
Hairdresser	1	0	0	0	0	0	0	0	1	0
Motor Eng	0	0	0	0	0	0	1	0	0	0
Financier	0	0	0	0	1	0	0	0	0	0
Lecturer	0	0	1	0	0	0	0	0	0	0
Res Chemist	0	0	0	1	0	0	0	0	0	0
Advert Agent	0	0	0	0	0	0	1	0	0	0

Central Synagogue - Tailors and Allied Trades

	Soho/ Fitzroy		M'bone		B'bury		Mayfair		WC2	
	M	W	M	W	M	W	M	W	M	W
1871-1900	21	8	4	0	9	0	0	0	2	0
1901-20	33	8	3	0	8	0	0	0	0	0
1921-35	34	20	3	0	7	0	0	0	0	0
1936-45	10	3	3	0	1	0	0	0	0	0

Central Synagogue - Other Trades 1871 - 1920

	Soho/ Fitzrov		M'bone		B'bury		Mayfair		WC2	
	M	W	M	W	M	W	M	W	M	W
Tradesmen	8	0	1	0	4	0	0	0	0	0
Merchants	8	1	4	0	33	0	0	0	0	0
Craftsmen	3	0	1	0	5	0	0	0	0	0
Salesmen	8	2	0	0	0	0	0	0	0	0
Tobacco	5	0	1	0	6	0	0	0	0	0
Jewellers	1	0	1	0	7	0	0	0	1	0
Hairdresser	2	0	0	0	0	0	0	0	0	0
Secretarial	2	0	0	0	0	0	0	0	0	0
Commercial	0	0	0	0	5	0	0	0	0	0
Teacher	3	1	0	0	0	0	0	0	0	0
Art/Antique	1	0	0	0	5	0	0	1	0	0
Medical	4	0	0	0	3	0	0	0	0	0
Furrier	3	0	0	0	0	0	0	0	0	0
Pawnbroker	0	0	0	0	2	0	0	0	0	0
Manufacturer	0	0	0	0	4	0	0	0	0	0
Stockbroker	0	0	5	0	5	0	0	0	0	0
Entertainment	4	0	0	0	3	0	0	0	0	0
Catering	1	0	0	0	0	0	0	0	0	0
Armed Forces	0	0	2	0	1	0	0	0	0	0
Artist	0	0	2	0	4	0	1	0	1	0
Solicitor	0	0	4	0	6	0	1	0	0	0
Engineer	4	0	0	0	0	0	0	0	0	0
Bookseller	0	0	0	0	1	0	0	0	0	0
General Broker	2	0	0	0	0	0	0	0	0	0
Barrister	0	0	1	0	1	0	0	0	0	0
Journalist	1	0	0	0	1	1	0	0	0	0
Banker	1	0	2	0	1	0	2	0	0	0
Diamond Mer	0	0	2	0	2	0	0	0	0	0
Shipping	0	0	1	0	2	0	0	0	0	0
Auctioneer	0	0	0	0	2	0	1	0	0	0

Central Synagogue - Other Trades 1921 - 1945

	Soho Fitzrov		M'bone		B'bury		Mayfair		WC2	
	M	W	M	W	M	W	M	W	M	W
Tradesmen	5	0	0	0	3	0	0	0	0	0
Merchants	1	1	3	0	5	0	0	0	0	0
Craftsmen	7	0	0	0	0	0	0	0	0	0
Salesmen	3	7	2	0	2	2	0	0	0	0
Tobacco	0	7	0	0	0	0	0	0	0	0
Jewellers	1	0	1	0	0	0	1	0	0	0
Hairdresser	6	0	0	0	0	0	0	0	0	0
Secretarial	0	0	1	0	1	4	0	0	0	0
Commercial	0	0	0	0	0	0	0	0	0	0
Teacher	0	0	0	0	0	1	0	0	0	0
Art/Antique	1	0	1	0	0	0	0	0	0	0
Medical	3	1	2	0	1	0	0	0	0	0
Manufacturer	0	0	0	0	6	0	0	0	0	0
Entertainment	7	0	0	0	2	0	0	0	0	0
Catering	1	0	2	0	0	0	0	0	0	0
Solicitor	0	0	3	0	0	0	0	0	0	0
General Broker	0	0	0	0	1	0	0	0	0	0
Milliner	2	0	0	0	1	1	0	0	1	0
Publican	2	0	0	0	0	0	0	0	0	0
Car Dealer	1	0	0	0	1	0	0	0	0	0

West End Talmud Torah & Bikkur Holim and Beth HaSepher
All Trades 1917 - 1945

	Soho		M'Bone		B'bury		Fitzrovia	
	M	W	M	W	M	W	M	W
Tailoring	52	42	5	2	7	7	31	23
Tradesmen	3	0	0	0	0	0	3	0
Merchants	1	0	0	0	0	0	2	0
Craftsmen	7	1	1	0	0	0	3	0
Salesmen	7	7	0	0	3	2	5	2
Hairdresser	5	0	0	0	2	0	9	2
Secretarial	0	4	0	0	0	0	4	0
Commercial	1	0	1	0	1	1	1	2
Entertainment	1	1	0	0	0	1	1	0
Catering	2	0	1	0	0	0	3	0
Milliner	0	9	0	0	0	1	0	2
Publican	0	0	0	0	0	0	1	0
Dealer	1	0	0	0	0	0	1	0
Artist	0	0	0	0	1	0	0	0
Furrier	1	0	0	1	0	0	1	2
Engineer	1	0	0	0	0	0	0	0
Dispenser	0	0	0	0	0	0	1	0
Pugilist	0	0	0	0	0	0	1	0
Civil Service	0	0	0	0	0	0	0	1
Cab Driver	0	0	0	0	1	0	0	0
Coach Driver	0	0	0	0	0	0	1	0
Silversmith	0	0	0	0	1	0	0	0
Accountant	0	0	0	0	1	0	0	0
Labourer	0	0	0	0	0	0	1	0
Medical	0	0	0	0	0	0	1	0
War work	0	0	0	0	0	0	0	1

Maiden Lane Synagogue - Occupations

	Soho/Fitzrovia	Marylebone	Bloomsbury
Tailoring	1	0	0
Tobacco	2	0	0
Clothier	0	0	1
Publican	0	0	1
Dentist	0	1	0
Clerk	0	0	1

THE RESIDENCES OF WEST END JEWRY

The records of the earlier marriages show that from 1837 the district most thickly populated with Jews was Bloomsbury, followed closely by the Covent Garden/Strand area, Soho, Fitzrovia, Marylebone and Mayfair in that order. This applies to the Western and Maiden Lane Synagogues, the West London and the Central Synagogues, the exception being the West End Talmud Torah and Bikkur Holim Synagogue which attracted most of its marriage celebrants from Soho and Fitzrovia.

The Western was a popular synagogue for weddings from the Bloomsbury Jewish community, as were the West London and the Central Synagogues. The Bloomsbury squares and adjacent streets are given often as the addresses of the brides and/or bridegrooms. Tavistock Square, Bedford Square and Russell Square appear frequently, as do Woburn Place, Gower Street and Southampton Row. East of Southampton Row, Queen's Square, Lamb's Conduit Street and Red Lion Square together with the surrounding area are also mentioned. The area between Gower Street and Tottenham Court Road also housed many Jewish families and businesses. The Bloomsbury Jewish community extended southwards to the Parish of St Giles which is shown to have a strong Jewish presence.

Changes occur after 1914, noticeably in the Haymarket/Strand district. The connection with this area was diminishing, only in the marriage records of the Central and Western Synagogues are addresses given from here in the 1930's and 1940's. The Jews of this district were spread throughout Covent Garden and the Strand and in the vicinity of St Martin's Lane.

Soho and Fitzrovia are strongly represented in the marriage registers of the Central, Western and, as already mentioned, the West End Talmud Torah, less so in the records of the West London Synagogue. Almost every thoroughfare in Soho and Fitzrovia had Jewish residences and businesses. Some streets were more densely Jewish than others, but the records show a wide coverage throughout the two districts situated north and south of Oxford Street in which many Jews also lived.

Marylebone figures strongly in the records of the Western Synagogue from 1837, in those of the West London Synagogue from 1842 and at the Central from 1871. Only 10 marriages from the Marylebone area are recorded at the West End Talmud Torah 1917-44. This contrasts with 64 at the Central and 35 at the West London Synagogue over a comparable period. The relocation of the Western Synagogue from the Haymarket to Bloomsbury in 1914, and the delay in the building of the new synagogue and its subsequent destruction by enemy action in the early 1940's, could have caused the drop in the number of marriages from Marylebone, only 11 being recorded in this period. Marylebone was and is a district composed of important squares and wide thoroughfares, the homes of lawyers, doctors, bankers and 'gentlemen', also of streets with small shops and craftsmen. The Jewish community established itself everywhere, not only in Gloucester Place, Weymouth Street, Harley Street, Portland Place and Park Crescent, Portman Square and Montagu Square, but also in Chiltern Street (then called East Street), Paddington Street, Marylebone High Street and Crawford Street.

It is in the marriage registers of the Western, West London, and Central Synagogues that Mayfair is shown as an area of Jewish domicile. One marriage is recorded at the West End Talmud Torah. The number of marriages giving a link with Mayfair was never large numerically.

The pattern of marriages shows changes over the years examined. Various reasons can be found. These include more marriages between those living within the area of the Jewish West End to people living outside it, the ceremony taking place in the synagogue in which the other worshipped, whether or not a particular synagogue was thought fashionable, and also the movement of people through the years.

I wish to thank the following for their assistance and for allowing me to work in their respective offices:

Mr David Massel, Executive Director, Board of Deputies of British Jews.

Mr Charles Tucker, Archivist, The Office of the Chief Rabbi.

Mrs Coral Jowell, Administrator, the Central Synagogue.

Mr Stanley Levy, Secretary, West End Great Synagogue.

Mr Maurice Ross, Executive Director, West London Synagogue of British Jews.

Mrs Joanne Parker, Assistant to Mr Maurice Ross.

To Dr Amy Gottlieb and Mr Raymond Kalman for their encouragement and Mrs Ruth Meek for deciphering my handwriting and transcribing it.

APPENDIX III

The following extracts from the Post Office Directories of 1900, 1910, 1920, 1930, 1939, and 1950 provide a guide to the percentage of Jewish-owned shops or businesses in a few of the better known streets of Soho and Fitzrovia, but they are not comprehensive and must be treated with caution. How is one to be certain that they were Jewish owned? Apart from a few obvious examples, such as those which are described in the Directories as kosher butchers or kosher restaurants, the selection has been based mainly on Jewish sounding names, or on the type of business which was almost exclusively Jewish, such as trimming shops. The process of selection became more difficult as the century progressed. There was an increase in the number of limited liability companies. Names like 'Fashion Dresses Limited' or 'Novelty Trimmings Limited' provide no firm evidence one way or the other. And more Jews anglicised their surnames. However the extracts provide a guide.

Perhaps the most prominent street was Berwick Street - in 1900 12 per cent of the shops were Jewish-owned, in 1910 30 per cent, in 1920 57 per cent and in 1930 71 per cent.

A few non-Jewish businesses have also been included for nostalgic purposes only, for example the Welsh Dairies.

Berwick Street (Peter Street to Oxford Street)

Post Office Directory 1900

5/6	Marcus Erdman - fancy draper
9	Morris Herzfeld - linen draper
11	Harry Landau & Co. - glass and china dealers
12	John Krakower - fancy draper
16	Kate Freeman - oil dealer
22	Blue Posts - Chas Schnauber
23/4	Three Doves - Louis Herman Mikesch
30	Fred Zeller - Hairdresser
36	Mrs Laura Franklin - tobacconist
49	Samuel King - woollen rag merchant

49	Samuel M. Bull - dealer in tobacconists' sundries
50	C T & G Fox - manufacturing silversmiths
79	William Lazarus - hairdresser
	[13 Jewish entries out of 104 : 12.5%]

Post Office Directory 1910

5	Footring Bros - fancy draper
8	Morris Herzfeld - linen draper
11/12	John Krakower & Co - fancy drapers
22	Blue Posts - Ignace Wieger
23/24	Three Doves - Leopold Cline
30	Florence Jacobs & Sons - butcher
34	Solomon Stein - broker
35	Samuel Lewis - dining rooms
38	Bernard Danzig & Co. - wine merchants
39	Mrs Kate Mazareck - chandler
46	Madame Rose Friedman - milliner
47	Barnet Shombrot - cycle dealer
50	C T & G Fox - manufacturing silversmiths
60	Samuel King - woollen rag merchant
61	Bela Bloom - foreign provision dealer
65	Comman Shoolman - tailor
66A	Joseph Ackerhalt - hairdresser
69	Joseph Kutock - butcher
70	David Solomon - corset maker
71	Barnet Cohen - tailors' trimmings
72	Jacob Goldberg - tobacconist
77	Solomon Weinstein - tailor
78	Abraham Keltz - greengrocer
79	William Lazarus - hairdresser

80	Solomon Milbour - tailor
81	Samuel Blank - tobacconist
83	Joseph Appel - gas fitter
84	Philip Kerner - tailors' trimmings
86A	Barnett Gronfein - tobacconist
89	Mrs Annie Nieman - butcher
93	Samuel Frankel - butcher
	[31 Jewish entries out of 104: 30%]

Post Office Directory 1920

1A	Louis Courte - horse butcher
1	London Blouse Co - draper
1	Walter Bennet - fishmonger
4	Elias Pishnoff - hosier
11	Israel Franks - draper
12 & 47	Isaac Weingarden - costumier
14	Isidore Nieman - butcher
20	Davis Rosengard - bootmaker
21	Mrs Margaret Weinblatt - milliner
22	Blue Posts - Harry Joel
23 & 24	Three Doves - Leopold Cline
26	David Goldesgeyme - jeweller
26	Max Weintrop & Son - boot master
30	Mrs Flora Jacobs - butcher
31	Harris Gold - tailors' trimmings
33	Jacob Sokolov - provision dealer
34	Lilian Share - milliner
34A	Taboriski & Stein - tailors' trimmings
35	Samuel Lewis - dining rooms
36	Harris Vetchinsky - fishmonger

38	Bernard Danzig & Co - wine merchants
39	Mrs Kate Lazareck - chandler
40	Valkows & Edelman - corset masters
44	L & A Friedman - printers
45	Rosette Kingly - milliner
46	Miss Jane Lewis - dressmaker
47/12	Isaac Weingarden - costumier
47	Alex Krasnow - artificial teeth manufacturer
50	C T & G Fox - manufacturing silversmiths
51	Arnold Heilport M.D. Brux - physician
58	Frederick Augustus Sahnow - tailor
60	Samuel King - woollen rag merchant
61	Bela Baruch Bloom - foreign provision dealer
65	Max Fritz Michael - furniture dealer
66	David Silverstone - tobacconist
66A	Albert Sternkiel - hairdresser
68	Woolf Goody - restaurant
69	Barnet Cohen & Co - tailors' trimmings
70	Abraham Feinman - umbrella man
71	Nathan Nyman - trimmings dealer
72	Jacob Goldberg - tobacconist
74	Hyman Warshawsky - tailor
75	Daniel Harris - chandler
76	Abraham Lewis - chandler
77	Madame Dora Lewis - dressmaker
78	Abraham Katz - greengrocer
79	William Lazarus - hairdresser
80	Milbour Solomon - ladies' tailor
81	Samuel Blank - tobacconist
83	Morris Taffel - chandler

84	Meyer Cohen - costumier
86	Madame Mannetta - ladies' tailor
86A	Jacob Brill - tobacconist
87	Jacob Bick - chandler
89	Max Watermann - butcher
90	Nathan Hyman - bootmaker
93	Harry Sarpinsky - draper
94	Jacob Jacobson - butcher
95	Herman Yankowich - draper
	[59 Jewish entries out of 104: 57%]

Post Office Directory 1930

1	Gilbert & Simons - milliner
1A	London Blouse Co - draper
3/63	B Alex Ltd - silk merchants
5	Madame Max - ladies outfitter
8	Coleman & Cherns - linen draper
9	Daniel Landau - lace dealer
10	Charles Freeman - butcher
11	I & P Franks - ladies' hosiers
12	V Falber & Sons - silk merchants
14	Joseph Krichefsky - silk merchants
15	Mrs K Nurik - ladies' hosier
16	David William Davies - dairy
17	Madame Annie Franks - milliner
18	Julius Stalbow - draper
19	Philip Cohen - ladies' hosier
20	Davis Rosengard - boot maker
21	Samuel Weinblatt - draper
23	Morris Klar - ladies' outfitter

24	Berwick Arcade Ltd - costumiers
24	J Packter - gown manufacturer
25	Jacob Sugar - costumier
26/38/42	Hyman Parnes - costumier
28/29	Eker & Albert - silk manufacturers
30	Monique - costumier
31	Irene - costumier
32	Barnet Goodman - costumier
33	Marcelle - costumier
34/35	Handel's Arcade - costumier
36/43	Mrs Lilian Share - costumier
37	D Harris Ltd - costumier
38	Parnes - costumier
39	Leslie - costumier
40	Ann - milliner
41	Morris Green - shoemaker
42	Parnes - costumier
43	Share - milliner
45	Madame Rosette Kingly - costumier
46/47	Isaac Weingarten - costumier
46	Madame Jane Lewis - dressmaker
48/72	Marks Blankfine - costumier
49	Madame Rosa - costumier
50	Maison Nettie - costumier
51	Madame Eda - costumier
52	Mrs Sarah Goodman - costumier
52	Maison Sylvia - ladies' hairdresser
57	Green Man - Alf Lavender
58	Augustus Fredk Sahnow - tailor
60	S King - costumier

61	Bela Baruch Bloom - foreign provision dealer
63/68	Alex B. Ltd - silkmen
63	H Simmons - cigar manufacturer
64	Pauline - milliner
65	Rose Fiber - costumier
65	Maurice Silver - restaurant
65	Abraham Miller - hairdresser
65	Hyman Saunders - tailor
66A	Bernard Danzig & Co. - wine merchants
68	Woolf Goody - restaurant
69	Barnett Cohen & Co - wholesale tailors' trimmings
70	Sadie - costumier
70	Itzlovitch & Feigenbaum - hairdressers
70	Hotston & Myers - hairdressers
71	M Weintrop - boot dealers
72/48	Marks Blankfine - costumier
73/74	Joseph Freeman - costumier
73	A Helfond - ladies' tailor
73	Album & Morgenstein - manufacturing furriers
74	Aug Levan - lapidary
76	Abraham Lewis - chandler
77	Madame Lewis Ltd - dressmakers
78	T Katz - greengrocer
79	Joanna - costumier
79	Freeman Marks - accordian pleating manufacturer
80	S Milbour - costumier
81	S & M Blank - costumier
83	Morris Taffel - chandler
84	Meyer Cohen - costumier
85	L & L Harris - milliner

86	- Phillips - costumier
87	Jacob Bick - chandler
88/89	Luck Bros - wholesale drapers
93	Z Kopelovitch - hosiery merchants
94	Jacob Jacobson - butcher
95	Herman Yankowich - silk mercer
100	Elias Ashnoff - hosier
	[85 Jewish entries out of 120: 71%]

Post Office Directory 1939

1	Berwick Millinery Stores
3/4	Berwick Silk Stores
5	Madame Max Ltd - ladies' hosiers
9	D Landau & Son Ltd - lace manufacturer
10	C F Freedman Ltd - butcher
11	Franks (West End) Ltd - ladies hosiers
12	V Falber & Sons - silk merchants
13	Half & Guinea Gown Shop
15	Gerrard Silk Co Ltd - silk merchants
16	Sol Borovick - silk merchants
17	Madame Anne Franks - milliner
18	Eker & Albert Ltd - silk merchants
21	Samuel Weinblatt - draper
23	A Klar - knitwear specialist
24	Anjo Modes Ltd - costumier
27/29	Colman's - gown specialist
27/29	H & N Gowns - wholesale gown manufacturers
27/29	H Emanuel - mantle manufacturers
28/29	T Phillips - mantle maker-up
31	Phillip Hyman - boot and shoe dealer

33	Marcelle - costumier
36	Lilian - gowns
37	D Harris - costumier
37	Silver[S] and Gordon [J] - waistcoat makers up
38	Betty - ladies hairdresser
38	Jack Fox - working tailor
42	Doreen - milliner
44	Max Rosen - furrier
45	Kingly Rosette Ltd - costumier
46	Madame Jane Lewis - dressmaker
46/47	Madame Lena - mantles
48/49	Millicent (Berwick Street) Ltd - gowns
55	Goody's Original Kosher Restaurant Ltd
58	Hyman (Floorcoverings) Ltd
58	Augustus Frdk Sahnow - tailor
60	D Oser & Sons - tailor
61	Bela Baruch Bloom - foreign provision dealers
62	Ackerman & Berger - ladies' manufacturing tailors
64	Renette - milliner
65	Wyner's - Ladies' manufacturing tailors
65	Stern's Kosher Restaurant
65	Moss I Frank - ladies' tailor
66A	
	Bernard Danzig & Co - wine merchants
68	Harvey Helen Ltd - milliner
69	Barnett Cohen & Co - wholesale tailors trimmings
70	Marion - milliner
70	Simons Itzcovitch - ladies dresses
71	Weintrop M - boot dealer
73/74	I Freeman - costumier
73	M Klein - milliner

75	Montrose Ltd - milliner
76	Abraham Lewis - shopkeeper
77	Madame Deby - gowns
80/48 as 48	
80	M Blank (London) Ltd - wholesale mantle manufacturer
82	Patisserie Bruxelloises Ltd - baker
82	Lewis - ladies manufacturing tailor
83	Morris Taffel - grocer
85	Mrs Minnie Harris - milliner
87	J Lyons & Co - cafe
91	Nathan Kerner - gown manufacturer
91	Antoine Gowns -
92	Z Kopelovitch Ltd - lace manufacturer
93	Quality Egg Store
94	Jacob Jacobson - kosher butcher
95	H Yankowich Ltd - silk merchants

[66 Jewish entries out of 120: 55%]

Post Office Directory 1951

1	Rachelle - ladies' shoes
3	Berwick Silk Stores
10	C F Freeman - butcher
12	C Fisner (London) - ladies' handbag manufacturer
14	D Landau & Son Ltd - lace manufacturer
15	S Zarywacz - tailor
16	S Borovick Ltd - silk merchants
21	Samuel Weinblatt - baker
24	E Harris - Mantles Manufacturing Co Ltd
25	B & P Traeger - costume makers up
26	David Siegalman - button holing

28/29	J & G Waxman - working ladies' tailor
28/29	Dolphin Dress Co - gown makers up
30	Louis Mankin Ltd - tailors; trimmings dealer
31	Philip Hyman - boot and shoe dealer
32	Manfield (West End) Store - china dealers
33	Nick Brodin Ltd - silk mercers
34/35	Trimfit Ltd - dress ornaments
35	Wilbru Ltd - ladies belt manufacturers
36	Ascot Fashions (West End) Ltd - mantle manufacturers
36	B. Alton - button manufacturer
36	J & P Waldman Ltd - woollen merchant
37	Carfax Gowns Ltd
37	I Schneiderman & Sons - tailor
38	S K S Fashions Ltd - gown manufacturer
39	A Klein (Trimmings) Ltd - trimmingsmerchant
39	Leslie Shaw - mantle maker up
41	Youngwear Ltd - children's dress manufacturer
41	West London Button Co Ltd - button manufacturer
41	Jack Mazin - book dealer
42	Debby Ltd - gowns
42	Miriam and Edith - dressmaker
43	Simmons J & S Ltd - rayons
44	Louis Bund Ltd - feathers, flowers and novelties
44	K Martin & Co Ltd - millinery manufacturer
46	H Rockman Ltd - mantle manufacturers
47	Eden Hat Co Ltd - manufacturing milliner
47	Erith Ollrom - ladies' handbags
51	R Alexander Ltd - woollen merchant
52	Rich Rose & Co Ltd - tobacconist
52	Frederick Palman - ladies' tailor

55	Goody's Original Kosher Restaurant Ltd
57	Green Man - George Benjamin
59	Glenclad Fashions Ltd - gown manufacturing
60	Sam Arkus - men's outfitter
61	
	Bela Baruch Bloom - foreign provisions dealer
62	Alfred Lewis (London) Ltd - mantle manufacturer
64	A & L Fried - coat manufacturer
64	West End Trimmers Ltd - button merchant
66	Lewis Rosenfeld - ladies' dresses
66A	B Danzig & Co - wine merchants
68	A C Noorden Ltd - imitation jewellery
69	Morris Greenberg Ltd - tailors' trimmings merchants
69	Victor & Sons - working tailors
71	Alfred Weintrop - boot dealer
72	H A Heller - furrier
74	Lenora Gowns - makers up
76	Abraham Lewis - shopkeeper
77	S & B Lesser Ltd - cafe
79	Joseph Miller - fruiterer
80	M Blank (London) Ltd - mantle manufacturer
81	Harry Newman - wholesale gowns
82	Patisserie Bruxelloise
82	W Greenwood & Sons - manufacturing tailor
82	William Cohen - Ladies' manufacturing tailor
82	Jack Spiegel - gown maker up
84	David Lewin - paper bag merchant
92	Z. Kopelovitch Ltd - lace manufacturers
93	S.Shaw - snack bar
94	Jacob Jacobson - kosher butcher
100A	Frederick Korn - hairdresser

[71 Jewish entries out of 118: 60%]

Charlotte Street

Post Office Directory 1920

3	Matz Bros - tobacconists
7	Isadore Zarach - manufacturing clothiers
9	Anatole Dublin - shirt and collar dealer
17A	Jacob Blackman - tailor
17A	Jacob Walters - tailor
19	Celeste Bertorelli - refreshment rooms
21	John David Richards - dairyman
23	David Prosser & Son - builders
27	George Bruschweiller - butcher
29	Charles Feldman - tobacconist
35A	Solomon Grodzinsky - draper
43	Thomas Morgan Jones - dairy
45	Sydney Laudag - boot dealer
49	Mark Michael - ladies' outfitter
55	Davis Landau - hosier
57	French laundry
63	Benjamin Risky & Co - cigarette manufacturers
65	Welsh dairy
79	Eoleslas Raczynski Schulz - teacher of the zither
85	Edward Caplin - foreign provision dealer
107/109	Communist Working Men's Club & Institute
111	Frank King - antique furniture dealer
113	Barnett Abrahams - tailor
117	Leighton Waud - artist
121	Mrs Louisa and Elizabeth Barnett - feather dressers

4	Sydney Hyman Butwick - antique furniture dealer
6	Marks Berliner - milliner
10	Harp makers
12A	Victor Lucas - boot repairer
14	Sarar Levenson - tobacconist
16	FITZROY - Judah Morris Kleinfeld
16A	Abraham Raphael - butcher
18	David Leon Hyman - grocer
24	P Leon - tailor
28	Louis Model - oriental warehouse
34	Mrs Edith Stern - cooked meat shop
44	Max Schliephak Ltd - chemist
46	Philip Landau - hosier
52	Harry Landau - hosier
56	Foreign Circulating Library
	SCALA THEATRE
64	Two artists
66	Solomon Herzfeld - outfitter
74	Swiss Club
90/92	Y W C A - Hostel for theatrical employees
98	Mayfair Working Girls' Club

Post Office Directory 1930

9	Anatole Dublin - shirt and collar dresser
23	David Prosser & Son - builder
29	Mrs Jennie Losowsky - tobacconist
35	Harold Isaacs - jeweller
35A	A Freedman & Son - tailors' trimmings
37	Max Raznick - butcher
45	David Myers - manufacturing furrier

51	Rosen & Schneider - ladies tailor
79	Eoleslas Schulz - teacher of the zither
81	Herman Berman - tailor
81	Hyman Swern - ladies tailor
83	Isidore Ferdman - boot repairer
85	David Miller - foreign provision dealer
89	H Phillips & Son - dental instrument maker
101	Philip Traeger - tailor
111	R Lomberg - ladies tailor
113	Barnett Abrahams - tailor
117	Mrs Becky Silver - gown manufacturer
121	Miss Eliz Barnett - feather dresser
12	Michael Freedman - printer
16	FITZROY - Judah Morris Kleinfeld
18	Aaron Zeidman - grocer
24	Samuel Holstein - ladies tailor
26	Hooper Struve - table water manufacturer
32	Sol Jacobovitch - tailor
34	Lazarus Ruback - provision dealer
44/16	Philip Landau - hosier
66	Mrs Flora Schindler - tobacconist
70	John Horowitz - fancy leather goods maker
90	Joel Jay Wolff - antique furniture dealer

Post Office Directory 1939

1/3	Glicksman & Schneider - mantle manufacturers
19	Bertorelli
23	David Prosser - builders
25	Hyman Brick - gown manufacturer
27	George Brushweiler - butcher

29	Mrs Jeannie Losonsky - tobacconist
31A	L Horowitz - watchmaker
37	Max Raznick - butcher
39	George Fox - tobacconist
43/45	Barnett Bros (Sportswear) Ltd
43/45	Frederick Midda - gown makers
43/45	Arlen - Sportswear
59	Mrs Nita Goldblatt - gown maker
59	Samuel Winograd - ladies' handbag manufacturer
63	Max Rubin - tailors' trimmings
73/75	Jay the Jewellers - jewellery
79	Eoleslas Schulz - teacher of the zither
91	Mrs P Fischel - fruiterer
101	Philip Trager - tailor
111	Harry Ansell - antique furniture dealer
115	Frederick Naser - working tailor
117	Mrs Becky Silver - gown manufacturer
119	United Ladies' Tailors Trade Union
16	FITZROY - Judah Morris Kleinfeld and Charles Allchild
18	Aaron Zeidman - grocer
24	Hyam Jacob - tailor
24	Samuel Holstein - tailor
26	Hooper Struve
32	Solly Jay - tailor
34	Philip Morris - provision dealer
44	Philip Landau - hosier
48	Bernstein & Kalb - manufacturing furriers
56	Mrs Lucie Buhler - newsagent
66	Mrs Frances Levene - tobacconist
66	Sidney Ponder - cabinet maker

74	Swiss Club
90	Philip Hackman - ladies' tailor
96	
	Cohen - sportswear

Post Office Directory 1951

1/3	Glicksman & Schneider - mantle manufacturers
	Bertorelli at 19
23	David Prosser - builders
27	George Brushweiler - butcher
29	L Horowitz - watchmaker
37	Max Raznick - butcher
39	George Fox - tobacconist
59	Mrs Nita Goldblatt - gown maker
63	Max Rubin - tailors' trimmings
73/75	Jay the Jewellers - jewellery
119	United Ladies' Tailors Trade Union
16	FITZROY - Judah Morris Kleinfeld and Charles Allchild
18	Aaron Zeidman - grocer
26	Hooper Struve
34	Philip Morris - provision dealer
48	Bernstein & Kalb - manufacturing furriers
66	Mrs Frances Levene - tobacconist
74	Swiss Club

OTHER STREETS

Post Office Directory 1920

Saville Street (later changed to Hanson Street)

12	Julius Herrmann - hairdresser
13	Lazarus Lazorovitch - kosher butcher
21	Harry Rees - butcher

22	SHIP - [public house]
23	Barnett Shapiro - foreign provision dealer
41	Reuben Lassarson - linen draper
42	Mrs Sarah Epstein - chandler
43	Morris Pozcaimski - tin plate worker
44	
	John Draper - boot repairer

Windmill Street   Only 42 buildings

About 10 of the 52 entries Jewish.   Trades include opticians, stationers, electrical engineers, restaurants, out metal worker, trunk maker, grocery shops, engravers, tailors, cabinet makers, builders, antique furniture dealers, gold and silver casters, working jewellers, brass founders, boot repairers, coppersmiths, public house, upholsterer, carriage lamp japanner, dental instrument maker, carver and gilder, blouse maker, bakers, dairyman, hairdresser, laundry and French laundry, plate glass merchants, gold and silver casters.

Cleveland Street

Of the 113 entries a minimum 31 were Jewish including boot and shoe repairers [3] fishmonger [1] tailor and allied [2] fruiterer [1] plate glass merchants [1] tobacconist [1] confectioner [1] butcher [2] laundry [1]

Bromley Arms - Solomon Lipman. hairdresser [2] dairy [2] watchmaker [1] baker [1] hosier[1] draper[2] grocers [2].   Mrs Emily Vallan - cats meat dealer.

D'Arblay Street

39 entries plus 8 in Wardour Mews. 14 Jewish including:

5	Samuel Bergman - restaurant
8	BRITANNIA - Reuben Rosenthau
9	Sam Sugarman - butcher
25	Mrs Annie Jacobs - grocery shop
30	Joseph Fulberg - fishmonger

Manette Street

No obvious Jewish traders, only West End Talmud Torah and Bikur Holim.

Broad [wick] - Broad Street

41 entries, 15 Jewish. Hairdresser [1] corset manufacturer [1] grocer/ greengrocer [4] china and glass dealer [1] tailoring and allied [3] confectioner [2] bootmaker [1] furniture [1]

Wardour Street

About 200 entries - only 22-25 could with confidence be said to be Jewish, but there was a heavy film industry presence under limited company names, and many of them were Jewish.

TWO SHIPS - Louis Canter

Post Office Directory 1930

Saville Street (later changed to Hanson Street)

12	Jack Prozzer - hairdresser
13	Lazarus Lazarovitch - kosher butcher
14	Joseph Fulberg - fishmonger
21	Harry Rees - butcher
22	SHIP - E J Rose & Co Ltd
23	Shapiro Barnett - foreign provision dealer
24	Herschel Harris - bootmaker
29/30	Charles Irish - decorator
41	Mrs Fanny Lassarson - confectioner
42	Mrs Sarah Epstein - chandlers shop
43	Mrs Annie Nudel - draper
44	Harris Vetchinsky - fishmonger

D'Arblay Street

1	GEORGE - Mrs Bessie Larholt
2/3	Madame S Siegler - costumier
4	Harry Greenfield - electrical engineer
5	Victor Woolf & Sons - costumier
6	Abraham Taylor - tailors' trimmings
8	BRITANNIA - Reuben Rosenthau
9	Sam Sugarman - kosher butcher
10	Hy Rose - builders' materials
10	Benjamin Harris - embroiderer
11	G Garbe & Son Ltd - tortoiseshell workers
11	Davies, Garbe & Co - ivories
12	Harcourt Corset Co Ltd
13	A horse collar manufacturer
14/15	M Choimacky Ltd - costume manufacturer
14/15	H J Jenner & Co Ltd - embroiderer
29	D Harris - costumier
30	Joseph Fulberg - fishmonger
31	Mark Kutock & Son - butchers
32	Alec Spero - news vendor
33	I Wainstain - tailor

7 Wardour Mews - Charles Ray, barrow lender

Windmill Street

About 16 Jewish traders,   Still wide variety of trades in street.

Cleveland Street   36 Jewish traders

Wardour Street   There was a J Lyons and Co at 56/58.   Comparatively few Jewish names, but an increasing number of film companies and limited companies which could be Jewish.

Post Office Directory 1939

Hanson [formerly Saville] Street

Previous entries were from 21 Foley Street to 17A Upper Marylebone Street. The following entries are from 21 Foley Street to 19 Carburton Street.

East Side

18	Mrs Nancy Lazarovitch - kosher butcher
20	Joseph Fulberg & Sons - fishmonger
30	Harry Rees - kosher butcher [here is New Cavendish Street]
32	Mrs Fanny Solka - baker
34	Ralph Church - locksmith [Clipstone Street]
68	A Bennett & Co - wholsesale cabinet makers
80	Cecil Frederick Myles - shopkeeper
90	Frank Albert Box - newsagent
92	LORD NELSON - James Ernest Hardwick

West side

1	Gladys Harper - fruiterer
3	Paul Cura - fried fish dealer
5	Mrs Sarah Epstein - chandler
7	Mrs Fanny Lasserson - confectioner
27	Hershell Harris - bootmaker
29	Barnett Shapiro - foreign provision dealer
31	SHIP - E J Rose & Co Ltd [New Cavendish Street]
33	Miss B Levine - confectioner
40/48	Working Boys' Home [Clipstone Street]
67	Meawick & Co - upholstery manufacturers
77	Reinforced Glass Co Ltd - optical lens laminators
77	Quiddington & Son Ltd - carpet planners

77	H Gulson & Co - upholsterers
77	H Khaan - cabinet makers
77	Walter Moss - upholsterer
77	Geo Miller - cabinet makers
77	International Tyre Distributors
77	Vigor Permanent Waving Co
87	Frank Stanley Vincent - cafe
91	Leib Rosenkranz - hairdresser

D'Arblay Street

9	Sam Sugarman - kosher restaurant proprietor
30	Joseph Fulberg & Sons - fishmonger
31	Marks Kutock - kosher butcher

Cleveland Street   At least 35 Jewish firms.

Post Office Directories 1951 and [1960] (if still there in 1960)

Hanson Street

10	Chris Panani - gown maker-up
18	Marks Lazarovitch - kosher butcher [1960]
20	Electrosonic Ltd - radio engineers
30	J S Richards - baker
34	Clef Music Publishing Co Ltd
33/34	Atlas Equipment (London) Ltd - bakery engineers
40/48	Latimer House
40/48	Homes for Working Boys in London (Incorporated)
68	William Jones Clifton & Co Ltd - rubber stamp m/f [1960]
76	J D Beardmore - architectural ironmongers
80	Frederick Myles - shopkeeper
90	Frank Albert Box - newsagent

92   LORD NELSON - Percy Beard [1960]

1   Miss Gladys Harper [1960]

3   R Seiden - wholesale gown manufacturers [1960]

5   Mrs Sarah Epstein - shopkeeper

7   Mrs Fanny Lasserson - confectioner

19   M & S Cooperman - mantle makers up [1960]

27   Mrs Marie Katsaiss - draper

29   Barnett Shapiro - foreign provision dealer

31   SHIP - E J Rose & Co Ltd [1960]

33   B Levene - confectioner

63A   Meawick & Co - upholstery manufacturers

67   Speedy Cables Ltd - speedometer repairs [1960]

67   Aro Batteries - electrical

67   Silshine Candle Co Ltd

77   J & M Tyres - tyre factors [1960]

77   Charles Algernon Brooks - boot and shoe repairers to the trade [1960]

77   Masters Engineering Ltd - precision engineers

87   Edward Thomas Peace - fruiterer [1960]

91   Leib Rosenkranz - ladies dresses [1960]

APPENDIX IV

In 1898 a book was published by the Clergy of St Anne's Church, *Two Centuries of Soho, Its Institutions, Firms and Amusements.* Lily Montagu provided the entry for theWest Central Jewish Girls' Club. It is reproduced here almost in its entirety, and readers who attended the club in the 1920's and 1930's may be surprised to recognise how much of the basic form and principles of the club as they knew it were already in place before the end of the last century:

TheWest Central Jewish Girls' Club, 8A Dean Street. [By the Honorary Secretary, Lily Montagu].

The West-Central Jewish Girls' Club was founded some ten years ago by Lady Battersea, assisted by Miss Emily Harris. [Lily was here referring to the earlier religious classes. It is more accurate to date the Club from 1893]. It was primarily a religious institution, and met on the Jewish Sabbath eve for prayers. Gradually more ladies became interested in the work of the Club, and having regard to the needs of the large Jewish population in Soho, it was deemed advisable to re-organise the Club and establish it on a larger basis. Membership now numbers 210 girls, and the evening attendance averages 60.

The Club consists of one large hall, suitable for musical drill, dancing, concerts or lectures; two class-rooms, one fitted with sink and dresser, suited and used for cooking and laundry classes, the other containing the lending library, and used for evening school. In addition to these rooms the elder girls have a small drawing room where they sit and talk when too tired or unwilling to join classes.

The Club is managed by a General Committee, consisting of i) the three officers, Pres, Hon Treasurer, and Hon Sec ii) of nine workers i.e. ladies who visit the Club in regular rotation to instruct or amuse the girls and iii) of six members of the Club.

Ten workers (from among whom an Hon Sec is annually elected) and the six representative members are elected annually by the general body of members over sixteen years of age.

The following are the present members of the Committee:

Miss Emily Harris (President), 23 Clifton Gardens, Maida Vale

Miss Nathan (Hon Treasurer), 11 Pembridge Square, W

Miss L H Montagu (Hon Sec), 12 Kensington Palace Gardens

Workers:

Miss E Franklin, 35 Porchester Terrace

Miss M Franklin, 69 Elgin Avenue, Maida Vale

Miss Lewis, 34 Leinster Gardens

Miss Lucas, 5 Westbourne Terrace

Miss Montagu, 12 Kensington Palace Gardens

Miss Amy Schloss, 120 Westbourne Terrace

Miss M Samuel, 80 Onslow Gardens, S. Ken

Miss Waley, 22 Devonshire Place, Portland Place

Miss Alice Schloss, 17 Leinster Gardens

Representative members:

Miss Dora Blumenthal, 27 St Anne's Court, Dean Street

Miss Rachel Bloom, 13 Princeton Street, Red Lion Square

Miss Rose Davis, 13 Broad Street, Bloomsbury

Miss Lily Jacobs, 64 New Compton Street, C.X Rd.

Miss Phoebe Rosenbloom, 57 Old Compton Street, Soho

Miss Sara Trenner, 14 Gt Coram Street, WC

The superintendent (Miss Julia Kauffman) 28 Goodge St, Tottenham Court Road, attends the club every evening, marks the registers, collects the subscriptions, and by sympathy and kindness, tries to secure a good and quiet tone throughout the Club.   The Hon Sec, assisted by three ladies, visits members in their homes, and tries to obtain the sympathy and interest of parents in the work of the Club.   She endeavours to find the girls work when they are out of employment, and apprentices girls as they leave school.   The superintendent furnishes her with an absentee list every fortnight, and she visits the homes to discover the cause of absence. Every member is expected to attend one working evening a week. Should she, on two consecutive evenings, miss a class for which she has enrolled her name, she is expected to retire in favour of another member.

In April last, the Club was recognised by the Education Department as an evening continuation school, and grants will be claimed for instruction in musical drill, French, literature, English reading, and composition, singing, cooking, laundry, and ambulance (ambulance and laundry given under the auspices of the Technical Education Board). Every evening foreign girls are instructed in English reading and writing. These classes are assisted by the Russo-Jewish committee. Classes are also held for Hebrew, basketwork, and brush drawing. Before the Club closes every evening, a prayer is recited, or a psalm sung, by the members, and on alternate Sunday evenings the Rev Gerald Friedlander visits the members and talks to them on scriptural and religious subjects. Every Saturday Miss Harris holds a Sabbath class at the Westminster Jews' Free School, Hamway Street, and the service is largely attended by members of the club.

Saturday evenings are given up to recreations. Members dance amongst themselves, and have music and recitations. Ladies and gentlemen visit the Club regularly on these evenings and act as hostesses and hosts. On the first Saturday in every month, a debate is held, for which two members read papers, and several others join in the discussion.

Every Sunday evening a tea is given. A few members, assisted by the superintendent, act as hostesses and prepare the teas and wait on the others. After tea, an address (religous or lay) is generally given and the rest of the evening is spent in dancing. The Club is open every evening except Friday (which is the Sabbath eve) from 8 till 10 and on Sundays from 6.30 till 10.00. The Club library is well used, and managed by Miss Amy Schloss, assisted by two sub-librarians chosen from the members. This library has recently been federated to the Central Club Library, organised by the Women's Industrial Council, and the exchange of 30 new books every quarter is expect to add much to its interest.

About 25 girls have joined the club branch of the London Medical Provident Asssociation; and the Club's Savings Bank is well used by many members.

The members of the West Central Jewish Girls' Club include representatives of many different trades, but the great majority are tailoresses and work in the district of Soho, chiefly in domestic workshops. There are also dressmakers, milliners, cigar-makers, stationers, home-helps, cap makers, waistcoat makers, and wig makers.

The members subscribe one penny per week, and pay twopence as entry fee; the main source of income is in outside subscriptions and donations.

The Hon Sec endeavours to arrange country holidays for all members who apply for assistance. With the help of the Factory Girls' Holiday Fund, 117 holidays were organised this summer. One farm was rented at Bishops Stortford, and another at Sevenoaks, and parties of 12 and 8 girls spent two weeks together in the country.

The West Central Jewish Girls' Club, since its reorganisation in January 1896, has taken girls as they leave school, while it still retains many of the original members.

Women, the circumstances of whose lives are different from those of the members, spend evenings among them sympathising with the joys and sorrows of their lives, and seek to draw them to themselves by ties of friendship.   As years pass, the committee and members hope to see a spirit of mutual help and love general among workers and girls, so that they may all rejoice in a broader and happier life.

SELECT BIBLIOGRAPHY

The *Jewish Chronicle* is always a good starting point for any research into Anglo-Jewish history from 1841 onwards, and considerable use has been made of its pages. There is some archival material held at the Greater London Record Office concerning Westminster Jews' Free School, Pulteney School and Upper Marylebone Street School. The London Museum of Jewish Life has copies of the Girls' Club magazine, *Link,* and as a result of the Jewish West End Project extensive oral history and photographic archives relating to the Jewish West End.. The Jewish Studies Department at University College some annual reports of the Boys' Club. The *Jewish Year Books* from 1896 are invaluable for general information and for educational information in particular. *Post Office* and other directories were of course useful sources.

Bailey, N, *Fitzrovia* (1984)

Barnett, Arthur, *The Western Synagogue through Two Centuries* (1961)

Bermant, Chaim, *The Cousinhood* (1971)

Black, Eugene C, *The Social Politics of Anglo-Jewry 1880-1920* (1988)

Black, Gerry, *Lender to the Lords; Giver to the Poor* (1992)

Bunt, Sidney, *Jewish Youth Work in Britain* (1975)

Cardwell, J H, *Two Centuries of Soho* (1898)

Colby, Reginald, *Mayfair - A Town Within London* (1966)

Colquhoun, P, *Treatise on the Police of the Metropolis* (1800)

Endelman, Todd M, *The Jews of Georgian England 1714-1830* (1979)

Gartner, Lloyd P, *The Jewish Immigrant in England 1870-1914* (1960)

Hyamson, Albert M, *Jews' College London* 1855-1955 (1955)

Kershen, Anne, (Ed), *150 years of Progressive Judaism in Britain* (1990)

Levy, Nellie G , *The West Central Story and its Founders 1893-1968* (1968)

Lewis, Chaim, *A Soho Address* (1965)

Lindsay, Paul, *The Synagogues of London* (1993)

Lipman, Vivian, *Social History of the Jews in England 1850-1950* (1954)

Lipman, Vivian, The Rise of Suburbia, *Transactions of the Jewish Historical Society of England, Vol XIX* (1956)

Montagu, Lily, *My Club and I* (1941)

Newman, Aubrey, *The United Synagogue 1870-1970* (1976)

Pollins, Harold, *Economic History of the Jews in England* (1982)

Rimbault, E F and Clinch G, *Soho and its Associations* (1895)

Roth, Cecil, *Records of the Western Synagogue* (1932)

History of the Great Synagogue London 1690-1940 (1950)

Summers, Judith, *Soho* (1989)

CONTRIBUTORS

Alphabetical list of text and archival contributors, oral history recordings, interviewers, interviewees and researchers

Every effort has been made to include all who helped, and to spell names correctly. Sincere apologies are offered to anyone who has been inadvertently omitted or whose name is incorrectly given.

Albert Aarons, David and Jolene Abrahams, Annie Allchild, Michael Ambrose, Moss Amias, Rev Saul Amias, B Andrusier, Jack Anthony, Sylvia Anthony, Jacky Arnold, Jean Austin.

Mannie Bacrac, David Bailey, Jasmine Bandel, Mr and Mrs Banks, Kitty Barber, Nat Barker, Eileen Barnett, Joe Barnett, Mrs M Barnett, Peter Barnett, Sam Barnett, Zvia Ben-Horin, Anne Benjamin, Betty Benjamin, Samuel Bennett, Doreen Berger, Stanley Berman, Ziggy Bernstein, Sonia Birnbaum, Gerry and Anita Black, Mrs E Blankover, Rivy Blau, Ben Boskin, Kenneth Brown, Maurice Brown, Sidney and Sylvia Budd, Rickie Burman, Rabbi A Burns.

Beryl Caplin, Brian and Joel Chalfen, Barry Chapman, Barbara Clauson, Jean Cohen, Renee Cohen, Tony and Francis Colton, Janet Colton, Madelaine and Reginald Conick, Eric and Sheila Conrad, Josie Conway, Constance Cowan, Rae Cowen.

Donald Daniels, Millicent Davis, Sophie Dean, Fay Delmonte, Fanny Denbin, Lily Denbin, Nat Denbin, Judith Devons, Sydney Diamond, Gene Dorff, Iris Dove, D Droznika, Maureen Duck.

Betty and Joe Eisen, David Eison, Ronald and Ruth Erickson, Freda and Harry Errington.

Leni Faith, Alf Fegan, David and Sheila Fegan, Kitty Fegan, Hannah Feldman, Jack Feldman, Louis Feldman, Wolf Feldman, Sylvia Fernstein, Sally and Arthur Fiber, David Fielding, Rita Fihlebohn, Celia Finkle, Lily and Betty Fireman, Harold and Pamela Fisher, Alex and Trudie Flinder, Pearl Forman, Helen Franks, Phil Franks, Rosie Freedman, Steffen Frölich, S Fueurstein.

Fay Gilbert, Joe Gilbert, Jacqueline Gill, Percy B Gold, Manny Goldberg, Alex Goldstein, Esther Goldstein, Ettie Gontarsky, Anne Goodman, Jack and Muriel Goodman, Woolfie Goodman, Kitty Graber, Markus Grafenburg, Benny Green, Helena Green, Vicki and Moss Green, Arnold Greenwood, Michi Groos, Tilly Gross, Naomi Gryn, Rose Gutty.

Rosalie Haydorf, Judi and Steve Herman, Loveday Herridge, Maurice Hildebrand, Oscar Hildebrand, Evelyn Hill, Esther House, Tilly Hyman.

Max Jaffa, Cyril and Sheila Jacobs, Mr and Mrs P Jacobs, Faye Joseph.

Anne Kahn, Jack Kahn, Rachele and Raymond Kalman, Morris Kay, Joan Kaye, Mr and Mrs Kemlet, Edith Kendler, Anne Kershen, J Klausner, Maureen Kons, Millie Kopelman, Rita Koss.

Phillip Ladwith, Dora Landau, George and Daphne Lang, Maurice and Lily Leaderman, Joella and Wally Leaf, Marcia Lebon, Frank Lee, Jill Leigh, Mr J Lennard, Harold Lester, Mary Levrant, Stanley Levy, Mr Lewin, Chaim Lewis, D Lewis-Barned, Ian Lillicrapp, C Lipman, Celia Lyons.

Henry Mager, Mr and Mrs I Maltz, Trudie Mannaseh, Cissie Martin, Mr and Mrs Martin, Rosalie Maydorf, Alf Mendleson, Lily Mendleson, Rita Mendoza, Bea Miller, Louis Miller, Max Minkoff, Berta Mintz, Lola Monk, Maurice Monitz, Bryan Montagu, Harry Moore, Henry and Anne Morris, Jack and Sadie Morris, Marjorie Morris, Sidney Morrison, Doris Mozer.

Jean Nathan, Reg Needlemen, David Osmond, Estelle and Jack Patterson, David Paul, David Pela, Hugh Petrie, Gertie Phillips, Laura Phillips, Dame Shirley and Sir Leslie Porter.

Winnie Radstone, Daphne Redplatt, Albert Rose, Esther Rose, Harry Rose, Jack Rose, Robert Rose, Debbie Rosnika, Alex Rosenzsweig, John Rubens.

Edgar Samuels, Martin Savitt, Debbie Seedburgh, Jeffrey and Rose Segal, S Selby, Cyril Selinger, Celia and Jack Shaw, Edna Sherman, Morris Sherman, Daniel Shine, Miriam Silberberg, Lily Silver, Dr I Silverman, Millie Silverston, Cyril Silvertown, C S Simmons, Louis Simmons, Lily Simons, Susan Sinclair, Gerald Smith, Sidney Spellman, Doris Spencer,

Sophie Spitalnick, Sadie Starr, Evelyn Steinman, Hetty Stephens, Sadie Stern, Ronald Stein, Jack Stern, Mick and Leah Stollar, Judith Summers, Mr and Mrs H Sunshine, Mr and Mrs S Sunshine.

Sheila Trup, Arnold and Helen Tucker, Charles Tucker, Dennis and Hazel Tuhrim.

Mrs Evelyn Waley, Barry Weinberg, Henry Wildman, Debbie Winston, Marcia Woolf, Netta Woolfson, Sylvia Wright.

Phyllis Yates.

Nate and Mildred Zamet.

SPONSORS

We are grateful to the following who have sponsored the publication of this book of the Jewish West End, and who have dedicated their sponsorship in memory of loved ones who lived or worked in the West End.

David and Jolene ABRAHAMS of USA; family connection Joseph Victor (Master Tailor) of Shaftesbury Avenue (1889-1916). *To the memory of David's great grandfather*

Mrs Tessa ALTERMAN of Finchley; family connection Abrahams (Master Tailor) of Tottenham Court Rd (1929-44). *In loving memory of our grandparents Fanny and Barnet Abrahams, killed by enemy action*

Rev Saul AMIAS of Edgware. *In loving memory of my father, Rev Alexander Amias, Minister / Chazan of West End Talmud Torah Synagogue for forty years*

Mrs Sylvia ANTHONY of Brighton; family connection Goldstein (Grocery) of 35 Broad St which became 55 Broadwick St (1883-1942). *In loving memory of my parents Sam and Cissie Goldstein*

Jacky ARNOLD and Liz GOLD of Nottingham; family connection Cohen (Green Man Public House) of Union St which became Ridinghouse St (1910-30). *In loving memory of our parents, grandparents, and great-grandparents Prissie and Jacob Cohen*

Jeanne AUSTIN of Regent's Park; family connection Barnett (Barber Shop) of Ingestre Place, Golden Square (1900-38). *In fond remembrance of the founders - Miss Lily and Miss Marian (Montagu), the helpers and the members of the West Central Girls' Club*

Mr David BAILEY of Ilford; family connection Bailey (Tailor) of Cleveland St and Robert St (1916-50). *Remembering my mother, Katie Bailey (1882-1971) with compassion and sadness*

Mrs Eve BANKOVER of Woodside Park; family connection Geduld of Napier House, Union St, which became Ridinghouse St (1928-36). *In memory of the members of the West Central Boys' Club who sacrificed their lives in the Second World War*

Mrs Zvia BEN-HORIN of Haifa; family connection Jack Wolf Weintroub (my father) who worked as teacher and headmaster at West Central Hebrew National Institute, 26a Soho Square (1910-19).

Dr Alan BENNY of Godalming; family connection Benny (Tailor) at several West End addresses (circa 1870). *In loving memory of 'Aunt Frances'*

Mr Emmanuel BERG of Wembley; family connection Berg of 37 Hanson St (1928-56). *In loving memory of my parents Esther and Morris Berg*

Mrs Sonia BIRNBAUM of Stanmore; family connection Raznick (Kosher Butcher) at 37 Charlotte St (1907-56). *In loving memory of our dear parents, Rose and Max Raznick*

Mr Kenneth BROWN of Marylebone; family connection Brown (*Rose & Crown* Public House) 85 Dean St (1920-59). *In loving memory of my grandparents, and of my parents Sam and Annie Brown*

Mr Reuben (Buddy) BUDD of Canada; family connection Yarnitsky of 24 and 36 Broad St which became Broadwick St (1910-42). *In loving memory of my parents Maier and Rachel Yarnitsky, and of my wife Cissie (née Warshawsky)*

Dr Sidney BUDD of Edgware; family connection Budd (Yarnitsky) of 48 and 60 Howland St and 66 Berwick St (1928-1944). *Remembering with affection my grandparents, and especially my mother Cissie who loved her West End*

Mrs Zena BULLMORE MBE of Hemel Hempstead; family connection Blau (Tailor) of 4 Dufours Place (1919-72). *Max and Rosie Blau remembered with deep affection by their children and grandchildren*

Mrs Beryl CAPLIN of Hackney; family connection Rendlick of Gt Tichfield St, Windmill St and Hanson St (1900-77). *In loving memory of the Rendlick family - West End residents for over seventy years*

Mr Joe CHILTON of Wembley; family connection Cibulia (Tailor) of Broad St and West St, which became Newburgh St (1910-58). *In loving memory of my grandparents, and of my parents Harry and Freda Cibulia*

Mrs Madelaine CONICK of Finchley; family connection Lipman (Tailor) of 7 Little Tichfield St and 35 Goodge St (1935-). *In memory of my parents Fanny and Emanuel Lipman, and Monte - all such wonderful people*

Mr Malcolm COOPER-SMITH of Reading; family connection Adler of 86 Berwick St and 21 Dean St (1920-). *In memory of my parents Phoebe and Victor Cooper-Smith*

Mrs Betty EISEN of Finchley; family connection King (Trimming Shop) of 60 Berwick St (1880-1938). *In memory of my father Moishe King - one of the characters of Berwick St*

Mr Harry ERRINGTON GC of Bloomsbury; family connection Ehrengott of 35 Broad St, which became Broadwick St (1914-). *In loving memory of our dear parents Baila and Shepsel Ehrengott*

Mr David FEGAN of Northwood; family connection Feigenbaum of Berwick St and Rothberg (Hardware) of Cleveland St (1920-1940). *In loving memory of the Rothberg and the Feigenbaum families*

Mr Wolf FELDMAN of Ealing; family connection Feldman of 42 Berwick St, 48 Howland St and 23 Nassau St (1912-55). *In loving memory of my mother Annie Feldman and my sister Fay Jacobson*

Mr Arthur FIBER of Northwood; family connection King (Trimmings Shop) of 60 Berwick St (1880-1936). *In loving memory of my grandparents, Kate and Samuel King, Vice President of Talmud Torah, and of my mother Rose Fiber, President of West Central Ladies' Guild*

Mrs Sally FIBER of Northwood; family connection Kleinfeld of 4 Phoenix St - the *Fitzroy Tavern* and Ridgmount Gardens.. Residents of Fitzrovia for over 85 years. *In memory of my grandparents Jane and Judah Kleinfeld, and of my parents Annie and Charles Allchild. Their lives have inspired this project*

Mr David FIELDING of Ruislip; family connection Feigenblatt (Grocery) of 6 St Annes Court (1921-70). *In loving memory of my parents Isaac and Bella Feigenblatt*

Pamela and Harold FISHER of Harrow; family connection Kazinoff (Military Tailor) of Wardour St (1910-17). *In memory of Edward and Bertha Kazinoff (Kay), the parents of Anne Benjamin*

Mr Alex FLINDER of Hampstead; family connection Flinder (Barber Shop) of 37 Marshall St (1885-1938). *In loving memory of Harry and Bessie Flinder, from their children Alex and Tilly*

Mrs Golda FREEDMAN of Muswell Hill; family connection Diamond of 151 Oxford St (-1926). *In loving memory of our Dad Simon (Shimshe) Diamond*

Mr Percy GOLD of High Wycombe; family connection Gold of 27 Clipstone St and New Cavendish St (1918-47). *In loving memory of my parents Rachel and Lewis Gold*

Mrs Norma GOLDMAN of Marylebone; family connection Levy (Ladies Outfitter) of 36 Store St (1907-20). *In loving memory of my grandparents Louis and Pauline Levy*

Mr Alec GOLDSTEIN of Southgate; family connection Goldstein (Tailor) of 65 Poland St (1909-45). *In memory of the West End Philanthropic Society*

The GOLDWATER grandchildren remember Harris and Sarah Goldwater (Tailor) and their family, who lived in Poland St, Maple St and finally Gt Tichfield St (1890-1926) before migrating to the north and west of London

Miss Ettie GONTARSKY of Soho; family connection Gontarsky, who lived at four addresses on Soho (1912-84). *In loving memory of my parents Benjamin and Katie Gontarsky*

Mrs M GOODMAN of Wandsworth; family connection Goodman (Grocery) of 2 Livonia St *In loving memory of Esther, Jack and Annie, and their Boobah*

Audrey and Arnold GREENWOOD of Bristol; family connection Bacrac (Grocery / Fishmonger) of 14 Livonia St (1904-87). *In memory of the Bacracs*

Mr Lionel GURVITZ of Hendon; family connection Gurvitz (Waistcoat maker) of 102 Gt Tichfield St (1921-65). *In memory of my dear father, Harry Gurvitz, and the Hirsch family*

Mr Philip HELMAN of Brighton; family connection Helman (Tailor) of 54 Broad St (1900-34). *Remembering our parents Mark and Mary Helman and two of our brothers, Harry and Bert*

Mrs Evelyn HILL of Southgate; family connection Antrich (Master Tailor) of 33 Howland St (1920-). *In loving memory of my parents Henry and Antoinette Antrich*

Sheila and Cyril JACOBS of Hove. *In memory of grandparents Rose and Joseph Victor of Shaftesbury Avenue*

Mr Jack KAHN of St John's Wood; family connection Kahn of 4 Charlotte St and Kahn's Kosher Restaurant of 5 Sherwood St (1915-50). *In memory of my parents Kever and Rose Kahn*

Mrs Rachele KALMAN of Hendon; family connection Morris Magar (Tailor) of 17 Tottenham St and Henry Magar (Hairdresser) of 8 Marchmont St (1920-). *Remembering my mother Marie Magar from Paris who settled in Bloomsbury and loved it*

Mrs Anne KERSHEN of Mill Hill; family connection Spero (Tobacconist / Confectioner) of 32 D'Arblay St (1926-92). *In loving memory of my maternal grandparents Alec and Leah Spero*

Mrs Jacqueline KING-CLINE of Woodside Park; family connection Rosin of Berwick St (1910-50). *In memory of my grandfather, Max Rosin, a great Zionist who raised money for the purchase of the first WIZO ambulance*

Mrs Maureen KONS of St Albans; family connections Wiseman of 15 Brewer St and 4 Soho Square (1930-60) and Cohen of Gt Pulteney St *In loving memory of Lilli and Sam Wiseman*

Mrs Daphne LANG of Wembley; family connection King of 60 Berwick St *In loving memory of my father Isaac (Ike) King 1894-1975*

Miss Bella LEADERMAN of Highgate; family connection Leaderman of 13 Carburton St (1920-38). *In loving memory of my parents Abraham and Rose Leaderman, and my sister Ruth*

Joella and Wally LEAF of Wembley; family connections Carolin, Grad and Stein of Soho and Russell Square (1897-1976). *With fond memories of Anne Stein.*

Mr Frank LEE of U.S.A.; family connection Leaderman of 52 Tottenham St and Carburton St (1924-38). *In loving memory of my wife Shirley, my in-laws Hetty and Nate King, and my brother Maurice Leaderman*

Mr Nathan LEWIN of Greenford; family connection Lewin (Tailor) of 106 Bolsover St (1903-55). *In loving memory of my parents Harris and Annie Lewin*

Mr Colman LIPMAN of Elstree; family connection Lipman (Gents Tailor) of 8 Middleton Buildings, Langham St (1901-59). *In loving memory of Sarah and Solomon Lipman*

Mrs Celia LYONS of Hendon; family connection Wainstain (Master Tailor) of 33 D'Arblay St (1899-1939). *In loving memory of my father and mother, Lazarus and Fanny Wainstain, and my husband George Louis Lyons - both of the men were officers at the Dean St Synagogue*

Harold MATZ and Bessie SAKTREGER of Harrow; family connection Matz of 115 Cleveland St (1927-42). *In loving memory of our parents Deborah and Robert Matz*

Mrs Cissie MERKIN of Maida Vale; family connection Freedman (Newsagent) of 66 Cleveland St . *With happy memories of my mother Jane Freedman's delicious ice cream, and my brother Alf's cheerful personality*

Mr Joseph MORRIS of Stepney. *In loving memory of my wife Celia - from Joe*

Mr David PELA of St John's Wood; family connection Pela (Master Tailor) and Plaskwa, of 36 Berwick St (1911-46). *In loving memory of my parents Annie and Wolfe Pela, and of my grandparents Gittel and Lewis Plaskwa*

Mr Anthony RADSTONE of Willesden; family connection Radstone (Master Tailor) of 9 Greek St (1906-42). *In loving memory of our family*

Mrs Winnie RADSTONE of Edgware; family connection Lipman (Master Tailor) of 134 Wardour St (1910-50). *In loving memory of our family*

Miss Frances RAVDEN of Mayfair; family connection Ravden of Carburton St and Abrahams of Hanson St. *In memory of happy days*

Marion RINGLE of Hendon; family connection Goodman of Wardour St (1905-20). *In loving memory of my mother, Annie Fiber (nee Goodman)*

Mr Robert ROSE of Stanmore; family connection Denbin (Master Tailor) of 16 Arthur St and Dean St (1914-30). *In loving memory of my grandparents Rose and Malech Denbin*

Mr Joseph ROSEN of Finchley; family connection Rosen of 52 Wells St (1914-28). *In memory of all the members of my family who have passed away*

Mr David ROSENBLATT of Edgware; family connection Rosenblatt (Grocery) of 34 Clipstone St (1923-40); *Remembering Jack's Stores, the Fortnum and Mason of the Gt Portland St area*

Mr Martin SAVITT of Finchley; family connection Savitt (Shopfitter) of D'Arblay Mews (1918-35) and Savitt (Office Equipment) of 20 Brewer St (1945-85). *For my parents, Edith and George, in fond memory*

Mrs Debbie SEEDBURGH of Hendon; family connection Levine of 35 Broad St and 55 Carnaby St (1895-1923) and Goldstein of 102 Cleveland St and 1 Albert St (1890-1914). *In memory of our parents Sollie and Esther Goldstein who loved the West End*

Mrs Celia SHAW of Stanmore; family connection Waterman (Kosher Butcher) of Clipstone St and Charlotte St (1921-33). *In loving memory of my father, Sam Waterman*

Mr Ronald SHELLEY of Edgware; business connection Shelley (Chartered Accountant) of 45 Mortimer St (1958-)

Mr Sidney SPELLMAN of Highgate; family connection Spigelman of 23 Hanson St (1910-70). *In loving memory of my parents Hyman and Bella Spigelman and of my grandparents Maurice and Rebecca Needleman*

Mr Benjamin STANTON of Highgate; family connection Silverstein of Goodge St *In loving memory of my parents Davis and Rose Silverstein*

Mr Ronald STEIN of West Hampstead; family connection Stein (Newsagent / Tobacconist) of 29 Rathbone Place (1906-46). *Remembering 'Bubu' Bertha and her children, especially my dear father Harry Stein*

Mrs Hetty STEPHENS, Chairman of the West End Great Synagogue Ladies' Guild, on behalf of the Guild: *In fond remembrance of all the members of the West End Great Synagogue Ladies' Guild over so many years*

Mr Sam STOLLER of Golders Green; former Secretary of the West End Great Synagogue (1966-83). *In loving memory of my dear and devoted wife, Leah*

Mr Dennis TUHRIM of Edgware; family connection Tuhrim (Gents Tailor) of 95 Charlotte St and Ehrengott of 4 Phoenix St (1920-37). *In memory of our family - the Tuhrims and Ehrengotts*

Mrs Ruth WARREN of Enfield; family connection Beiny of 27 Baker St and 49 George St (1930-60). *In memory of our father - Beiny, the well known photographer*

Mr Sam WITZENFIELD DSO of Woodford; family connection Silver (Tailor) of 65 Whitfield St (1910-36). *In loving memory of grandparents Israel and Betsy Silver, and my parents Michael and Kitty Witzenfield*

Mr Nathan ZAMET of Finchley; family connection Zamet of 32a Rupert St (1898-1930). *In loving memory of Esther and Morris Zamet*

* * * * * * *

No history of the West End would be complete without mentioning those who managed the WEST CENTRAL BOYS' CLUB. These men were not necessarily residents of the West End but were instrumental in so many ways in forming the character of the boys who lived in the West End. We dedicate this to the memory of Harold Samson, the leader of the Club, his very able assistants Hillier Field, Ronald Kaufman, Dickie Norton, and so many others. On behalf of the West Central Old Boys we thank you for all you did for us - H Errington and A Tucker

CHRONOLOGY OF EVENTS

1698	Wolf Liepman born in Germany
1699	St Anne's Boys' School founded
1739	*Blue Posts* public house opened at 22 Berwick Street
1745	Middlesex Hospital founded in Windmill Street; moved to its present site 1755-75
1750's	Rate books show Jews living in districts of Soho and Covent Garden
1761	Western Synagogue founded in house of Wolf Liepman in Great Pulteney Street
1765	Western Synagogue moved to Denmark Court, on site of present Strand Palace Hotel
1797	St Anne's Girls' School founded
1808	Western Synagogue entered into "non-poaching" treaty with City synagogues
1810	Group of members seceded from Western Synagogue; later settled in Maiden Lane
1811	Levi Graeditz employed by Western Synagogue to teach children of its poor members in his home - started with 14 pupils
1815	Western Synagogue purchased cemetery at Queen's Elm, Brompton
1820	Westminster Institution for Educating Indigent Jewish Children (later Westminster Jews' Free School) founded
1822	Westminster Benevolent Institution founded by Western Synagogue
1825	Sir Moses Montefiore moved to Park Lane, and Nathan Meyer Rothschild purchased 107 Piccadilly

1826	Western Synagogue moved to St Alban's Place, Haymarket
1827	Westminster Benevolent Institution reorganised and renamed Western Jewish Philanthropic Society. Levi Graeditz died
1829	George Shillibeer started cheap omnibus route from Paddington Green to Bank of England
1837	Westminster Jews' Free School rented premises in Stanhope Street
1840	Meeting of Reform group at Bedford Hotel, Russell Square
1841	Chief Rabbi Solomon Hirschell pronounced *herem* (excommunication) on Reform movement
1842	West London Synagogue of British Jews (Reform) opened in Burton Street, Bloomsbury. Jewish Ladies' West End Charity formed.
1843	Westminster Jews' Free School moved to Greek Street West London Synagogue of British Jews acquired burial ground at Ball's Pond Road, Islington
1845	Reform movement opened Boys' School
1846	Reform movement opened school for girls in Little Queen Street (in August). Western Jewish Girls' School opened in Dean Street (in October)
1847	St Anne's Infants' School formed
1849	West London Synagogue of British Jews moved to Margaret Street
1853	Boys' School and Girls' School amalgamated at 60 Greek Street under title Westminster Jews' Free School Bevis Marks opened branch synagogue in Wigmore Street

1855	Great Synagogue opened branch, the Central Synagogue, in Portland Street
1861	Western branch of Bevis Marks moved to Bryanston Street
1863	Bayswater Synagogue consecrated
1868	Marian Montagu born
1870	New building of Central Synagogue consecrated in Great Portland Street
	West London Synagogue of British Jews moved to Upper Berkeley Street.
	United Synagogue formed by Act of Parliament
1872	St Anne's School (combined boys, girls and infants) opened in Dean Street
1873	Lily Montagu born
1876	St John's Wood Synagogue consecrated
1879	New West End Synagogue (St Petersburgh Place) consecrated
1880	West End Talmud Torah founded at 10 Green's Court
	Samuel Lewis became first Jew to live in Grosvenor Square
1883	Consecration of new Westminster Jews' Free School building in Hanway Place
1885	Jews' College moved to Tavistock Square
1893	West Central Jewish Girls' Club founded at 71 Dean Street
1894	West London Hebrew Loyal United Brethren Friendly Society formed
1896	Bevis Marks branch moved from Bryanston Street to Lauderdale Road, Maida Vale

1898   West Central Jewish Working Lads' Club founded at 38 Fitzroy Square

West Central Hebrew Tontine and Benefit Society founded

Lord Rothschild Lodge of Order of *Achei Brith* founded

1900   Fourth Zionist Conference (first outside Basle) held at Queen's Hall, Langham Place

West Central Zionist Association founded

Oxford Circus Tube station opened

Baron Ferdinand de Rothschild Lodge of Order *Achei Ameth* founded

1901   Thomas Burberry opened his shop in Haymarket

1902   First public service of Jewish Religious Union (Liberal) held at Wharncliffe Rooms, Marylebone Road

Emily Harris Home for Friendless Jewish Girls opened at 60 Frith Street

1903   West End Radom Hebrew Tontine and Benefit Society founded

1904   West London Hebrew Benefit and Divisional Society founded

1905   West Central Jewish Working Men's Club founded at 113 Tottenham Court Road

1907   Maiden Lane Synagogue closed, and rejoined Western Synagogue in St Alban's Place

Coventry Street Corner House opened

1910   West Central Jewish National Institute (later Beth HaSepher) founded

West End Talmud Torah merged with Bikkur Holim (synagogue at 41 Brewer Street)

Palladium opened

1912	Bloomsbury Synagogue founded in Lamb's Conduit Street
	Regent Palace Hotel opened
	Strand Corner House opened
1913	Rabbi Zvi Ferber installed as rabbi of West End Talmud Torah / Bikkur Holim at £2 per week
1914	Upper Marylebone Street School opened
	West Central Jewish Girls' Club opened new premises in Alfred Place
	Poland Street Refuge opened for Belgian refugees
1915	West End Talmud Torah / Bikkur Holim purchased burial ground at Streatham
	Foundation Stone laid of Western Synagogue in Alfred Place
1916	Beth HaSepher opened Shivat Zion Synagogue at 82 Berwick Street
	West End Talmud Torah / Bikkur Holim took premises at 14 Manette Street
1918	Beth HaSepher moved to 26a Soho Square
1923	Oxford Street Corner House opened
1924	Rev Arthur Barnett appointed Minister of Western Synagogue
1925	Strand Palace Hotel opened
1926	Scala Theatre first used for High Holyday overflow Services by West End Talmud Torah / Bikkur Holim
1927	Western Synagogue formed its own burial society
1928	West Central Synagogue established in Alfred Place
1932	Mocatta Library opened at University College
1933	Cumberland Hotel opened
1937	Victor Rothschild sold the family mansion at 148 Piccadilly

1941	Central Synagogue, Western Synagogue, West Central Synagogue and West Central Jewish Girls' Club destroyed by enemy action
	Harry Errington awarded George Cross
1943	Western Synagogue's temporary premises at Grotrian Hall, Wigmore Street destroyed
	West Central Jewish Girls' Club Golden Anniversary pageant at Scala Theatre
	West London Hebrew Congregation founded
1948	Beth HaSepher merged with West End Talmud Torah / Bikkur Holim under new title of West End Great Synagogue with premises in Dean Street
1949	Religion classes of Central and West End Great Synagogues merged
1950	Bloomsbury Synagogue and West London Hebrew Congregation merged under title West London and Bloomsbury Synagogue
1957	Western Synagogue moved to Crawford Place
1958	Rebuilding of Central Synagogue in Great Portland Street completed
1960	Rebuilding of West End Great Synagogue in Dean Street completed
1961	Marble Arch Synagogue founded in Great Cumberland Place
1963	Lily Montagu died
1965	Marian Montagu died
1991	Western Synagogue merged with Marble Arch Synagogue at Great Cumberland Place under title Western Marble Arch Synagogue

GLOSSARY

Aliyah	a 'calling-up' to read the Scroll of the Law in synagogue
Ashkenazim	Jews of German, French and Eastern European origin.
Bima	dais or platform in synagogue where reading desk is placed
Brocha	blessing
Chazan	Cantor
Cheder	Hebrew school
Chuppa	wedding canopy
Dayan	ecclesiastical judge
Daven	pray
Drosha	sermon
Frum	religious
Goyim	non-Jews
Haftorah	reading from the prophets
Haggadah	story of the Exodus from Egypt read aloud at the Passover Seder
Heim	original homeland
Heimishe	friendly, homely
Heremex-	communication
Landsleit	people from the same part of the old country
Lockshen	vermicelli
Lulav	palm branch, used ceremoniously on the Fast of Succoth
Matzo	unleavened bread
Mikvah	ritual bath
Minyan	quorum of ten men required for religious services
Mishpocha	family, relatives
Mitzvah	good deed, commandment
Pentateuch	the Written Law
Pesach	Passover
Rachmonos	pity
Rosh Hashonah	The Jewish New Year

Sephardi	Jews of Spanish and Portugese origin
Seder	ceremonial Passover meal
Shabbos	Sabbath
Shema	prayer recited in daily prayers proclaiming unity of God
Shidduch	arranged marriage, match
Shiva	seven day period of mourning
Shlepper	tout enticing customers into a shop
Shnorrer	professional cadger
Shammas	beadle or sexton in synagogue
Shochet	ritual slaughterer
Shtetl	Jewish village community in Eastern Europe
Shtiebl(or chevra)	small informal synagogue, often just a room in a house
Shul	synagogue
Siddur	daily prayer book
Sidra	portion of the Pentateuch read in the Synagogue on the Sabbath
Simcha	celebration, such as an engagement or wedding party
Succah	booth erected during the festival of Succoth
Succoth	festival of the Tabernacles
Yarmulka	skullcap
Yeshiva	academy for Jewish study
Yom Kippur	Day of Atonement
Yom Tov	festival

THE LONDON MUSEUM OF JEWISH LIFE

The London Museum of Jewish Life was founded in 1983 with the aim of rescuing and preserving the social and cultural history of London's Jewish community. The Museum has a large and growing collection of objects, photographs, documents and oral history recordings.

The Museum's permanent exhibition traces Jewish immigration and settlement in London, with reconstructions of a tailoring workshop and an immigrant's home. In addition, the Museum has an active programme of temporary exhibitions, and provides Education Programmes and Travelling Displays for a wide range of organisations.

The Museum also organises family history workshops, research seminars, guided walks and cultural events. It provides advice and resources for those interested in researching Jewish history.

A "Museum Friends" organisation has been launched to provide support for the Museum. Members receive a regular newsletter, invitations to exhibition previews and information on all the Museum's activities.

The Museum would welcome offers of material and assistance, both practical and financial.

Opening hours: Monday -Thursday 10.30am - 5.00pm. Sundays 10.30am - 4.30pm (except August and Bank Holiday weekends) Closed on Jewish festivals and public holidays.

For further information please contact: The Curator, The London Museum of Jewish Life, The Sternberg Centre, 80 East End Road, London N3 2SY. Tel: 0181-346 2288 or 0181-349 1143. The Museum is an independent registered charity, No. 293248. Registered Museum No. 36

Index

C

D

E

F

DONORS

The London Museum of Jewish Life and the Jewish West End Project gratefully acknowledge the financial assistanceof the following individuals and organisations towards the research and production of this book and the associated exhibition, "Living Up West"

The Area Museums Service for South-East England

The Clore Foundation

Beatrice and David Gluckstein

Helen and Larry Kleinfeld

Frances and Percy Gold

The London Boroughs Grants Committee

The Montagu Jewish Community Trust

The Porter Foundation

Living Up West - Jewish Life in London's West End is available as a Touring Exhibition from The London Museum of Jewish Life, 80 East End Road, London N3 2SY. Tel: 0181 349 1143

OTHER PUBLICATIONS BY
THE LONDON MUSEUM OF JEWISH LIFE

Museum publications currently available include:

THE JEWS OF ADEN

Published in association with Kadimah Youth Movement, 1991. 48 pp.

150 YEARS OF PROGRESSIVE JUDAISM IN BRITAIN 1840-1990

Edited by Anne Kershen, 1990. 72 pp.

OFF-THE-PEG: THE STORY OF THE WOMEN'S WHOLESALE GARMENT INDUSTRY 1880's to the 1990's.

Edited by Anne Kershen, 1988. 72 pp.

BORIS - THE STUDIO PHOTOGRAPHER

1986, 36 pp.

MAP OF THE JEWISH EAST END

(reproduced from *The Jew in London,* 1901). Coloured shading to indicate the proportion of Jewish settlement in different streets.

WANDERING STARS

Video documentary on the history of Yiddish theatre in London, produced by Ruth Shulamith Cohen, 1987, 35 minutes, colour VHS.

RESEARCH PAPERS

Published by the London Museum of Jewish Life in association with the Department of History, University of Leicester.

No 1   *Trade Unionism amongst the Jewish Tailoring Workers of London 1872-1915* by Anne Kershen, 1988. 32 pp.

No 2   *Hopeful Travellers: Jewish Migrants and Settlers in 19th Century Britain* by Harold Pollins, 1989. 50 pp.

No 3   *The Heymishe Front: Jews in War-time Britain* by Tony Kushner, 1992. 16 pp.

NEWSLETTER

A newsletter is published three times a year, available to Friends of the Museum.